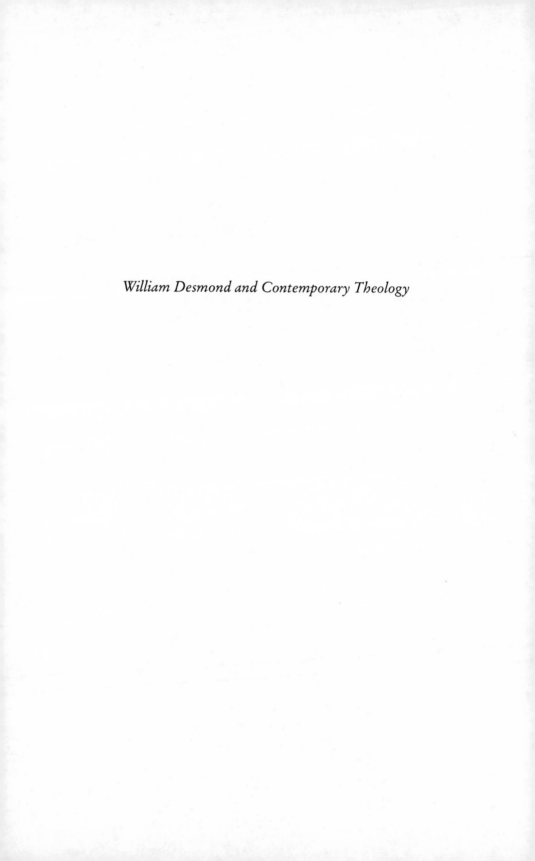

William Desmond and Contemporary Theology

WILLIAM DESMOND

and

CONTEMPORARY THEOLOGY

Edited by

CHRISTOPHER BEN SIMPSON
and **BRENDAN THOMAS SAMMON**

University of Notre Dame Press

Notre Dame, Indiana

University of Notre Dame Press
Notre Dame, Indiana 46556
www.undpress.nd.edu

Manufactured in the United States of America

Library of Congress Cataloging-in-Publication Data

Names: Simpson, Christopher Ben, 1973– editor.
Title: William Desmond and contemporary theology / edited by Christopher
   Ben Simpson and Brendan Thomas Sammon.
Description: Notre Dame : University of Notre Dame Press, 2017. | Includes
   index.
Identifiers: LCCN 2017030353 (print) | LCCN 2017040539 (ebook) |
   ISBN 9780268102234 (pdf) | ISBN 9780268102241 (epub) |
   ISBN 9780268102210 (hardcover : alk. paper) | ISBN 026810221X
   (hardcover : alk. paper)
Subjects: LCSH: Desmond, William, 1951- | Philosophical theology. |
   Philosophy and religion. | Metaphysics. | Theology.
Classification: LCC BT40 (ebook) | LCC BT40 .W535 2017 (print) |
   DDC 230.092—dc23
LC record available at https://lccn.loc.gov/2017030353

∞ *This paper meets the requirements of ANSI/NISO Z39.48-1992*
(Permanence of Paper).

CONTENTS

ABBREVIATIONS

AA   *Art and the Absolute: A Study of Hegel's Aesthetics*. Albany: SUNY Press, 1986.

AOO   *Art, Origins, Otherness*. Albany: SUNY Press, 2003.

BB   *Being and the Between*. Albany: SUNY Press, 1995.

BHD   *Beyond Hegel and Dialectic*. Albany: SUNY Press, 1992.

DDO   *Desire, Dialectic and Otherness*. New Haven, CT: Yale University Press, 1987.

EB   *Ethics and the Between*. Albany: SUNY Press, 2001.

GB   *God and the Between*. Oxford: Blackwell, 2008.

HG   *Hegel's God*. Aldershot: Ashgate, 2003.

ISB   *The Intimate Strangeness of Being: Metaphysics after Dialectic*. Washington, DC: Catholic University of America Press, 2012.

IST   *Is There a Sabbath for Thought? Between Religion and Philosophy*. New York: Fordham University Press, 2005.

PO   *Philosophy and Its Others*. Albany: SUNY Press, 1990.

PU   *Perplexity and Ultimacy*. Albany: SUNY Press, 1995.

Introduction

BRENDAN THOMAS SAMMON AND
CHRISTOPHER BEN SIMPSON

The task of appropriating William Desmond's original and constructive philosophical insights for the work of Christian theology is at its beginning. This volume represents possible contributions that the philosophy of William Desmond makes to various areas of contemporary theological discourse.

Modernity, in the wake of Kant, saw a retreat of metaphysical thinking. Desmond's work can be located within several post-Kantian streams of nineteenth- and twentieth-century philosophy that arose to respond to this eclipse. The tradition of German Idealism in general and Hegel in particular saw a combination of a focus on the dialectical and unfolding nature of thought with a definite metaphysical ambitiousness—a drive to address ultimate questions. Desmond stands within this particularly continental post-Hegelian stream. In the twentieth century, phenomenology sought to uncover stable structures in the rich ground of given experience and consciousness (variously reduced), and Desmond (longtime professor at the phenomenological nodal point of the Institute of Philosophy in Leuven) has been sympathetic to this mode of persistent philosophical attentiveness. Following in this vein is the tradition of existentialists such as Heidegger and Sartre (and Desmond takes up differently many of their emphases) who revive the question of "being," yet as disclosed in the privileged locus of lived experience as especially disclosed in "moods"—in the previously often discounted domains of the otherwise than discursive emotions and passions. Finally, Desmond's work has drawn from and developed in conversation with postmodern thought, with its principled reticence and resistance to claims to finality, permanence, identity, and universality, and instead seeks to hold out a fundamental place for difference and otherness—for irreducible ambiguity, uncertainty, and equivocity.

In this philosophical context, Desmond has done the work of retrieving and showing the necessity of metaphysics from within the languages, impulses, and concerns of these often anti-metaphysical philosophical traditions. In this way he contributes to the recovery of the potential for a common ground of intelligibility after the "postmodern" critiques and dissolutions of such and so contributes to the recent revival of metaphysics and realism in continental philosophy (with the likes of figures such as Alain Badiou and Quentin Meillassoux).

This volume assumes that there is an essential, and not merely accidental, bond between theology and metaphysics, a bond that is both discernible in and verified by historical analysis. From its earliest origins, theology has always had metaphysical blood running through its veins, animating, sustaining, and expressing its essential aspirations to think the relation between the finite and the infinite, the natural and the supernatural, creation and the Creator, the human and the divine. If God is the proper subject/object of theological inquiry and if at the same time this inquiry is expressed through finite categorical and linguistic forms, then it seems that theology cannot avoid implicating a metaphysics of some kind or another. The study of what comes after, or lies beyond (*meta*), the natural order (*physis*) always already gestures toward a "space" wherein an account (*logos*) of the divine (*theos*) may take form. For like theology, which is always and intrinsically a discourse in between the human and the divine, Desmond's metaxological metaphysics, as he himself writes, is "a *logos* of the *metaxu*, the between"; it is a "discourse concerning the middle, of the middle, and in the middle." As a metaphysics that comingles in equal measure a systematic dimension and a poetic dimension, it renews the kind of *Denkform* that was born when Christian theology first took shape as the human aspiration to think, speak, and live the Word spoken by God.

Desmond's metaphysics offers a unique mode of mindfulness to the Christian theologian tasked with communicating the excessive truth of Christian mystery. The history of this communication has resulted in a number of diverse theological kinds often identified with the figure who has been most influential over a given theological approach. Consequently, theologians will identify themselves as Platonists, Aristotelians, Thomists, Bonaventurians, Scotists, Rahnerian, Balthasarian, and so on, or, as is most often the case, a hybrid of one or more of these. It is the contention of this volume that the adoption of Desmond's thought not only allows one to remain a Platonist, Aristotelian, or Thomist, but to do so with greater clarity in an age when metaphysics has become suspect. There are other theological kinds that, conceding the contemporary suspicion of metaphysics, distance themselves from the aforementioned associations. For those who reject the metaphysical requirement, it is the contention of this volume that Desmond's thought may also provide tremendous benefit because it embraces and augments, without ever reducing, thought forms not normally associated with metaphysics. Consequently, Desmond's thinking grants these thought forms metaphysical status not by enlisting them into the metaphysical camp but by expanding the metaphysical reach to include thought forms other to itself, thought forms that as other come to constitute the very identity of a metaphysics that is between. Within both alternatives, Desmond provides to theological discourse a wealth of treasures that serve to enrich its essentially middle, or metaxological, nature as thought standing in between creation and Creator, finite and infinite, human and divine.

As theologians continue to struggle with the question of metaphysics, its place in and significance to the theological enterprise,

Desmond's donation to this struggle includes furnishing them with a number of benefits. These are a hermeneutic that can bring clarity to past thinkers; a powerful critique of certain ways of thinking that obscure important theological issues; principles for thought that provide a new way of understanding the mysteries of Christianity; a method that serves to continually keep theology's others as an indispensable dimension of theological discourse; a poetics that serves the speculative dimension of theology married to a systematics that serves the dogmatic dimension of theology; an experientially based mode of thinking that serves to prevent theological discourse from neglecting or even downplaying the importance of praxis and concrete realities; an emphasis on vocation that serves to prevent theological discourse from neglecting the indelible dimension of commitment; and, perhaps most important, a reminder to keep theological discourse from becoming too self-interested to the point of neglecting the wonder and awe of the mystery of God.

This volume begins with an essay by Brendan Thomas Sammon, who argues that Desmond's metaxological philosophy can be read as reawakening the intimacy between reason and being that was, prior to the modern period, secured by the phenomenon of beauty. The essay opens with an autobiographical account of Sammon's experience of developing as a student of Desmond. But more than extraneous praise, this opening account provides a glimpse into the link between Sammon's own experience of Desmond and the eventual reading of his thought that comes to light. As Sammon argues, Desmond's metaxology narrates an account of being that, corresponding to the theological tradition of beauty, configures it as an excess of intelligible content that precisely as an excess perpetually attracts the inquiring intellect into its mysterious content. Drawn in by the beauty of being, or in Desmond's terminology, the "between" of being, human reason begins in a state of wonder where it opens itself to the mysterious other that attracts it. Thus attracted, reason is brought more and more into this source that attracts it not in order to solve a metaphysical riddle but, as the human experience of beauty recapitulates, in order to celebrate the mystery through intimate union. This is much more than fanciful rhetoric for Sammon, whose experience of the figures he brings together—Dionysius, Aquinas, and Desmond—reflects this very dynamic. Thus, Desmond's contribution to the theological tradition, as Sammon narrates it, is to bring back into theological discourse a metaphysics that remains true to the beauty of being.

Of course, such claims seem to neglect or ignore the fact that ours is an age that, as the story goes, has unmasked metaphysics as nothing but a kind of discursive hegemony that reduces otherness to sameness, diversity to identity, plurality to unity, and past and future to mere presence. It is this alleged unmasking that has led much of contemporary continental philosophy to declare the death of metaphysics. Theologians who rely on metaphysics, then, end up being little more than onto-theologians, hopelessly confusing God with being and, becoming metaphysical morticians, endlessly adorning a dead body. Unless, of course, the whole charge of the so-called death of metaphysics is greatly exaggerated, which is the argument fiercely advanced by John R. Betz. In an essay that critically examines the accusations leveled against metaphysics, especially from Heidegger and his posterity, Betz unmasks the alleged unmasking as itself guilty of the very charges brought against metaphysics. Caught up in the enthusiasm of their postmetaphysical declarations, the heralds of the postmetaphysical, so Betz argues, have themselves forgotten or misremembered metaphysical modes of mindfulness that not only remain vital to philosophical inquiry but also simply remain, no matter how loudly one may proclaim otherwise. What is most forgotten is also that which is most basic to those philosophies that float to the surface in the wake of Heidegger's pretensions to the end of metaphysics: the real distinction between essence and existence. Heidegger's own interest in the question of being, as Betz demonstrates, is profoundly indebted to the very Christian metaphysics that he alleges is guilty of forgetting the question that grows out of this distinction. What all this means is that for contemporary philosophical and theological discourse it is not a question of either metaphysics or not; all thinking, as Betz contends, is of its very nature metaphysical precisely because, like being itself, thinking erupts in the space opened up by the real distinction between essence and existence. Instead, it is a question as to which metaphysics gets it right. Desmond, it turns out, is simply a better Virgil to our Dante-like odysseys through existence than Heidegger and his posterity could ever be because Desmond understands that metaphysics is an endowment of our created nature and an indelible sign of our origin. There is no "getting beyond" metaphysics because both the "beyond" and the "getting" implicated in such an effort are themselves already deeply metaphysical.

If Betz's essay demonstrates the paramount significance for all philosophical inquiry of the task to always bear in mind the real distinction between essence and existence, Corey Benjamin Tutewiler's essay considers the equally significant task of bringing to conscious awareness the various presuppositions that inhabit all thinking about the indeterminate character of being, presuppositions concerning how mind relates to being and how being relates to mind. Bringing Desmond into conversation with the contemporary speculative materialist Quentin Meillassoux, Tutewiler argues that there is a complementarity between the two whose philosophical significance can be found in the way that each might contribute to bridging certain gaps—linguistic, conceptual, grammatical—between Christian theologians and speculative materialists. Both figures read metaphysical indeterminacy as the locus where reason is confronted by its hyperbolic other and consequently comes face to face with the limits of its self-sufficiency. Yet, despite this shared principle, Tutewiler recognizes a more significant difference in that Meillassoux, unlike Desmond, lacks the speculative courage to let go of the idea that reason is sovereign in its quest for knowledge. The true courage of thought, so Tutewiler argues with Desmond, comes from being en-couraged, from recognizing that although courage emerges from something immanent, its true source, as communicated from powers to which one must attend, can never finally be possessed as one's own. It is a courage to recognize that reason is given to be prior to its taking form in the process of self-determination.

What does it mean to say more specifically that reason is given to be? What sort of configuration or account of being does such language suggest? D. C. Schindler's essay proposes a response to questions such as these by offering an interpretation of Desmond's philosophy with a view toward theological engagement. For Schindler, Desmond approaches reason in a way that, reflecting much premodern thought, sees it aspiring after the ultimate, except that Desmond interprets such aspiration in light of reason's origination in being itself. Reason's original rootedness in the mystery of being means that not only is reason already open to being's otherness, but also that being's otherness implies a relation to divine transcendence not only at the end of reason's activity, but from the beginning and throughout the process. Being's presence throughout all of reason's operations and activities indicates a positivity to both being and reason, which for Schindler point to the positivity of religion. The positivity at the core of Schindler's essay identifies the givenness of being in the fullest sense, that is, the hyperbolic excess of being in the plurality of its giftedness, especially in the gift of reason. But because reason is rooted already in this hyperbolic excess of being, this positivity is also identifiable as the mystery that perpetually funds the desire that drives reason's activity. It is in fact in human desire, so Schindler argues with Desmond, where the positivity of being makes itself known and out of which springs the religious impulse. Within this positivity of being, then, reason merges with religious thought as a primordial love of being that is inherently open to the divine. Here, God communicates his presence, not as some foreign entity imposed upon the process of reason *ab extra*, but rather as the one who always already dwells intimately with reason.

As these first four essays all argue in one way or another, Desmond's metaxological metaphysics is a way of being and mind that reads reason's integrity, not as an atomized self-sufficiency, but always in relation to its ontological and divine other(s). Primordially rooted in the givenness of being itself, reason's attraction to being is already a way to God. As if drawing the lens into clearer focus on this particular issue, Joseph K. Gordon and D. Stephen Long examine in more specific detail what a theology of God would look like when constituted by metaxology. For Gordon and Long, the most appropriate articulation of such a metaxological theology is one that uses the language of "ways" to God modeled on more traditional theological accounts like Anselm's rather than modern approaches like Hegel's. Anselm, as Desmond himself has argued, represents a way to God where thought and prayer are intimately bound up, both springing spontaneously and authentically from the original excess of the agapeic origin—a characterization of the origin as a ceaseless act of giving. As Gordon and Long argue, however, Desmond is not so much concerned with affirming traditional attributes of God as articulating why the way of speaking about God that these attributes entail matters. Desmond's metaxological way to God, following in this way of speaking about God, matters because it enables us to see a God whose absolute power is revealed as enabling a letting be of being and beings; beings are given to be for themselves, for the good of their own being. Desmond's way to God, therefore, gets us beyond the Hegelian counterfeit double of God, whose act of creation is an act of self-othering, wherein beings are given to be for the sake of God's own act of self-determination.

One of the more compelling attributes of the Hegelian God, which perhaps accounts for its widespread acceptance through-out modernity, is that it secures the central place of God within the "whole show"; everything is ordered toward divine self-realization. But if beings are given to be for themselves, as Desmond contends, then where is there room for God to be with and in them? If God truly releases beings to be for themselves rather than for himself, then do we not arrive at an extreme that stands opposite Hegel? Are we not left with the deist God who simply does not interact with beings, having released them to be for themselves? Patrick X. Gardner's essay demonstrates that, in the same way that the Christian theological tradition avoided such extremes when it approached God within a metaphysics of analogy, Desmond's way to God flows from this same analogical wellspring. The analogical metaphysics that inhabited so much of premodern Christian theological thought (as well as contemporary theological thought even if not in a thematic, or explicit, way) in many significant ways is revivified in the thought of Erich Przywara. As Gardner argues, there is a kinship if not direct identification between the role that analogy performs in Przywara's thought and the role that the *metaxu* performs in Desmond's thought. For in both central principles—analogy and the *metaxu*—being is conceived both as that which enters into composition with creaturely existence, and so guides it on the way, and as that which infinitely exceeds creaturely existence, and so remains beyond it, ever drawing creatures higher and higher into its excess plenitude of intelligible content. Only a metaphysics that is attentive to the analogical or metaxological character of being as such can properly narrate the relationships that obtain among creatures, but also the relationship between creatures and the Creator. As Gardner demonstrates, only when the univocal sense of identities, the equivocal differences that erupt on account of them, and the self-mediating dialectics that emerge between all equivocities are properly located by a dynamic middle—whether such a middle is identified as analogy or metaxology—can the both/and mindfulness necessary to think the dynamics of relationship be most effectively approached. For this reason, Gardner proceeds to explain, to the extent that Przywara's own reasoning is accurate, it gestures not only toward how Desmond's metaphysics provides a natural theology derived from the purest sense of philosophy but also, by providing a Catholic metaphysics, how Desmond's metaxology provides rich resources for a fundamental theology.

The analogy, or metaxology, of being shows itself to be the only valid way of thinking the relation between being and mind in a context that views being as an excess, or plenitude. For the Christian metaphysical tradition, the excess of being was rooted in the divine substance itself, which, as St. Paul articulated very early on, is the substance in which we "live and move and have our being." For Desmond, this excess is identified as the "overdetermination" of being that establishes the conditions wherein beings come to be. This coming to be, then, happens in the midst of being's overdetermined plenitude. Sharing in this overdetermination of being, beings are at once integral selves that are also other to themselves insofar as their act of selving happens in relation to other beings and to being as other. One of the ways that Desmond articulates metaxological selving is through the symbol of the mask, and it is the theme that is taken up by Renée Köhler-Ryan. As Köhler-Ryan explains, the mask, which vivifies an ancient intuition concerning mediation, is profoundly metaxological in that it allows one to represent herself as something other to herself all the while remaining herself. Masks both reveal and reserve an excess or more to what rides in tandem with the revealed; it is founded upon a fundamental ontological porosity between self and being as other to the self. Masks, it might be said, are an essential dimension of human selving in the between. Exploring this theme for its theological significance, Köhler-Ryan sees its value especially for the way that the mask enables a mediation between the "always greater" of the divine substance (as recognized most famously by Augustine) and the nothingness that the divine substance precisely as "always more" can often seem to be to the finite mind (as Aquinas came to see at the end of his life). Examining both an Augustinian and a Thomist account of the God who is "always more" and for this reason "as nothing" to human finitude, Köhler Ryan considers the way that these two great thinkers of the "nothing more" of the divine are companions to Desmond's own dwelling in between the more and the nothing. Both figures excel at using masks as a way to communicate their own nothingness before the more of the divine being, enabling them to become passages through which the divine transcendence speaks itself. Indeed, this capacity for a person to become a mediation of divine speaking by means of the masks is what is found at the core of metaxological selving.

The theme of the mask as double—as a display of self and of what is other to self—reveals the porosity between the natural world and that which transcends it. It is a porosity that opens to transcendence all the while preserving the integrity of the natural, indeed constituting this natural integrity. In this sense, Desmond's metaxological metaphysics provides important if not indelible resources for every mode of natural theology, the theme explored in the next essay by Christopher R. Brewer. Bringing Desmond into conversation with Howard E. Root, Brewer argues that Desmond's donation to theology, among other riches, involves both diagnosing and remedying many of the contemporary problems surrounding the possibility, conditions, and practice of a natural theology of the arts. If Root is correct to recognize that the new starting point of a natural theology is not discursive argumentation but a developed awareness of the relationship between theology and its object on the one hand and the various arts that erupt in the human confrontation with being on the other, then Desmond's contribution to this concerns not only his account of being (metaphysics) but also his metaxology of art. As Brewer argues, Desmond's account of relational intermediation so very vital to his metaxological metaphysics provides not only insight, but principles for understanding how theology might better relate to and intermediate the various arts that constitute human creativity. Only by exploring the depths of this relational intermediation can theology, in a kind of rocking back, properly read the tradition of natural theology. And in the same way that a rocking back creates the conditions for a forward release, a metaxological reading of the tradition of natural theology releases possibilities for a faithful re-creation of that tradition.

One of the benefits, then, that metaxology offers to contemporary theology concerns the way it enables an authentic return of more traditional resources for thinking while attending patiently to the developments that constitute the present conditions in which any return can be enabled. But return always comes with risk, and Desmond's metaxological metaphysics also offers various ways to mitigate such risks. Cyril O'Regan's essay examines how Desmond's metaxology provides crucial insight into the contours of a possible return of Gnosticism in our late modern world especially insofar as it dwells in the shadow of Hegelian thought. It is an insight that O'Regan believes goes beyond what philology and what other modern thinkers interested in the topic have offered, as it is both arraigning and convicting. Foregrounding Desmond's notion of the counterfeit double—a notion that identifies how "doubling" (the concept Desmond prefers to "dualism," since the latter implicates an unmediated difference that the former overcomes) can often lead to a counterfeit form of what is doubled—O'Regan identifies in Desmond's account of Gnosticism the way that such counterfeit doubling takes the form of both an epistemic-ontological mode and a hermeneutical mode, modes that although distinct ultimately work together. The epistemic-ontological mode of counterfeit doubling identifies the way in which, for Gnosticism, the material, social, cultural, and historical worlds (ontological) are not only impediments to authentic knowledge (epistemic), but are spheres where value is evacuated as a new absolute (dis)value. The hermeneutical mode of counterfeit doubling identifies the elevation of an interpretive framework that repeats though in distorted ways prior forms of religious thought. O'Regan sees one of Desmond's more significant contributions to theological thought to be the way that he provides insight into the nature of Gnosticism: in one way by identifying the epistemic-ontological mode of doubling as a unique feature of Gnostic texts despite their variations and in another way by validating the claim that there are indeed modern forms of Gnosticism even if such modern forms are more world affirming than their ancient counterparts. In this light, as both Desmond and O'Regan have argued elsewhere as well, Hegel's God can be more carefully exposed as a Gnostic counterfeit doubling of the Christian God it supposes is at its center, thus opening significant vistas for contemporary theological thought in a world where Christianity is on trial if it has not already been condemned.

The final essay of the volume follows John Panteleimon Manoussakis as he explores one such vista that is opened by Desmond's thought but that Manoussakis claims is left unexplored by Desmond himself: the nature of sin. Asking whether Desmond's *logos*, which is a *logos* of the *metaxu*, might in fact be a philosophical identification of *the* Logos—Christ—Manoussakis recognizes metaxology's potential to inhabit a space where human and divine are intimately bound up. He thus reads metaxology as a mode of "daemonic" mind, first recognized by Plato, that dwells in between what is of God (or the gods) and what is "not," focusing on the way that metaxology enables us to see and even speak of the "not" in the light of the divine. What is revealed is the way in which this "not" all-too-easily deceives itself into thinking it is itself *the* light of the Logos, giving rise to the problem of sin. Manoussakis proceeds to explore the all-too-often unseen contours of the nature of sin, reading it in many senses: the denial of the origin; the denial of mediation and intermediation; a desire for immediacy such that one is averse to time and history and, unable to wait for the Other, is averse to human dependency; the refusal of continuity for the sake of the impulsive moment; and more. Yet, demonstrating the power of the metaxological, Manoussakis also exhibits how such a reading of sin necessarily involves a recognition of the ways in which the very conditions that allow sin to erupt in the world are the conditions that also put us on the path to sin's redemption: the mediation of time as a movement toward perfection and the intermediation of the other; and the Other, against whom sin is always committed and through whom forgiveness must be given. When sin is associated with the sundered association with the origin and the disordered obsession with the end, Desmond's metaphysics of that which stands between origin and end, as Manoussakis suggests in the performance of his essay, offers a clarity to one's vision and practices precisely by repositioning the human person in a more proper relation to origin and end.

The essays in this volume all share the conviction that Desmond's metaphysics offers something vital for the theological enterprise today. As its rich history illustrates, theological discourse never charts its course alone. From its inception until today, it has always traveled in the company of others. Most often, its others have been philosophical companions. Augustine traveled with Plato, Cicero, Plotinus, and others; Aquinas traveled with Aristotle, Dionysius, Avicenna, Averroes, and others; Rahner traveled with Kant, Heidegger, and others, to cite but a few notable examples. Today theologians continue to seek the company of philosophers as they navigate the murky waters of encounter with the divine. Foucault, Wittgenstein, Derrida, Lacan, and others have shown themselves to be worthy companions offering valuable contributions to a variety of theological complexities. It is hoped that this volume not only illuminates the benefit of traveling with Desmond, but that in Desmond one finds a companion par excellence, whose presence on the journey not only guides one across the roughest of terrains and enables one to ascend the steepest of slopes but also enables one to see along the way the Beauty that, as Augustine so gloriously declared, is "so old and so new."

CHAPTER 1

The Reawakening of the Between

William Desmond and Reason's Intimacy with Beauty

BRENDAN THOMAS SAMMON

A PREFATORY REFLECTION

I was an undergraduate theology major when I first encountered the work of William Desmond. I remember gathering in the small common areas of the humanities building at what is now Loyola University in Maryland to hear conversations between members of the theology and philosophy faculty about a variety of topics. When Desmond would speak, his words were like immense waves of thought that drenched my unformed mind, satisfying a thirst I didn't even know I had while simultaneously increasing that thirst. I found myself being opened, wooed even, into a mysterious depth of something that could not be defined, something as attractive as it was harrowing.

I had the great fortune of spending my junior year abroad in Leuven, where Desmond had recently received a faculty post. His gifts as a teacher and mentor not only made him popular among students, but alongside his philosophical work also generated a revered awe among them. There was a rotation of note takers and disseminators among those enrolled in his Philosophy of God course, a few of whom, playfully (though with no less respect for that) imitating the tradition of depicting the name "God" as "G_d," would spell his name "D_smond." This was emblematic of the awe that arose in that respectful distance that seemed to come with being a professor in Leuven. Unlike most professors, however, Desmond would "kenotically" cross that distance with an uncommon comfort and ease, often inviting students to continue the conversation over any one of Belgium's finest beers.

As I sat in his class week after week, knowing very little about philosophy or the philosophical tradition, his lectures were for me more like poetry readings than philosophical instruction. Although I could barely comprehend the content of his thinking, there was something beautiful in it that drew me ever closer, something profoundly enticing that made the increasing awareness of my own ignorance tolerable, perhaps even delightful. Here was a voice, it seemed to me, that sang from a depth of being that I had never before encountered. And it was a voicing that brought me to a place of harmony and balance with the world precisely because it did not try to make sense of existence; that is to say, it did not try to force existence to conform to human ways of thinking but rather opened thinking to the gift of existence.

And so it was the beauty of Desmond's thinking that continually sustained my struggle to see the breadth and depth that he saw. I was also fortunate to return to Leuven as a graduate student of theology, this time better prepared to continue to engage his thinking. The poetic sense of his thought did not withdraw, but as I became more familiar with and knowledgeable about the Western intellectual tradition, this poetic dimension of his thinking now opened itself to a more systematic side of philosophical thought, providing a balance between the two I had never before encountered. This unique balance of the poetic and the systematic became for me a mark—if not *the* mark—of thinking worthy of my attention.[1] Only this mark, rather than narrowing the field of my appreciation of thinkers, opened it to almost every thinker I encountered. Often it happens that a person beginning an advanced pursuit of the philosophical or theological tradition finds a thinker in whom that tradition makes sense because he or she narrows one's vision, allowing that person to perhaps dismiss figures who for whatever reason don't fit with that vision. For me, Desmond's impact was the opposite, because he provided me with a mark, not for excluding the figures I found unfitting, but for finding in them both a poetic and a systematic sense, ever increasing my capacity to appreciate them despite certain disagreements.

Nevertheless, choices had to be made. As I pursued my own studies, I found myself drawn to figures who I believed balanced better between the poetic and systematic dimensions than others. I was drawn to the work of Thomas Aquinas much in the same way I was drawn to Desmond. Desmond's own description of Aquinas expresses my experience with Aquinas and with Desmond himself. "Reading Aquinas," he writes, "one can have the feeling of standing in a cathedral and of not being able to make out the sense of strange sensuous language of signs and symbols. There is something enigmatic to the many different figures and yet also a kind of intimacy. In the strangeness there is the suggestion of immense significance, though what this is exactly is hard to say."[2] There is a sense of beauty in Thomas's simplicity and clarity, which like Desmond's thought sustained my every effort to see what he saw. I also found myself drawn to the work of Dionysius the Areopagite, a figure whose impact on Aquinas has all too often been eclipsed by Aristotle. This enigmatic figure, who has been receiving increasing attention in recent decades,[3] shares with both Desmond and Aquinas a beauty and simplicity in his thinking that is often camouflaged by the difficult nature of his language and style. But as Aquinas himself noted, for those who diligently read him, there is a great profundity of opinion despite the difficult nature of his language and style.[4] As I studied these figures more and more, I found a genuine kinship among them, and it is this kinship that provides the context for what follows.

INTRODUCTION

In this essay I want to argue that Desmond's *metaxology* offers something of paramount importance to contemporary theology—namely, a metaphysical foundation that reawakens reason's intimacy with beauty. His is not the only project to concern itself with reason's intimacy with beauty in recent decades. Von Balthasar is, of course, a companion in this, and it is possible to read Von Balthasar as harboring a nascent metaxology in his thought.[5] But I want to suggest that, although others like Von Balthasar have contributed to the reawakening of reason's intimacy with beauty, Desmond offers crucial insight into the metaphysical foundations common to any such reawakening. This commonality is not reductive of the plurality of possible forms such a reawakening may take. Instead, it is a commonality more akin to how Desmond understands the commonality of the original power of being: "it is common precisely because it constitutes the metaxological community of being and may indeed be said to necessitate a plurality of possible articulations in order to do justice to its own power."[6] The reawakening of reason's intimacy with beauty is a reawakening to a communal voicing, or "communivocity," to borrow Desmond's term, more primordial than any singular articulation.

Desmond's service to theology is in providing a means whereby a plurality of theological forms and practices can enter into community with each other by affirming an underlying shared unity in and through their differences and otherness. In this respect, metaxology moves in the space between a certain impulse in modern thought that implies unity requires a mitigating of difference and otherness, as well as a certain impulse in postmodern thinking that implies any effort toward unity is already a violence toward otherness and difference.

There are two key features to the wording of my thesis, which are significant to the working out of its content. The first concerns the notion of a "reawakening," which has a twofold sense. First, in terms of methodology, reawakening indicates a deepening of the sort of skeptical waking made most famous perhaps by Kant's declaration in the *Prolegomena* that Hume had awoken him from his dogmatic slumber. In Desmond's reading of this slumber, the dogmatist is said to fall asleep in determinate forms, resting comfortable in the univocal fixity apparent to the dogmatist. The skeptic, however, discomforted by his knowledge that such determinate forms fix something that is impossible to fix given the plurality, diversity, and difference of all that is, is alone capable of waking up from such a univocal dream.[7] Within such a state of waking, univocity, and thus unity and identity, dissolves in the morning light of plurality, diversity, and difference, existing only as the memory of dream. Yet, as Desmond proceeds to explain, such a waking is really a withdrawal from any affirmation, fearing as it does the univocity, unity, and identity that every affirmation entails, and thus even the skeptic's affirmation of plurality, diversity, and difference. As I attempt to show, beauty was once conceived as a unity-in-plurality, an identity-in-difference, and so, allied to reason, guarded against the equivocal tension between the dogmatist and the skeptic. Thus, in this first sense, the reawakening pointed to in this essay indicates the way in which Desmond's metaxology enables an awakening from skeptical waking. This is especially relevant to the sort of metaphysical skepticism that took hold of Heidegger, prompting him to misconstrue something called "the metaphysical" as a way to simplify a far more complicated tradition of thought, as Ricoeur incisively saw.[8]

Second, in terms of the object of inquiry, reawakening also indicates that to which one is being awakened. Further on in his analysis of skeptical deconstruction, Desmond remarks, "Can one just be woken up to the fact that one was asleep, or perhaps always must be asleep or half asleep? If we don't wake up to *something*, our being woken up is just another sleep—we wake from one 'dream' to another, and hence the entire point of waking up has no point."[9] In this sense, Desmond's metaxology, so this essay contends, reawakens us to the presence of beauty that has remained despite the slumber that took hold of the mind amidst many of modernity's more soporific skepticisms.

The second feature of the thesis's wording concerns the notion of *reason*'s intimacy with beauty. As it is used in this essay, *reason* identifies the rich diverse modes of mindfulness that constitute human thought. This is an intentionally general if not indefinite way of describing it. There is a tendency today, especially in the West, to identify reason, in the wake of the "Enlightenment," as almost exclusively a universal a priori fait accompli that is the same for all people everywhere. Reason in this sense tends to be synonymous with first principles: the principle of identity, the principle of the suspended middle, and the principle of noncontradiction. It is, in the wake of Kant, the transcendental reservoir

of all possible concepts and principles that the mind uses in its engagement with objects it must ever strive to represent to itself. Reason, in
this sense, is the instrument that provides clarity through a calculated
measure of what is empirically encountered.

All of this certainly identifies important dimensions of how
human beings reason. But when these dimensions were almost exclusively prioritized in the modern period, conditions arose in which
an emphasis of certain dimensions of reason were confused with the
whole of reason itself. As Alasdair MacIntyre has argued, reason is
culturally rooted because it is tradition-constituted.[10] How a person
reasons in one cultural tradition differs from how a person reasons in
another precisely because culture embodies the first stirrings of the
valuation system that engenders a particular emphasis on aspects of
rationality. This is not to dismiss that dimension of reason emphasized
in the Western world—what might be identified as "dimensions of the
head"—but rather to remind ourselves that it is in fact an emphasis of
a particular dimension of reason; that is to say, it is a way of identifying
human thought per se that derives from a more primordial value judgment, which judgment is not itself verifiable by the very mode of reason it advances. Consequently, as an emphasis it does not exhaust the
whole of human reason since nobody thinks only in his or her head.
What might be called "dimensions of the heart"—passions, emotions,
sensuality, memory, love—unavoidably enter into the mix of human
thought whether we want them to or not (as modern romanticism and
existentialism, for example, helpfully remind us). If we are to grasp
reason's intimacy with beauty, a more complete picture of reason that
includes the heart must be allowed to present itself. As we will see,
reason's intimacy with beauty at one point in time allowed the balance
between the matters of the heart and the matters of the head that is
vital to every theological enterprise.

This essay proceeds as follows. First, I exposit both thematically
and historically the way in which beauty once gifted reason with certain principles, and therefore powers or capacities, to think the mysteries of existence and God. It did this in large part by serving as the
excess of intelligibility that stands in between that which is perpetually
desired (the good) and that which is contracted into the categorical and

conceptual structures of thought (the true). Many of the scholastics, including Albert the Great and Thomas Aquinas following the Dionysian tradition, maintained that beauty is in part the good in its becoming received as truth. Broadly speaking, this meant that beauty served as a unifying force between desire and knowledge, establishing the analogical relationship (rather than a univocal, or equivocal) between the human and the divine. I suggest that this gift performed an indelible role in shaping the theological tradition well up until that tradition, for whatever reason, severed its focus into a putative unmediated difference between determinate cognition (the true as given over to science) and value (the good as given over to ethics). I focus on beauty as it is found within the Dionysian-Thomistic tradition both for the reason that, as noted above, Desmond shares a particular kinship with these two thinkers and for the reason that it has been one of the most influential for shaping the theological tradition of beauty. Second, I examine those areas of Desmond's thought that resonate with this tradition. I attempt to demonstrate how the most significant aspects of Desmond's metaphysics reawaken this tradition for contemporary theological discourse at a metaphysical level. Here I assume rather than argue that all theology is in some way tied to certain forms of metaphysics when metaphysics is taken broadly to identify a discourse between the physical world and what is beyond the physical world. But this assumption is measured by the argument that Desmond's metaphysics reawakens the tradition of beauty. Consequently, I close by gesturing toward the ways in which this tradition, as mediated through Desmond's metaphysics, is indelible to the practice of theology today.

BEAUTY IN THE DIONYSIAN-THOMISTIC TRADITION

The foundation for the reawakening of reason's intimacy with beauty concerns what in Desmond's project is called the *metaxu*, or the between. Those familiar with the works of Plato might recognize this as a shared principle. Toward the end of the *Symposium*, for example, Socrates relays his encounter with Diotima, who had introduced Socrates to a mode of thinking or discourse (*logos*) that recognizes a mode of being "between" (*metaxu*) the terms of various dyads: beautiful and ugly, learned and ignorant, and so on.[11] It is this kind of thinking that enables the recognition of the importance of both sameness and difference simultaneously. For Socrates, this becomes important because, having just argued that love is always oriented toward beauty, he now faces the difficulty that beauty poses to anyone who approaches it—a difficulty he declared at the end of the *Hippias major* when, after failing to define beauty, he confesses, "I now know the meaning of that ancient proverb, 'all that is beautiful is difficult.' "[12] Beauty's difficulty concerns the fact that, among other complexities, more than any other phenomenon it inhabits both the spiritual and the material, the universal and the particular, the abstract and the concrete. It is, one might say, a both/and phenomenon, inherently analogical and recalcitrant to exclusive either/or equivocation. Hence it requires a mode of mind that, without compromising these differences, can move about in the unifying "space" between them.

Desmond's own configuration of the *metaxu*, although perhaps sharing a kinship with Platonic thinking, goes well beyond Plato. It is a *metaxu* that is constituted by a number of philosophical principles and ideas that come to light within the philosophical tradition, and more important, invested with the riches of Desmond's own originality. I have more to say about Desmond's *metaxu* below. For now, I want to suggest that Desmond's *metaxu* reawakens the place that beauty once occupied for the theological tradition, especially as that tradition is communicated in the Dionysian-Thomistic reading of it.[13]

Beauty as the *Metaxu* I: Dionysius

For Dionysius, beauty was more than a spiritual principle and more than an attribute of concrete beings: it was a name for God. What exactly Dionysius means by a divine name is not clear in the texts that bear his name.[14] However, close examination of his works makes it possible to discern some attributes. A divine name is not identifiable with the divine essence itself, since nothing is. The divine essence remains forever hidden from all communication, as Dionysius had apparently explained in his lost treatise *Theological Outlines*. Nor, however, is a divine name an attribute derived from creatures that is then applied to God. Rather, as he explained in another lost treatise, *Symbolic Theology*, names derived from creatures are symbols we use to talk about the divine.

In between these two dimensions is where we can locate a divine name: it is a perfection of God that proceeds from his superessential plenitude and comes to constitute the formal attributes of creatures. Or to put it more concisely, a divine name is God's very presence in the constitution of a created entity.[15] As Aquinas would later clarify, it is a procession not of essence (like the procession of persons in the Trinity) but of similitude.[16] A divine name, then, is its own kind of *metaxu* between the incomprehensible and unknowable divine essence and the creatures through whom God communicates a similitude of himself.

Beauty as a divine name means both that God is himself beauty and that God gives his beauty to creatures. Dionysius's understanding of the finer details surrounding this double sense of beauty derives from both the biblical and Neoplatonic traditions. His bringing these two traditions together is one of the profound achievements of his work. Part of this synthesis involved the merging of the two Parmenidean hypotheses into the one God of Jesus Christ[17]—a move thought by some to have been original to Dionysius.[18] The first hypothesis, "the One is not," intends to establish the complete removal of the One from any other, while the second hypothesis, "the One is," establishes the inevitable relation to being that is implicated in any consideration of the One. The distinction between these two hypotheses leads to the distinction within Neoplatonism between the One in itself, derived from the first hypothesis, and the first emanated principle, *nous*, derived from the second hypothesis. Rather than identify these as two distinct principles, as Neoplatonism had done, Dionysius interprets these as two aspects of the one God. The first hypothesis identifies God as he is in himself, hidden from all comprehension, while the second identifies God's creative act of self-communication.

Beauty as a divine name identifies both aspects of God, providing a bond between God and creation as well as a bond between creatures. The order in which Dionysius presents the divine names has long been a subject of inquiry, though no decisive conclusions have arisen.[19] It is possible, though, to discern from this order the way in which beauty marks the most concrete point of encounter between God and creation.

In chapter 4 of *On the Divine Names,* Dionysius begins his account with the name *good,* which for Dionysius (unlike for Aquinas) is the most proper name for God. As that which all things desire, the good identifies God as the original principle of attraction for being and non-being alike. This means that the name "good" identifies the plenitude that funds the seemingly infinite restlessness of desire, as well as the ethos in which ontological emergence takes shape.[20] Admittedly this is somewhat abstract, but the interesting thing about Dionysius's account of the good is that it remains rather abstract.

As the sequence of names proceeds, one can detect a momentum toward more concrete articulations. The name that follows the good is "light," which identifies the good as the good gives itself over as the conditions of "visibility," both spiritual and material, intellectual and physical.[21] Light is in this sense not only illumination, but luminous content itself or light as the emergence of substance. As Robert Grosseteste would later explain, light is conceived as both the first of corporeal forms, and so the most noble and exalted of all essences, and corporeity itself.[22] As the emergence of substance, light identifies the primal energy of every being as it emerges into existence, which means that it is also the substance of all that can be made intelligible. Hence it is the excess of all intelligibility as a unified plenitude.[23] Light also provides a more concrete instance of how the good is endlessly self-diffusive; one simple flame could in theory spark an endless number of other flames, which is to say, the material form of light (fire) can, to paraphrase the Areopagite's observations concerning the divine light, "multiply itself and go forth, as becomes its goodness, while remaining firmly and solitarily centered within itself in its unmoved sameness."[24] The divine name "light," then, is the good as the good creates conditions wherein the good may begin to give itself to be perceived, known, and loved.

Dionysius follows light with the name "beauty," and his account of it is far more metaphysical than certain dominant theories of beauty in modernity, which is perhaps why it has received harsh judgment among historians of aesthetics.[25] Nevertheless, the Dionysian account of beauty furnished theological posterity with important principles and ideas for thinking the mysteries of the Christian faith. Above all, beauty identifies a transcendent plenitude of all substance. In this sense, beauty adds diversity to the unified content of the transcendent plenitude of light. That is to say, where light is an excess of intelligible content as a unified plenitude (without formal plurality), beauty now names this excess of intelligible content as a unity-in-plurality. Dionysius derived this in large part from Plotinus, who had identified beauty with *nous*. *Nous*, for Plotinus, is the first emanation of the One, and as such is being itself. But as it turns back to gaze on the One, it is also intellect. Hence, *nous* identified a unity-in-plurality, the fullness of all that is, was, and will be. Beauty, it might be said, identifies the good and the light as they begin to take form in more concrete ways by giving birth to color, shape, size, magnitude, and so on. This might seem to make beauty the same as being, rendering being as a divine name rather redundant. For Dionysius, however (and for Aquinas later), beauty adds the dimension of attraction both physical and intellectual, making it in some sense more primordial than being. The Greeks had many words for what we today call "beauty," but primary among them was the word *kallos*, meaning "call." So where being identifies what is, beauty identifies the power in all things that are to attract, or call, others toward themselves.

Since beauty identifies both God in himself and God in his creative self-communication, it is bound up with the transition between these two dimensions. Dionysius borrowed the Neoplatonic scheme of emanation to identify this transition, though he amends it to fit with Christian teaching. Where emanation had meant for Neoplatonism the necessary self-diffusion of the good out of itself, for Dionysius (as for other Christian Neoplatonists) God's act of emanation is not necessary but a freely willed act of love that gives birth to the otherness of creatures for their own sake.

It is not at all clear at what point in Western history the triadic structure of (Greek) emanation—*monos*, *prodos*, and *epistrophe*—becomes reconfigured as the (Latin) binary *exitus-reditus*, but the difference is significant.[26] As Proclus had explained in his *Elements of Theology*, the product of emanation (*prodos-epistrophe*) is neither a parceling out nor a transformation of the producer (*monos*), because the producer remains steadfast in its own ontological constitution while emanating derivative entities.[27] Moreover, because "all procession is accomplished through a likeness of the secondary to the primary," there is a sharing of the *monos* in all proceeding entities.[28] This means that not only does every proceeding entity harbor its own *monos*, by which it remains united to the absolute *monos*, but also that it is precisely on account of this plurality of *monoi* of all emanations held in the unity of the absolute *monos* that a true community of entities is enabled. Remaining always in the producer (*monos*), each procession shares an identity with it, while its procession establishes its difference, two relations—identity and difference—that are inseparable.[29] Procession for Dionysius (and Proclus), then, is the contraction of a fullness rather than a projection into a space of ontological indeterminacy. And it is the continued relation to the absolute *monos*, along with the unity between identity and difference, that allows the epistrophic return.

One primary point to bear in mind in all this is that the *monos*, the remaining plenitude, is a vital component of emanation that cannot be neglected, as the Latin binary *exitus-reditus* in some way seems to do. The *monos* identifies the good-light-beauty component of the divine identity as it gives itself to be in and as the otherness of creatures. And it is by virtue of emanation as a model of this procession that the beauty of creatures may be better understood. In sharing in the beauty of God, creatures recapitulate their own unique *monos-prodos-epistrophe*. And nowhere was this more clearly articulated than in Aquinas's account of beauty.

Beauty as the *Metaxu* II: Aquinas

Although in recent decades more attention has been given to Thomas's account of beauty,[30] much work remains to be done especially in terms of how the theological tradition of beauty as a divine name had an impact on other dimensions of his thought. Space does not allow me here to offer any extensive treatment of this impact, but I do want to suggest that in light of the preceding, beauty as a divine name in

Aquinas was, as it was for Dionysius, a metaphysical phenomenon that is best conceived as a *metaxu*.

We first find this *metaxu* sense of beauty in his *Commentary on the Divine Names*.[31] Here Thomas explains how beauty and the good—like all the so-called transcendental properties of being— are the same in substance while they differ in *ratio* for this reason: "beyond the good, the beautiful adds an order to the cognitive powers that the good (*illud*) is of such a kind."[32] In other words, beauty identifies the good, which in itself is in excess of all determinate form, as the good assumes a particular kind of form. Only when the good becomes "this" particular good can it become an object for the cognitive powers. In Thomas's view, beauty is that perfection of being that makes this transition possible. Later in the *Summa Theologiae* Thomas will reiterate this, elaborating a bit further:

> The beautiful is the same as the good only differing in *ratio*. For since the good is that which all things desire, concerning its ratio it is that in which the appetite comes to rest; but with respect to the ratio of the beautiful pertains that in which the appetite comes to rest in its cognitive aspect. Wherefore those senses especially provide for the beautiful, which are the most cognitive, viz. sight and hearing, *as ministering to reason*; for we speak of beautiful sights and beautiful sounds. But in reference to other objects of the other senses, we do not use the name "beauty," for we do not speak of beautiful tastes, and beautiful odors. And thus it appears that the beautiful adds up on the good a certain order to the cognitive powers, so that good is called that which is pleasing to the appetite; however, that, the apprehension of which itself gives pleasure, is called the beautiful.[33]

A couple of important points must be stressed in the above passage. First, Aquinas uses the language of "ministering" (*deservientes*) to describe the relationship between beauty and reason. Beauty serves reason by ordering the good to those senses that are closer to intellectual activity, namely, hearing and seeing. The good may come to rest in the lower senses by assuming forms that can be tasted, touched, and smelled, powers that all sentient beings share. It is *not* that these taste-able, touchable, and smellable forms are without beauty; should these forms also become objects of cognition, then their beauty as goods ordered toward the cognitive faculties will be foregrounded. How-ever, insofar as they come to rest in these lower senses, their beauty, although present insofar as these forms can be perceived and known at all, remains present in less definitive ways. These lower senses do not require the deliberation of the intellect since their evaluation—their "judgment" over the goodness of a given form—is immediate. The senses of seeing and hearing, however, have a more mediated evalu-ation over the good of the forms they receive. For the good to be taken in by those senses closer to reason, it becomes necessary for the good to assume the *ratio* of beauty.

Second, based on the preceding we can say there is a twofold sense in which beauty is a *metaxu*: transcendentally, beauty is in between the good and the true, ordering the good toward more determinate form where, in becoming intelligible and knowable, it can assume the *ratio* of truth; and predicamentally (i.e., on the horizontal level of categorical, predicamental, relations), beauty is in between the lower senses that respond to the good as such (taste, smell, touch) and the proper object of the intellect, namely, truth. Beauty orders the good toward cognition, which is to say that beauty is the good as the good is becoming contracted so as to fit into the categorical and conceptual requirements of the intellect whereby it is received as truth. To be sure, beauty is not identifiable with these categories or concepts but rather is the excess of intelligible content that allows these to emerge.

Third, beauty for Aquinas, then, has an integral place in the intel-lectual process, both in terms of how the intellect encounters intelli-gible objects and in terms of how objects-to-be-known give themselves to the intellectual process. In one of his more frequently quoted state-ments on beauty, Aquinas declared, "The beautiful, however, bears upon a knowing power: for things are called beautiful which please when they are seen."[34] In light of the preceding and in light of the first part of Aquinas's statement, it should be clear that seeing indicates the physical act of perceiving but also the intellectual act of cognition. And even though Aquinas does not specify exactly what pleases when seen, we might look to book 2, chapter 1 of his *Summa contra Gentiles*. Written around the same time as the *Prima Pars*, and around the completion of his *Commentary on the Divine Names*, there would have been a thematic continuity within these texts, making it instructive for our concerns.[35] Citing Psalm 142:5, Aquinas opens this book with the words, "I meditated upon all your works; I meditated upon the works of your hands." As Aquinas's own explanation clarifies, this excerpt distinguishes between God in himself ("all your works") and God in his act of creative self-communication ("the works of your hands"). It is a distinction that fit well with how Aquinas had read Dionysius's account of beauty in his *Commentary on the Divine Names*, having recognized both beauty as God's very self and beauty as God's creative causality. In short, it serves to suggest that every created thing at least has the potential to please when seen, that is, to serve as doorways through which the invisible things of God can become visible (Rom. 1:20). Dionysius had himself said that all things can become a help to contemplation,[36] and it would not at all be surprising if this idea had impressed itself upon Aquinas. So all things possess beauty insofar as they can become centers of contemplative thought. This does not mean a thing's beauty obligates a percipient to recognize it. Certainly two people can perceive the same object with two differing visions of its beauty. As Aquinas states, though, since the beautiful "bears upon a knowing power" (*pulchrum autem respicit vim cognoscitivam*), to perceive a thing's beauty requires one to perceive things rightly, requires a growth in intellectual capacity (though "rightly" should not be taken in a determinate, or univocal, sense). Too often, Thomas is read as if he were saying in his *placent* statement that there are beautiful things in the world and there are ugly things in the world, and the way we know the difference is because beautiful things please us when seen. But this reading of Thomas not only wrongly makes him a modern objectivist—as if for him beauty is purely in the object with no relation to the percipient—but more significantly it neglects his account of beauty in his *Commentary on the Divine Names*. For Thomas, beauty is neither something objective in the things of the world nor something deriving from subjective perception of things. Rather, it is a metaphysical middle by which the infinite good that is desired by all creatures is ordered to the cognitive faculties where it may enter the mind as the *ratio* of truth.

When we look to Aquinas's more theological account of beauty, we see the way in which, derived from the Son, it is a theo-metaphysical phenomenon that establishes beings in their own unique being by establishing them in the community of beings. This most well-known passage on beauty in Thomas's thought is found in his treatise on the Trinity, *Prima Pars*, question 39, article 8. In a part of his response, Thomas provides the necessary conditions (*tria requiruntur*) for beauty, which is to say, the conditions necessary for beauty both to manifest itself and to become perceivable. The "necessary conditions" formula was common among the schoolmen to designate conditions that, rather than being merely sufficient, establish the sine qua non for the particular phenomenon in question. Adopted primarily from Hillary of Poitiers, beauty in Thomas's explanation is most fundamentally a theo-metaphysical dynamic drawn from the second person of the Trinity, the Son. That is to say, Thomas does not apply beauty to the Son *ab extra*, as if the Son were simply the most beautiful of all in creation and therefore merits the highest position in the genus "beauty." Rather, *beauty is revealed in the Son* insofar as the Son's relationship as image of the Paternal Archetype gives to the world the three necessary conditions for beauty. The metaphysics of the image is here crucial, and Aquinas sees in the Son the origin of all image-archetype relationships. The Son is the perfect image of the Father, and hence the perfect image qua image. There is no outside notion of image that can then be used to measure the Son as image, just as there is no outside notion of beauty that can then be used to measure the Son's beauty.

Question 39 of Thomas's *Prima Pars* concerns the persons of the Trinity in reference to the divine essence. Thomas's final article of the question inquires whether or not the Holy Doctors—by whom Thomas means Augustine, Hillary, and the authors of scripture—fittingly appropriate the essential attributes to each of the persons of the Trinity. Commenting on Hillary's appropriation of the name "species" to the Son, Thomas writes the following: "For with regard to beauty, there are three necessary conditions. First, certainly, wholeness or completeness (*integritas*), for some things which are impaired are ugly because of this; second, due proportion or harmony (*pro-portio*); and third, clarity (*claritas*), from which some things have a bright color, and thus are said to be beautiful."[37] Many commentators have wrongly abstracted this statement from its place in Thomas's text and then proceeded to use it as if it were a formula for identifying instances of beauty. But when examined in the context of question 39, we can see this is a statement about beauty as a theo-metaphysical bond, which can then be translated as beauty as a *metaxu*.

First it is important to point out that this particular article begins with Aquinas foregrounding his guiding principle: "Now in considering any creature four things occur to us by a particular order. First, the thing itself is considered absolutely insofar as it is a certain being. Second, consideration of the thing insofar as it is one. Third, consideration of the thing according to what is in it by its power of operating and causing. Fourth, consideration according to its habitude toward what it causes."[38] This fourfold schematic echoes the fourfold causality of beauty that Aquinas had outlined in his *Commentary on the Divine Names*.[39] There he had described the causality of the beautiful as (1) concerns being (*esse*); (2) oneness or unity; (3) order, that is, action, or the act of existing in itself (power) and with others (causality); and (4) rest/motion. There is an obvious alteration of terminology in his *Summa*, especially with the fourth consideration. But, as he explains in the cited passage from his *Commentary on the Divine Names*, rest/motion concerns the relation that God has to what is caused by the beautiful, which means that the terminological alteration does not reflect an alteration of content. The point to be made here is that Aquinas's account of beauty in this question is deeply entrenched in the metaphysical structure of his thought, especially concerning the way creatures relate to God. It is, we might say, in between theology and metaphysics.

And so it is in this context of the preceding fourfold metaphysical scheme, alongside his trinitarian theology and the image/archetype relation, that Thomas's three necessary conditions for beauty ought to be read. *Integritas*, he explains, has a likeness to the property of the Son insofar as the Son has in himself truly and perfectly the nature of the Father. When we read this alongside other dimensions of perfection or completeness in his work, we can see how *integritas* identifies the completeness of a given thing's being at any moment it is considered. Thomas believed that what was unique to the person of the Son was his being sent.[40] Insofar as this sending was an immersion in time and space, it could be considered at any of those moments or places. *Integritas*, then, identifies the concrete particularity of a being that, in process of becoming more complete, represents that completeness at any given moment. But it is a completeness that, always in excess of this representation, is present at all times and made visible insofar as the concrete particular being images it. The image is a sending, or emanation, of the archetype communicating the archetype without merely reduplicating it. What does it mean, after all, for the Son to be sent from the Father? In proceeding from the Father, the Son stands as a complete communication from the Father without either being identical with the Father or exhausting everything of the Father. The Son precisely is the *integritas* of the Father because his concrete manifestation is a perfect showing of the Father. The perfection of its showing consists in its single, concrete communicated form but only as this form derives from the Fatherly plenitude to which it anagogically refers and upon which it ontologically depends.

So beauty requires *integritas*, which is to say, in order for beauty to appear and be perceived, it must do so through something whole at a given time and place. In other words, beauty requires the particularity of a concrete being, its unique ontological parameters that this particular being alone occupies. Beauty follows upon the particularity of form, which alone is able to "please when seen." This could even include abstract beings, like a universal category, but only insofar as that universal category is considered a being in its own right. For any given thing to be perceivable at all, it must be given in such a way to allow one's perceptive faculties to engage it as a whole. Otherwise, its beauty would be incapable of being perceived.

The second necessary condition, *proportio*, concerns the way in which a given thing's *integritas* is capable of being recognized at all. *Proportio*, Thomas explains, "agrees with the Son's property, inasmuch as he is the express image of the Father."[41] An image, Thomas implies, must convey both unity and difference at the same time in order for it to be a perfect representation. In other words, an image must be neither univocally identical with the archetype nor equivocally other to it but rather an analogical communication of the archetype's content in the uniqueness of the image's form (which is why a representation of even an ugly thing can be beautiful). The Son perfectly represents the Father by proceeding in distinction from the Father (indeed on the cross becoming the most distinct being from the Father) but with the complete nature of the Father. The Son, one might say, is image-ness itself, or subsistent image, by which any image can be known as such. As the image than which no greater image can be thought, the Son also perfectly communicates *proportio* as a perfect representation. The Son in his *integritas* is a perfect image of the Father by virtue of the perfect *proportio* between them. So to say that *proportio* is a necessary condition of beauty is to say that the image given as an *integritas* must be in a maximal relation to that which it images, must have a (relatively) perfect *proportio* to the archetype that sends it.

This archetype is what Aquinas identifies as the *claritas* of a given being. *Claritas* agrees with the Son insofar as the Son is the Word of the Father. Even here Aquinas is careful to follow the Dionysian distinction between God in himself, who remains forever hidden, and God in his act of self-communication, though the line does become more blurred. *Claritas* is, we might say, the fullness of a thing's intelligible content that is *proportio*nally communicated in its *integritas*. It is the *monos* in Dionysius's Christianized emanational schematic, the fullness of content that is contracted by a proceeding and returning image. Following John of Damascus, Aquinas explains that a word is "the light and splendor of the intellect."[42] Elsewhere Aquinas explains that a word is both that which is conceived in the mind and that which communicates what is thus conceived. As it is in the mind, a word is "representative of everything that is understood."[43] And although in the human mind many words are necessary to express all that is understood, in God's mind, according to Aquinas, "His one and only Word is expressive not only of the Father but of all creatures."[44] Although the Word's expressivity in God does not have a corresponding causal operation (the Word does not cause the Father to be), insofar as the Word is expressive of creatures it also causes creatures to be.

If, then, *claritas* agrees with the property of the Son insofar as the Son is the Word, and if as the Word the Son is expressive of the Father and causally expressive of all creatures, it follows that as a necessary condition for beauty *claritas* refers to that same dynamic in an analogous way: beauty identifies a given thing's communication of its intelligible content that generates creative causality. Perceiving a thing's beauty, then, is an encounter that stimulates an intellectual union between knower and thing known—or perhaps lover and thing loved—allowing the intellect to engage in causal activity of some sort. The intellect encounters a given thing's *integritas*, which is the concrete, particular communication that is "sent" from its greater fullness of substance (*claritas*). As a communication of a fuller intelligibility, a given thing's *integritas* is a perfect *proportio* with that given thing's *claritas*, which shines beyond it as its fullness of substance.

METAXOLOGY AS A METAPHYSICS OF CHRISTIAN BEAUTY: DESMOND'S REAWAKENING OF THE BETWEEN AND ITS SIGNIFICANCE FOR CONTEMPORARY THEOLOGY

As noted above, the language of reawakening implies a slumber, and indeed the claim in this essay is that the tradition of reason's intimacy with beauty falls into slumber during the modern period. It is not necessary here to consider the various reasons why this happened, especially since this has been done already in great detail.[45] Suffice it to say that our current condition, especially in the academic world, dwells within an overarching dichotomy between the good and the true, with ethics serving the discourse that examines the good and science the discourse that examines the true. Aesthetics continues to thrive but only as an independent field whose object is, for most, forbidden from crossing over into either ethics or science. Even within theology departments and faculties, the work of theology is being more and more displaced by the work of ethics and religious studies, the latter of which considers itself to be the only viably scientific approach to religious discourse.[46] What I want to suggest is that, insofar as these (and other) discourses harbor a nascent or unconsciously present mode of metaphysics—which all discourses in some way must, since discourses as such constitute the encounter between intellect and extra-mental existence, or mind and being—this tradition of beauty remains present although in a dormant, or slumbering, condition. Awakening this tradition from its slumber, and developing it in a number of significant ways, not only serves the internal work of theology, but provides immense benefit to its relation to its others, as well as the relations among these other discourses themselves. In what follows, I want to briefly and broadly examine some of the ways in which Desmond's metaxology reawakens some of the primary features of beauty noted above.

Beauty and the Metaphysical Milieu

One of the symptoms of beauty's slumber in the modern period involves the way in which many dominant figures presupposed the indeterminacy to what might be called the "metaphysical milieu": the conditions of being that, because they provide the context for thought, are themselves not subject to the thought they allow and so are assumed rather than demonstrably proffered. In the Christian theological tradition, this milieu was for the most part considered to be the very divine substance itself, in which, as Paul explained, we live and move and have our being. Beauty, as we saw, identified the good as the plenitude of intelligible content as that good gives itself to be known. All thought functioned within a metaphysical milieu that was believed to be an excess, or surplus, of substance available to the intellect as the intellect ascends more and more into this substance itself—what John Damascene, and later Aquinas echoing him, called an "infinite ocean of substance" (*pelagus substantiae infinitum*). But in the modern period, the metaphysical milieu is no longer seen as a fullness, excess, or plenitude of intelligible content but instead is conceived as an indeterminate emptiness into which the mind must project its own categories of determinacy.[47] Kant called it the "empty space of pure understanding," while Hegel referred to it as the "indeterminate immediate."[48] But such a conception was never something that was philosophically demonstrated. Rather, it was assumed, or held by a philosophic faith.[49]

Desmond's metaxology reawakens the premodern sense that the metaphysical milieu is a fullness, an excess of something that gives itself to be in and as the community of beings. There are two primary ways Desmond identifies this fullness or excess: as the agapeic origin and the overdetermination of being, which although identifying the same excess or fullness nevertheless are distinct in important ways.

The phrase "agapeic origin" identifies the source of all being not only as the primal giver of all that is, but as creative power whose giving is ceaseless and in excess of all finite determination.[50] "Creation is prodigal," writes Desmond, "a lavish spendthrift, nothing miserly; it gives and gives; it renews even when it takes into death; it is fire that burns and is rekindled in its burning."[51] The characterization of the origin as agapeic not only signifies an excess or fullness of substance— something akin to Damascene's *pelagus substantiae infinitum*—but also that this excess is willingly given to be as other in the form of all otherness. This metaphor signifies "origin as excess plenitude, transcendence itself as other; creation as finite concreteness, but not for the return of the origin to itself; the 'exitus,' if we call it such at all, is for what is given as other in the middle."[52] Not only is this otherness given to be from this excess, but it is given to be for itself as other; that is to say, the otherness of beings that arises from the agapeic origin is given, not for the sake of the origin (e.g., as its completion, or its own self-determination), but for the sake of that otherness itself. The origin is agapeic both in the sense of being a super-fullness and in the sense of being super-generous, where *super* indicates, in Dionysian-Thomist fashion, that which exceeds all genus or categories.[53] Understood in this way, the agapeic origin reawakens the (Neoplatonic) notion of the self-diffusive good but whose absolute generosity ushers in the (Christian) idea that the milieu is a freely willed gift.[54] Desmond does not give it a theological configuration, which makes his work as philosophy more valuable insofar as it has the capacity to inform various ways of theologically configuring this milieu.

As an excess, or plenitude, of intelligible content, the agapeic origin cannot itself be exhaustively determined by human reason. Reason emerges in the midst of the beings that erupt from the agape of the origin, which is to say, it emerges in between the excess of the origin and the eventual acts of determinate cognition that engage this excess to fit the limitations of reason-coming-to-itself. Thus the agapeic origin gives rise to, or makes possible, any and every act of determination wherein reason becomes more and more conscious of itself in its relation to its other(s). And, in making determination possible, the agapeic origin can be spoken of—with respect to the determination it makes possible—only in the language of fullness or excess: as an *overdetermined* origin. By "overdetermined," Desmond does not mean that the origin and its subsequent metaphysical milieu are the recipients of too much determination on the part of reason, or that it has been so determined as to have lost any remainder of mystery or ambiguity. Rather, it means that as the origin of all that is to be determined, it is itself a surplus, excess, or plenitude of determinable content; it is overdetermined in that it harbors the content of all that was, is, and will come to be determined by the act of reason. "As overdetermined plenitude," Desmond explains, "it is more than any definite whole. 'Mystery' is constitutive of its excessive being. No determinate intelligible structure could capture its 'essence.' Its 'essence' as plenitude is beyond every determinate why."[55] Similar to certain modern thinkers, Desmond sees the metaphysical milieu as indeterminate insofar as mystery is constitutive of its "essence." Unlike many of the moderns, however, he does not configure this indeterminacy as an emptiness or lack. Rather, "it is indeterminate but indeterminate in a positive and affirmative sense. This is why I prefer to speak of an overdetermination: such a sense of the indeterminate is not antithetical to determination. Rather it exceeds every determination we will later attempt, exceeds complete encapsulation in a definite and exhaustive definition."[56]

There are a few significant theological consequences in reawakening the beauty of the metaphysical milieu as an agapeic origin in the way that Desmond does. First, in reconfiguring the metaphysical milieu as a fullness, or plenitude, Desmond's metaxology accounts for the attraction that generates reason's efforts to know the world around it, that is to say, reason's act of determination. Why must this attraction be accounted for in the first place? Given the contrast between the original attraction to an overdetermined origin that characterizes both the premodern and the metaxological account of being, on the one hand, and the "pro-jection" onto an indeterminacy that marks a great deal of modern (and postmodern) thought, on the other, what justifies the contention that the former is a more valid condition? In one sense, there is no justification if such entails a univocally rational account of one option over the other. Reason is itself bound up with every account of the origin and so cannot get outside of the dynamic in order to somehow apprehend some higher mode of rational verifiability. Indeed, any attempt to approach the question of the origin in exclusively univocal terms is doomed to failure, though, as Desmond acknowledges, there is a place for univocal thought.[57] But such univocal thinking must be ordered metaxologically; that is to say, it must be thought in relation to the unmediated difference (or equivocity) that necessarily arises with every univocal claim, as well as the dialectic, or mediated difference, that every equivocity births.

And so the justification for "attraction" over "projection"— which is to say, justification for thinking within an original plenitude rather than an original emptiness—involves a mode of mind that is in between, that is to say, simultaneously rooted in determinate rationality while being porous to the plenitude that attracts it. In this sense, Desmond's metaxology also reawakens the need for theology and theological language to always walk a fine line in between negative (*apophatic*) and positive (*cataphatic*) thought. It is this line that alone prevents slipping into one of the two sides where lie the traps of idolatry (positive, *cataphatic*) and nihilism (negative, *apophatic*). Thought, it seems, engages its objects with greater clarity when it is not too "puffed up," as St. Paul says.

A reawakening of reason's intimacy with beauty in Desmond's metaphysical milieu not only provides reason with a necessary modesty before its interests, but it also serves to realign reason with love. Aquinas believed that "loving draws us into a thing more than knowing does,"[58] because knowledge of necessity reduces the thing to a thought of the thing. Knowledge abstracts the form in order to bring it into the mind, which is perhaps why St. Paul understood that knowledge "puffs up" the mind. However, when a person desires to know something she does not desire to have it as a thought but as a thing, as Aquinas maintained.[59] The antidote to reasoning that relies too much on its own power—puffed up as it is with abstractions, constructs, categories, and concepts—is love, because, as Aquinas again asserted, "love begins immediately where knowledge ends."[60]

The point to be stressed here is that love, among other things, gives reason a patience and a kindness before its object of interest. It enables reason to resist the urge to reduce the whole of a given object of inquiry so as to fit reason's already constructed categories where it may then more easily handle, and often manipulate, its object. Reasoning without love is only ever able to puff up its own categories and is destined to remain confined within itself. Putting the matter in poetic tones, Desmond offers an insightful reflection that captures well the loss of love in our late modern rationality and the sense of self-love it engenders:

> I sang to my love, when I was in love. Now I am not in love, and so I analyze the song. And now I love my analysis, perhaps my clever self, and no longer my love. I no longer sing. Alas, my old song cannot be voiced by my new transcendental language. My new . . . language speaks about itself and not the adored other that once turned my head."[61]

As this passage implies, reason without love closes itself off to seeing its object in new and perhaps vital ways, content instead to simply love itself. Desmond's metaxology is a continual reminder of this need to think with love, that is, with patience, with openness to the otherness of any object of inquiry, but also with a conscious giving of oneself to objects of inquiry. His is a call to think the other in love, and so to "sing the other" as a melody in one's own symphonic existence.[62] Contrary to much of so-called postmodern thought, which privileges the other to the neglect of the role that every self plays in the being of the other, Desmond's metaxology recognizes the role of the self. It reminds us that every object of inquiry has more to its intelligibility, which ought to chasten every rational effort to know it but also any laissez-faire approach to otherness. In a word, it unites knowledge with love, providing a mode of mindfulness that is vital to theological inquiry.

Between *Conatus* and *Passio*

In the Dionysian-Thomist tradition, beauty as the fullness of all intelligibility compels a more contemplative receptivity to what is being given in and as this beauty than models that presume an indeterminate metaphysical milieu. For Desmond, the metaphysical milieu that derives from the agapeic origin as overdetermined also compels a more contemplative receptivity in the form of what Desmond calls the *passio essendi*. Emergent in the midst of an embracing fullness or excessively generous wellspring of being, human reason is rocked back on itself into a state of what Desmond calls "agapeic astonishment."[63] This is the primordial state of illumination, or porosity to the origin, prior to any activity of reason wherein the otherness of being as agapeic begins to reveal itself. Standing in relation to this newly revealed agapeic overdetermined source, reason is opened, made passive (*passio*) or porous to the act of being (*essendi*). Of course, reason participates in the coming to be of all beings, and Desmond recognizes a form of the (Spinozan) *conatus essendi*, or the co-birthing of being. But, as Desmond explains, "we are *passio essendi* before we are *conatus essendi*, passion of being before striving to be."[64] Human activity, that is to say, the participation in the "birthing" of being in and through beings, is always derivative from the origin as agapeic and overdetermined. We are "in between" precisely because our being, and the being of all beings, emerges out of a plenitude that attracts and uplifts our emergent being. We are neither the nothingness out of which we are called by this plenitude, or agapeic overdetermined origin, nor are we this origin itself.

Reawakening reason's intimacy with beauty helps theological discourse to better navigate the murky waters between the *conatus essendi* and the *passio essendi*. More than any other discourse, theology has both a *conatus* and a *passio* dimension. Like any discourse as such, its *conatus* dimension derives from its active inquiry into its object: inquiry into any given object requires the constructs of thought like concepts or categories. But unlike any other discourses theology concerns itself directly with the act of revelation, which means its *passio* side is more fundamental than its *conatus* side. Again, speaking in general terms, Desmond's metaxology brings both dimensions to greater consciousness by going between them. Being between demands a conscious vigilance to never finally privilege either the *conatus* or the *passio* against the other, even though it does recognize the primordiality of the *passio*. But even then, the very fact of thinking the *passio* is itself a kind of *conatus*, insofar as every use of language, concepts, and categories is. In turn, the thinking of the *conatus* itself requires a kind of *passio* insofar as *conatus*, as a construct, requires something given to enable construction in the first place. Here is where the between begins to open itself, revealing depths that can only be properly engaged by means of a metaxology. The many indelible and vital couplings within theological discourse—grace and nature, spirit and matter, God and creation, Heaven and Hell, nature and will, substance and relation—require a similar kind of reasoning if they are to be properly thought.

Beauty, the Between, and Consciousness

Desmond's metaxology is a *logos* of the *metaxu*, an account, discourse, or thinking of "the between." Like beauty, the between cannot be reduced to one definition as if it were an object alongside other objects with limits to its scope. Rather, the between identifies the emergence of the original energy of existence that gives itself to be in the plurality of beings. As noted, there is both a transcendental and a predicamental (although Desmond does not use this latter term) level where the between may be recognized. We only encounter "being as such" (*ens inquantum est ens*, to borrow Thomist terminology) in the concrete beings before us. But, as both Aquinas and Desmond recognize, this does not mean that we are not at all in touch with being itself. It only means that we cannot abstract a positive concept of being from beings. Were we to do this, we would not be thinking about being as such but merely our "present" abstraction, laden as it is with the limitations of our experience, as a popular critique of metaphysics contends. Desmond and Aquinas (and perhaps Dionysius) are not unaware of this problem, and consequently are able to avoid its trappings. Where abstraction fails to provide a positive concept of being, one is still able to recognize that "that whereby something enjoys this particular kind of being" is not the same as "that whereby it enjoys being as such." Aquinas referred to this as *separatio*, which identifies a fundamentally negative kind of thinking that allows one to become porous to being as such beyond any of its contracted modes.[65] For Desmond, "that whereby a thing enjoys being as such" is the between as it identifies the fullness of being that, although contracting itself into diverse modes, remains in excess of all such modes. And insofar as it is in excess of all contracted modes or particular beings, it remains "in between": both predicamentally in between particular being, and transcendentally between the Origin and all other beings.

If for Dionysius and Thomas beauty identified that *ratio* of being where the good gives itself to be known as particular form such that it orders the good to the cognitive faculties, then beauty is the common condition in which we live and move and have our being. Beauty identifies the happening that takes place as human persons pursue the good in an effort to order that good more toward their cognitive faculties. No one lives directly and fully in the good, and no one fully cognizes all there is. But all persons live in the midst of pursued goods and assimilated truths. One might even say that life is a constant struggle to assimilate desire into knowledge, or the good into truth. Desmond's metaxology continually reveals that being is an event happening in this middle space where a confrontation with the good in and through goods provokes a desire for cognitive capture of the good, or "truth."

As history more than makes clear, staying in this between of beauty is difficult. Ordering the good to the cognitive faculties carries with it the risk of either tending toward the side of complete cognitive mastery or the side of complete abandonment of cognition. Such tendencies have taken many forms throughout history: rationalism and fideism; essentialism and romanticism; naturalism and nihilism; determinism and skepticism, to name a few. Desmond's metaxology serves to diagnose one of the primary problems that throws mindfulness off balance in the between. Describing what he sees as a perennial metaphysical prejudice, he explains how for a great many in the Western intellectual tradition "to be is to be intelligible, and to be intelligible is to be determinate. Hence, being is identified with determinate intelligibility."[66] In this way, Desmond also identifies an important distinction generating the triad of "being, intelligibility, and determinate intelligibility." This reawakens the Dionysian-Thomist notion that there is being that is beyond intelligibility (God in himself), there is intelligibility beyond current determinations (e.g., beauty, goodness, faith, love), and every act of determination moves within these. In other words, the assumption that whatever *is* must conform to our cognition completely collapses the rich space of ambiguity—which admittedly is often also beguiling—in between being as such (*ens inquantum est ens*) and human cognition. That is to say, it is a metaphysical prejudice that evacuates being of beauty, and no longer can being's excess intelligibility call to us or invite us to know it more deeply. With such a loss, so too does human knowledge lose its potential perspicacity over being, and we are left having to project ourselves onto the screen of being as absence or nothing. We are left reconstructing our past constructs.

Desmond's metaxology reawakens us not only to the dangers of such a loss but also to the perspicacious sense of being that comes from a *logos* of the *metaxu*. His is a metaphysics, then, also of consciousness that goes well beyond Hegelian self-consciousness. It is much closer to the type of consciousness that could be derived from the Dionysian-Thomist account of beauty, not only because this account of beauty identifies an excess of intelligible content, but because, in ordering the good to the cognitive faculties, it simultaneously elevates the cognitive faculties more and more into the inexhaustible plenitude of the good. As bound up with the intellect but also always in transcendent excess of intellectual capacity, beauty identifies a transcendent plenitude of intelligible content that on the one hand gives itself over to categories and concepts of human discursion but on the other hand withdraws from discursion in its transcendence. And insofar as this withdrawal continually attracts the intellect beyond itself into a transcendent other, beauty identifies an *anagogical* power to elevate the human person more and more into this transcendence itself, and so indicates the way in which beauty can be considered a power to elevate human consciousness.[67] Of course, consciousness as we know it was never a theme treated explicitly by premodern thinkers. Nevertheless, it remains valid to recognize the way in which beauty was a locus where being and thought merged, and so where a theological account of consciousness was waiting to be born. In many ways, Desmond's metaxology serves this effort. His metaxology gives rise to what he calls the fourfold sense of being, which describes not only the metaphysical milieu itself but also an account of consciousness in relation to the metaphysical milieu. And it is in such an account where we find Desmond's metaxology enabling the kind of community of being found in the Dionysian-Thomist tradition of beauty. I will bring this essay to a close by examining this and drawing out its significance for contemporary theological discourse.

The Community of Being and Beauty

Derrida famously remarked that "every other is absolutely (or 'wholly' or 'entirely') other,"[68] representing one of the ways in which postmodern thought tends toward an ontology of unmediated difference. But if every other is wholly other in the way Derrida indicates, then could this condition even be recognized to be the state of affairs? An otherness that is capable of being recognized—even as "absolutely other"—is an otherness that is capable of being known and hence loved. And an otherness that can be known and loved is not *only* wholly other in the way Derrida's remark suggests. For how is it that what is "absolutely other" remains nevertheless hospitable to a rational grasp of its otherness, such that Derrida can proclaim its fundamental nature as 'other'? What accounts for the sharing of this, allegedly, absolute otherness?

Neither the theological tradition of beauty nor Desmond's *metaxu* dismisses the otherness of beings that Derrida wants to secure. But where Derrida, and a great deal of postmodern thought, neglects the place of union, unity, identity, and univocity within the community of beings, Desmond's *metaxu* is a community in which the otherness and differences among beings are shared by virtue of the order of beings that includes both difference and identity, both otherness and unity, both plurivocity and univocity. Metaxology is a metaphysics of communion, that is to say, a metaphysics that aspires to think difference and identity simultaneously. Nowhere is this articulated better than in Desmond's fourfold sense of being, which bears a remarkable similarity to Aquinas's account of the necessary conditions for beauty.

The fourfold sense of being, in short, constitutes an ordering of the univocal, equivocal, dialectical, and metaxological ways of being and thinking. It is an order that bespeaks not only the way in which human consciousness emerges in its encounter with existence but also the state of existence as such. That is to say, the senses of being as they come to realization in thought reflect the diversity within being itself. And this diversity communicates the unity that follows in tandem with it, such that being as such is most fundamentally a comm-unity, a unity-in-plurality, a plurality-in-unity.

The fourfold sense of being emerges out of the fundamental con-figuration of being as overdetermined. Because being is in excess of reason's capacity to exhaustively determine it, there is a movement of thought as thought engages being itself. As Desmond explains, "Our understanding of what it means to be comes to definition in a complex interplay between indetermination and determination, transcendence and immanence, otherness and sameness, difference and identity."[69] Rocked back onto ourselves by the seemingly endless giving of being, we are brought to a place of astonishment, which then brings us to a realization of our lack, or emptiness. Here, astonishment gives way to perplexity, which triggers the fundamental desire to know existence itself. In contrast to the agapeic sense of astonishment—astonishment caused by the excess of what is given—perplexity, deriving as it does from the consequent realization of one's emptiness before the overde-termination of being, is "erotic." That is to say, our perplexity derives from our being other to, and so lacking, the origin. The fourfold sense of being emerges within the space between agapeic astonishment and erotic perplexity, where reside all efforts to mediate one with the other. The act of mediating the otherness of being and beings yields, in Desmond's view, a fourfold order:

Very broadly and first, the univocal sense of being stresses the notion of sameness, or unity, sometimes even immediate sameness, of mind and being. Correlative to the univocal sense of being is the search for determinate solutions to determinate problems, impelled by specific curiosity. Second, the equivocal sense accentuates diversity, the unmediated difference of being and mind, sometimes to the point of setting them in oppositional otherness. Perplexities in its restless encounter with troubling ambiguities can be correlated with this sense of the equivocal. Third, the dialectical sense emphasizes the mediation of the different, the reintegration of the diverse, the mediated conjunction of mind and being. Its mediation is primarily self-mediation, hence the side of the same is privileged in this conjunction. . . . Fourth, the metaxological sense gives a logos of the metaxu, the between. It puts stress on the mediated community of mind and being, but not in terms of the self-mediation from the side of the same. It calls attention to a pluralized mediation, beyond closed self-mediation from the side of the same, and hospitable to the mediation of the other, or transcendent, *out of its own otherness.*[70]

I have added the emphasis at the very end to stress that the metaxological derives from more than a hope to do justice to the other. Rather, it derives from Desmond's own insight into the otherness within identity itself. That is to say, beings are constituted not only by their unique univocal identity but also by an otherness that is bound up with that identity. This otherness derives from the fact that every being, emergent as it is from the overdetermined origin, recapitulates in its own way this sense of being overdetermined. Metaxology, then, allows us to repurpose Derrida's observation of otherness. It is not that, pace Derrida, "every other is absolutely other," since putting it in this way absolutizes the unmediated differences among beings, which begins to fall apart when deconstructed. Rather, when considered in light of metaxology, it is more accurate to say that *every other is an overdetermined other.*[71] Articulating it in this fashion allows us to preserve the postmodern concern with the integrity of otherness without having to abandon the communal nature of that integrity. The overdetermination of the other invites a community of beings into its coming-to-identity; that is to say, it opens the way for its being to be constituted by community. In fact, it almost necessitates a communal intermediation for its coming into its own identity. The overdetermination of the other means that even that other's own unique identity as a communication of its overdetermination is not itself capable of realizing—as in "making real"—its own being. Rather, it needs the community of beings in which it first comes into itself. But this need in no way trumps its unique integrity as truly other. In other words, with Derrida the metaxological other remains uncompromised in its otherness. Yet this otherness does not assume absolute difference such that unity violates it. And here, perhaps, is where the kinship between Desmond's fourfold way and Aquinas's necessary conditions of beauty might bring some clarity.

Elsewhere, Desmond explains the fourfold sense of being in tones that we will see closely echo Thomas's account of *integritas*, *proportio*, and *claritas*. Here is what Desmond writes:

> If univocity stresses sameness, equivocity difference, dialectic the appropriation of difference within a mediated sameness, the metaxological reiterates, first a sense of otherness not to be included in dialectical self-mediation, second a sense of togetherness not reached by the equivocal, third a sense of rich ontological integrity not answered for by the univocal, and fourth a rich sense of ontological ambiguity not answered for either by the univocal, the equivocal, the dialectical.[72]

Beginning with the fourth reiteration, we have in Desmond's account an echoing of the plenitude, or excess of intelligible content, that marks both the Dionysian and Thomist accounts of the divine similitude as it gives itself to be as *ens inquantum est ens*. The richness and the ambiguity that cannot be accounted for by the univocal, equivocal, and dialectical ways of being and mind precisely is the excess of being, the plenitude of determinate content that constitutes the givenness of being itself. It is too much for these ways of being and mind, and therefore transcends their mediating capacity. Consequently, in its transcendence it perpetually provokes a richer, communal intermediation.

Moving back to the first reiteration, the "sense of otherness" that cannot be included in dialectical self-mediation reawakens Thomas's notion of *claritas*. *Claritas*, as we saw, is the excess of a being's substance that shines beyond its constituent parts. It is the depth of a given being, its ontological rootedness in the plenitude of being itself. As such, it is recalcitrant to attempts exhaustively to mediate it; it is the more of a being that cannot be finally determined by human cognition. The second reiteration, the "sense of togetherness not reached by the equivocal," reawakens beauty's *proportio*. *Proportio* is the necessary condition that accounts not only for the relation between a being's *integritas* and its *claritas* but also for the relation between beings themselves. The fullness of unity among beings is located in the ontological depth that is beyond mediation where a given being's *claritas* opens to the plenitude of being itself, wherein it is united with the *claritates* of other beings. Community in this sense is an act rather than a thing, an event rather than a fait accompli. And what allows the comingling among the various *claritates* of beings derives from the condition of *proportio*. Equivocity, as Desmond contends, cannot reach the togetherness issued within this *proportio* because, as metaxology allows us to identify, this togetherness is where unity and plurality are in perfect proportion. It therefore cannot be mediated by absolutizing difference or unity. Rather, it must hold both together simultaneously. In this way, a given being articulates the third reiteration—a sense of integrity not answered for by the univocal. This is because where univocity stresses sameness, metaxological integrity—like Thomist *integritas*—stresses a sameness-in-otherness, an identity-in-community with others. For Desmond, the between is "charged with an aesthetic effulgence that comes to be embodied both communally and singularly."[73] As he explains, there is an "integral open wholeness"[74] that marks this aesthetic show of being's beauty, echoing the way Thomist *integritas* opens, via *proportio*, to otherness. That is to say, it is an integrity that is in proportion to its own overdetermined substance (*claritas*) which accounts for its ontological bond with all other beings. As Desmond himself puts it, "Aesthetic happening shows the enabling ethos as a togetherness of splendid beings. Beauty here is not something subjectivistic: aesthetic show communicates the beings themselves and their togetherness in terms of integral harmony and community with others."[75]

Throughout the second part of this essay, I have tried to establish the ways in which Desmond's metaxology contributes to theological discourse. I have argued that metaxology reawakens reason's intimacy with beauty. In the first part of this essay, I tried to demonstrate the ways in which beauty as a *metaxu* gave shape to significant dimensions of the Dionysian-Thomist reading of the Christian tradition. For both, beauty not only identified God in himself and God in his creative self-communication, but it also served as that middle space where the good is ordered to the cognitive faculties, that is to say, where desire is continually transformed into knowledge. And for this reason, it is the space of true communion where integrating selves realize the depth of their unique *claritates* through proportion with other integrating selves. Reason's intimacy with beauty, in this sense, secures and safeguards a unifying and integrating adhesive necessary to all discourses since, contrary to a certain posture common to our late modern context, there is ultimately no such thing as knowledge devoid of desire. This is not to say that the relationship between them is an easy or unambiguous one. Quite to the contrary, it is perhaps one of the most complicated associations confronting us today. In reawakening the *metaxu*, Desmond's metaxology reawakens the space once served by beauty. And reawakening beauty may prove to be the most significant step taken for contemporary theological discourse, not only with respect to its own internal relations and complexities, but more important with respect to the way it relates to its others.

Notes

1. For more on the poetic and systematic in Desmond, see, e.g., Thomas A. F. Kelly, ed., *Between Systematics and Poetics: William Desmond and Philosophy after Dialectic* (London: Routledge, 2007); and *ISB*, 34–43.

2. *ISB*, 233.

3. Among the more notable contributions are Stephen Gersh, *From Iamblichus to Eriugena: An Investigation of the Prehistory and Evolution of the Pseudo-Dionysian Tradition* (Leiden: Brill, 1978); Paul Rorem, *Biblical and Liturgical Symbols within the Pseudo-Dionysian Synthesis* (Toronto: Pontifical Institute of Medieval Studies, 1984), and *Pseudo-Dionysius: A Commentary on the Texts and an Introduction to Their Influence* (New York: Oxford University Press, 1993); Sarah Coakley and Charles M. Stang, eds., *Rethinking Dionysius the Areopagite* (Oxford: Blackwell, 2009); Eric D. Perl, *Theophany: The Neoplatonic Philosophy of Dionysius the Areopagite* (Albany: SUNY Press, 2007); Andrew Louth, *Denys the Areopagite* (London: Geoffrey Chapman, 1989); Fran O'Rourke, *Pseudo-Dionysius and the Metaphysics of Aquinas* (Notre Dame, IN: University of Notre Dame Press, 1992). Among the now-classic works are Jan Vanneste, *Le Mystère de Dieu: Essai sur la structure rationelle de la doctrine mystique du pseudo-Denys l'Aréopagite* (Brussels: Desclée de Brouwer, 1959); Eugenio Corsini, *Il trattato De divinis nominibus dell Pseudo-Dionigi e I commenti neoplatonici al parmenide* (Turin: G. Giappichelli, 1962).

4. Thomas Aquinas, *In de Divinis nominibus*, proemium.

5. Von Balthasar's trilogy is well known at this point and hardly needs citing. Instead, for the ways in which Von Balthasar gets beyond Hegelian dialectic, which is where his thinking interlaces with metaxology, see Cyril O'Regan, *The Anatomy of Misremembering: Von Balthasar's Response to Philosophical Modernity*, vol. 1: *Hegel* (New York: Herder & Herder, 2014). O'Regan does not make any explicit mention of Desmond's project in this work, but the analysis of Von Balthasar's relationship with Hegel is revealing for any nascent metaxology in Von Balthasar.

6. *PO*, 6.

7. *ISB*, 129–30.

8. Paul Ricoeur, *The Rule of Metaphor: Multi-Disciplinary Studies of the Creation of Meaning in Language*, trans. Robert Czerny with Kathleen McLaughlin, and John Costella, S.J. (London: Routledge, 1975, 2004), 311: "The unity of 'the metaphysical' is an after-the-fact construction of Heideggerian thought, intended to vindicate his own labor of thinking and to justify the renunciation of any kind of thinking that is not a genuine overcoming of metaphysics."

9. *ISB*, 130.

10. Alasdair MacIntyre, *Whose Justice? Which Rationality?* (Notre Dame, IN: University of Notre Dame Press, 1989).

11. Plato, *Symposium*, 202a–e, in *Platonis Opera*, ed. John Burnet (Oxford: Oxford University Press, 1903).

12. Plato, *Hippias major*, 304e, in Burnet, *Platonis Opera*.

13. For a more complete account of beauty as a divine name in the Dionysian-Thomist tradition, see Brendan Thomas Sammon, *The God Who Is Beauty: Beauty as a Divine Name in Thomas Aquinas and Dionysius the Areopagite* (Eugene, OR: Pickwick, 2013).

14. Editions consulted include the following: *Corpus Dionysiacum I: Pseudo-Dionysius Areopagita, De divinis nominibus*, ed. B. R. Suchla, Patristische Texte und Studien 33 (Berlin: De Gruyter, 1990); *Corpus Dionysiacum II: Pseudo-Dionysius Areopagita, De coelesti hierarchia, de ecclesiastica hierarchia, de mystica theologia, epistulae*, ed. G. Heil and A. M. Ritter, Patristische Texte und Studien 36 (Berlin: De Gruyter, 1991) (cited below as *DN = On the Divine Names*; *EH = Ecclesiastical Hierarchy*; *CH = Celestial Hierarchy*; *MT = Mystical Theology*); John Parker, *The Works of Dionysius the Areopagite*, 2 vols. (London: James Parker, 1897–99); *Dionysius the Areopagite: On the Divine Names and the Mystical Theology*, trans. Clarence Edwin Rolt (Mineola, NY: Dover Publications, 2004).

15. See also Perl, *Theophany*, 65; O'Rourke, *Pseudo-Dionysius and the Metaphysics of Aquinas*, 9; John Jones, "Mis-Reading the Divine Names as a Science: Aquinas' Interpretation of the Divine Names of Pseudo-Dionysius the Areopagite," *St. Vladimir's Theological Quarterly* 52 (2008): 157–62.

16. Thomas Aquinas, *Commentary on the Divine Names*, proemium.

17. Cf. Louth, *Denys the Areopagite*, ch. 5; Rorem, *Pseudo-Dionysius*, 164 ff.

18. See Gersh, *From Iamblichus to Eriugena*, 155.

19. The order of presentation of the Dionysian corpus has been considered in a few different ways. Vanneste, *Le Mystère de Dieu*, argued that the *DN* and the *MT* exposited the ascent of the individual mind, while the *EH* and the *CH* exposit a mode of 'theurgy' (divine work) mediated by hierarchies. In contrast to this splitting of the *CD*, Rene Roques, "Denys l'Areopagite," *Dictionnaire de Spiritualité* 3 (1957): 243–86, and *Structures théologiques de la Gnose à Richard de Saint Victor: Essais et analyses critiques* (Paris: Presses Universitaires de France, 1962), suggested a more unified sequence that follows the order *DN*, *MT*, *CH*, and *EH*. Most recently, Rorem, *Biblical and Liturgical Symbols within the Pseudo-Dionysian Synthesis*, followed Roques but argued that there is a single argument threading its way through all of the treatises, showing "signs of a conscious arrangement which itself reinforces the argument they contain" (127).

20. It is perhaps worth noting that in some sense this is how Albert the Great had also characterized the name "good" in Dionysius's text. See *De*

Pulchro et Bono, q. 1, a. 1, in *Albertus Magnus, Super Dionysium De Divinis Nominïbus* (*Opera omnia*, tom. 37); nn. 71–92, ed. P. Simon (Bonn: Editio Coloniensis, 1972), 180–95.

21. Catherine Pickstock explains the *metaxu* in terms of light. See her "What Shines Between," in Kelly, *Between Systematics and Poetics*, 107–22.

22. Robert Grosseteste, *De Luce* (*De Inchoacione Formarum*), trans. Clare C. Riedl (Milwaukee, WI: Marquette University Press, 1942, 1978), 10; see also L. Bauer, *Die Philosophischen Werke des Robert Grosseteste, Bischofs von Lincoln* (Münster: Aschendorff, 1912), 51.

23. Cf. Dionysius, *On the Divine Names*, c. 2, §4.

24. Dionysius, *The Celestial Hierarchy*, c. 1, §2. It should be noted that Dionysius is here referring to the divine light, though throughout his corpus he uses this imagery for other light forms.

25. See, e.g., Wladyslaw Tatarkiewicz, *History of Aesthetics*, ed. C. Barret, trans. Adam and Ann Czerniawski (London: Continuum International Publishing Group, 1999), vol. 2, 28; Katharine Everett Gilbert and Helmut Kuhn, *A History of Esthetics* (New York: Dover Publications, 1972), 120.

26. I know of no studies on the historical developments concerned with this issue. Scholars, it seems to me, tend to uncritically speak of the triad *monos-prodos-epistrophe* and the binary *exitus-reditus* as if there is no significant difference.

27. See Proclus, *The Elements of Theology: A Revised Text*, trans. E. R. Dodds (Oxford: Oxford at the Clarendon Press, 1933), prop. 25–27.

28. Proclus, *Elements of Theology*, prop. 29.

29. Proclus, *Elements of Theology*, prop. 30.

30. To date, the single most important work on Thomas's views of beauty is Francis J. Kovach, *Dei Ästhetik des Thomas von Aquin: Eine genetische und systematische Analyse* (Berlin: De Gruyter, 1961). Other contributions include Winfried Czapiewski, *Das Schöne bei Thomas von Aquin* (Fribourg: Herder, 1964); Leonard Callahan, O.P., *A Theory of Esthetic According to the Principles of St. Thomas Aquinas* (Washington, DC: Catholic University of America Press, 1927); Umberto Eco, *The Aesthetics of Thomas Aquinas*, trans. Hugh Bredin (Cambridge, MA: Harvard University Press, 1988); Thomas Gilby, O.P., *Poetic Experience: An Introduction to Thomist Aesthetics* (New York: Sheed and Ward, 1934); Jacques Maritain, *Art and Scholasticism and the Frontiers of Poetry*, trans. Joseph W. Evans (New York: Charles Scribner's Sons, 1962); Armand A. Maurer, C.S.B., *About Beauty: A Thomistic Interpretation* (Houston, TX: University of St. Thomas, 1983).

31. For an extensive analysis of the material and formal development of beauty in Thomas's thinking, see Kovach, *Dei Ästhetik des Thomas von Aquin*, 1–83.

32. Aquinas, *In de Divinis nominibus*, bk. 5, l. 4. The phrasing *nam pulchrum addit supra bonum, ordinem ad vim cognoscitivam illud esse huiusmodi* is not without a degree of ambiguity. To what exactly does *illud* refer? Some translations take it as a reference to *the particular* thing that is known (e.g., Eco, *The Aesthetics of Thomas Aquinas*, 31; Jan Aertsen, *Medieval Philosophy and the Transcendentals: The Case for Thomas Aquinas* [New York: Crossroads, 1996], 343). But the word's case, gender, and number align it with the good in the antecedent clause. If one takes *illud* to be a reference to a thing known rather than the good, one ends up interpreting Thomas to be saying that beauty adds to the good a capacity to know *a given thing* is of a certain kind. This seems to raise a difficulty, however, since it implies that the good somehow already contains a multitude of already determined discrete things that are merely awaiting cognitive reception. Interpreted this way, it is very unclear how beauty differs at all from truth. But for a thing to be known as a thing at all, it must already be of such a kind; that is to say, it must already be a determined "this." Translating *illud* as a reference to *particular things* introduces into Thomas's explanation a redundancy that is not there. There simply are no indeterminate *things* presented to the intellect in its quest for knowledge—"thing" is already a determination. The good, however, exceeds all determination not as indeterminate but as too-determinate, or *overdeterminate*; it is an excess of being-yet-to-be-determined. Therefore, in order for the good to be known it must in some way be ordered toward the determinative capacity of the cognitive powers. This is precisely what Aquinas understands is unique to beauty: it is between the hyper-determination (or *overdetermination*, in Desmond's language) associated with the good and the cognitive determination associated with truth. The *illud* therefore makes more sense when taken as a reference to the good, a view that is supported by other texts in Thomas (e.g., *Summa Theologiae*, I-II, q. 27, a. 2, ad. 3), as well as scholars like Maritain, *Art and Scholasticism*, 167–70; Tatarkiewicz, *History of Aesthetics*, vol. 2, 259; Edgar De Bruyne, *Etudes d'esthetique medievale* (Bruges: Éditions De Tempel, 1946), vol. 2, 281–86.

33. Aquinas, *Summa Theologiae*, I-II, q. 27, a. 1, ad. 3. Emphasis added.

34. Aquinas, *Summa Theologiae*, I, q. 5, a. 4, ad. 1.

35. Cf. Jean-Pierre Torrell, *Saint Thomas Aquinas*, vol. 1: *The Person and His Work* (Washington, DC: Catholic University of America Press, 2005),

102; James A. Weisheipl, O.P., *Friar Thomas D'Aquino, His Life, Thought, and Works* (New York: Doubleday, 1974), 359–60. Kovach recognizes these texts as occupying the same writing period in Thomas's career; see his *Dei Ästhetik des Thomas von Aquin*, 33–41.

36. Dionysius the Areopagite, *On the Celestial Hierarchy*, ch. 2, §4.

37. Aquinas, *Summa Theologiae*, I, q. 39, a. 8, resp.

38. Ibid.

39. Aquinas, *Commentary on the Divine Names*, bk. 4, lect. 6.

40. Aquinas, *Summa Theologiae*, I, q. 34, a. 2, ad. 3.

41. Aquinas, *Summa Theologiae*, I, q. 39, a. 8.

42. Ibid.

43. Aquinas, *Summa Theologiae*, I, q. 34, a. 3.

44. Ibid.

45. See Hans Urs von Balthasar, *The Glory of the Lord: A Theological Aesthetics*, vol. 1: *Seeing the Form* (San Francisco: Ignatius Press, 1984), 45–56, 70–78.

46. Something that is more and more being called into question. See, e.g., Timothy Fitzgerald, *The Ideology of Religious Studies* (Oxford: Oxford University Press, 2000).

47. See William Desmond, "God, Ethos, Ways," *International Journal for Philosophy of Religion* 45 (1999): 17.

48. Immanuel Kant, *Critique of Pure Reason*, trans. Werner S. Pluhar (Indianapolis: Hackett, 1966), Introd., III, A5, B9; G. W. G. Hegel, *The Science of Logic*, trans. A. V. Miller (Amherst, NY: Humanity Books, 1999), 82/1: 83 [195]; for a more in-depth account of this in Hegel, see O'Regan, *The Anatomy of Misremembering*, 103.

49. For Hegel as an instance of this kind of assumption, cf. O'Regan, *The Anatomy of Misremembering*, 103.

50. See esp. *PU*, 229–232.

51. *BB*, 230.

52. *PU*, 229.

53. Cf. Dionysius, *On the Divine Names*, c. 4; Aquinas, *In de Divinis nominibus*, c. 4, l. 5.

54. *BB*, 256–57: "What would this be? Such a radical origination would not be the shaping of preexistent matter through the superimposition of form, that also might be preexistent, as in the making of the Platonic demiurge. Such origination need not look to persuade necessity, but would give out of unconditional freedom. It need not create with conditions, for all derivative determination of being . . . [o]rigination rather would be the surplus of the

origin, its free, releasing generosity. Origination would be an absolute giving of being. If one wants to say that the origin gives being out of an internal necessity, this is true, if we mean by internal necessity that it is its being simply to give. But then, of course, freedom and necessity will mean something other than their more standard significations. This necessity, whose being is simply to give for the good of giving, would be absolute freedom, indeed absolute freeing. For this giving would free, release, absolve the given from the giver."

55. *PU*, 231.

56. William Desmond, "Being, Determination, and Dialectic: On the Sources of Metaphysical Thinking," in *Being and Dialectic: Metaphysics as a Cultural Presence*, ed. William Desmond and Joseph Grange (Albany: SUNY Press, 2000), 8.

57. *BB*, 233: "I do not want to say that this train of thought is simply false. I do want to say that the thought of the origin as univocal cannot be the final word. There are hits on the truth here, but the hits also produce inevitable misses."

58. Aquinas, *Summa Theologiae*, I-II, q. 22, a. 2.

59. Cf. Thomas Aquinas, *De Veritate*, q. 22, a. 4, ad. 3.

60. Aquinas, *Summa Theologiae*, I-II, q. 27, a. 4, ad. 1.

61. *GB*, 69.

62. On thought "singing the other," see *PO*, ch. 6.

63. See, e.g., *BB*, 7–11.

64. *AOO*, 271.

65. Cf. John F. Wippel, *The Metaphysical Thought of Thomas Aquinas, from Finite Being to Uncreated Being* (Washington, DC: Catholic University of America Press, 2000), 48–52.

66. *BB*, 16; "Being, Determination, and Dialectic," 6; *PU*, 12.

67. It is worth pointing out here that in this explanation there are three modes of transcendence being employed, which correspond to Desmond's own trinity of transcendence. This trinity of transcendences can be found in a few different primary texts, but the most concise summary is in *GB*, 22–26: "First transcendence (T^1): The transcendence of beings as other in exteriority. . . . Second transcendence (T^2): The transcendence of *self-being*, self-transcendence. . . . Third transcendence (T^3): original transcendence as still *other*—transcendence itself, not as the exterior, not as the interior, but as the superior." See also *BB*, 231.

68. Jacques Derrida, *The Gift of Death*, trans. David Wills (Chicago: University of Chicago Press, 1995), 82.

69. "Being, Determination, and Dialectic," 28.

70. Ibid.

71. Cf. *ISB*, 33: "In other words, I am not talking about a move from the overdetermined to the indeterminate to the determinate to the self-determined. I am talking of the overdetermined that is there always with all of these particular possibilities." Here we see in Desmond a reawakening of the notion—found in Proclus and Dionysius, and in a different way in Aquinas—that there is a *monos*, or *claritas*, which is a creaturely recapitulation of the original *monos* or Divine Light.

72. *BB*, 177.

73. *GB*, 134.

74. *GB*, 135.

75. *GB*, 135.

CHAPTER 2

Overcoming the Forgetfulness of Metaphysics

The More Original Philosophy of William Desmond

JOHN R. BETZ

To judge from a series of similar titles that have appeared in past years, from *Religion after Metaphysics* (2003) to *God after Metaphysics* (2007) to, most recently, *Theology without Metaphysics* (2012), the once-noble science of metaphysics, the science of being qua being, has seen better days.[1] Indeed, it would seem that its days are finally over, having been surpassed by a *meta* of its original *meta*, and that now dispensed from any further burden to think about it we can go on doing philosophy and theology without it. Whether or not this is a fait accompli, such titles also carry an implicit paraenetic message that metaphysics *should* be surpassed, and certainly avoided as a kind of contagious passion of the intellect, which is inimical to right thinking (about God, the world, and other people) and from which, therefore, should one be unfortunate enough to contract it, one needs to be delivered. It is, in any event, no longer an honored discipline in the modern academy (except perhaps in the world of contemporary analytic philosophy, where it has seen a remarkable resurgence); rather, it is something we are supposed to forget, like a bad dream, or get over, like a bad habit. And if we cannot forget it—like an ineradicable memory that "we did not make ourselves, [but] were made by him who abides for eternity"[2]—or if we cannot break the habit of thinking metaphysically, then we at least need a good therapist, who can help us cope with it, like an inveterate passion, or can provide alternative ways of thinking (perhaps a new mythology or a social-practical account of truth) as a form of psychic displacement. Such, it would seem, is the contemporary state of affairs: either we have arrived at the "end" of metaphysics (as the more radical would have it), or we are still working out its "ending" (as the more reflective would have it, who know that passions, whether of a moral or intellectual nature, are not necessarily cured overnight).[3] But *that* metaphysics should be overcome, and that one bears some moral responsibility to this end, few seem to question.

Of course, upon closer examination it turns out that such sensational titles proclaiming the "end of metaphysics" are not nearly as novel or provocative as one might at first (as their marketers no doubt intended) be led to believe. For, as Dominique Janicaud reminds us, the project of overcoming metaphysics is as old as metaphysics itself.[4] Indeed, to someone familiar with the history of philosophy and theology, such claims will appear rather passé: after nominalism's critique of universals; after Luther's claim to have been delivered from metaphysics as from a seductive temptation; after Descartes's radical skepticism and demolition of scholastic tradition; after Hume's famous exhortation to commit metaphysics to the flames; after Kant, who stripped it of any theoretical knowledge of ultimate reality (notwithstanding his own metaphysics of morals); after Karl Barth's demonizing of metaphysics, natural theology, and the *analogia entis*; after the postmodern deconstruction of metaphysics on the part of Nietzsche, Heidegger, and Derrida (the latter two trying to outdo their predecessors in terms of anti-metaphysical purity); after, on entirely differently grounds, the declared "elimination of metaphysics" on the part of Carnap and the logical positivists; after the "postmetaphysical" thinking of

Jürgen Habermas, the éminence grise of secular Europe; after Jean-Luc Marion's apophatic, postmetaphysical phenomenology; and, last but not least, after the deconstructive anti-metaphysical theology of John Caputo.[5] (For that matter, one could even regard today's postmetaphysical discourse as—more than any homage to Heidegger—simply another manifestation of the ongoing Enlightenment project: for just as we need to be liberated from monarchies and all traditional authorities, we also need to be liberated from the hierarchical systems of thought that justified them in the first place.) All of which goes to say that, while metaphysics was a common patrimony since Plato and Aristotle and enjoyed a certain prestige at least until the High Middle Ages, it has been on the decline for nearly seven hundred years—to the point that today, in certain circles of the academy, metaphysics is officially a term of opprobrium, and being against metaphysics is politically correct.[6]

What *is* surprising and provocative, however, given the increasingly fashionable and doctrinaire rejection of metaphysics, is William Desmond's courageous and almost singular defense of it. Indeed, at a time when nearly everyone else in the world of modern continental philosophy, including those theologians influenced by it, takes the end of metaphysics for granted (either as a fact or as an imperative), Desmond's philosophy stands, towering in its achievement, as an intellectually formidable exception. As he puts it in *Being and the Between*, the first work of his epic trilogy, "We must move beyond the paralysis and stultification generated by this rhetoric of the end of metaphysics."[7] In the following I hope to show why Desmond is right, and why his call for a renewed appreciation of metaphysics needs to be heard—not just by philosophers who think the age of metaphysics has past and now belongs in a museum of the history of (bad) ideas, but also by theologians who think that theology (without peril to the fundamental claims of the Christian faith) can do without it.

But if one is to defend the task of metaphysics today, following Desmond and the implicit mandate of *Fides et ratio*, one cannot fail to take the critics of metaphysics seriously, even if one cannot hope to address all of their concerns here. For this reason I intend to focus on one of their most common and frequently repeated allegations, namely, that metaphysics conceals something more basic, more real, more fundamental, which has been *forgotten*—whether for Reformed theologians this be divine revelation, which metaphysics ostensibly keeps from breaking through on its own sovereign terms (Karl Barth); or whether, for the triumvirate of postmodern philosophy, this be the will to power (Nietzsche), the truth of Being (Heidegger), or the play of *différance* (Derrida). In other words, I hope to respond to the charge, which is curiously common to Reformed iconoclasm and postmodern deconstruction alike, that the history of metaphysics is that of an extensive cover-up; that metaphysics is itself, ineluctably, a system of occultation that needs to be exposed and, if not entirely done away with, then at least "dismantled." Since I have dealt more extensively with Reformed criticisms elsewhere, however, my concern here is to address the standard postmodern charges, chiefly those of Heidegger.[8]

The Forgetfulness of Metaphysics

Before discussing the future of metaphysics, which is precisely in question, one thus has to deal with the question of what it has ostensibly forgotten. But immediately, before we can attempt to answer this question, we are confronted by several other questions. *First*, what exactly do these critics mean by "metaphysics"? As expedient as a univocal concept of metaphysics may be if one wants to dispense with it, can one really speak of a single metaphysics or even of *the* metaphysical tradition? Does the metaphysical tradition not comprise a host of, at best, analogically related philosophies and theologies, such that, in a way analogous to Alasdair MacIntyre's famous inquiry, one must ask, Whose metaphysics? or Which metaphysics? Perhaps by a stretch of the imagination, notwithstanding their obvious differences, one can put Plato and Aristotle in the same category. But can one conceivably do the same with Hegel and Pseudo-Dionysius? Do the philosopher of absolute knowledge (in the master concept) and the theologian of radical apophasis (in the dazzling darkness) really amount to the same thing? And if not, would it not be advisable to be more careful in one's use of terms?

Second, in critiquing metaphysics, essentially, for being superficial, for concealing something more basic, more fundamental—as
is implicitly the case mutatis mutandis with Nietzsche, Heidegger,
and Derrida—have they themselves not forgotten something? Are
they not themselves involved in the very task of metaphysics they
criticize? Are they not themselves willy-nilly metaphysicians in
search of a deeper ground or, if not a ground, at least some kind
of transcendental = x, which is the condition for the possibility of
all (comparatively superficial) foregrounds? Famously, in his two-
volume work on Nietzsche, Heidegger alleged that this was the
case with Nietzsche's doctrine of the will to power—that even here
we have a residual metaphysics; indeed, Nietzsche is the "last"
and "consummate" metaphysician.[9] But can the same not be said
of Heidegger's Being (however many times he may have crossed it
out) and of Derrida's *différance* (even if he alleges it to be a figure of
ultimate in-significance)?[10] To employ a good old trope of Platonic
(and Augustinian) metaphysics, which for them is most in question,
do they not in some sense *abide* beneath the surface—this abyssal
nonground of Being in Heidegger, this ἀρχή of *différance* in Derrida? Are we really to believe that they have finally led us into some
brave new, postmetaphysical world? Or, in view of their archaeological search for something more basic, more fundamental, and
more ultimate (than God), which no one has yet uncovered, have
they not simply replaced one kind of metaphysics with another?[11]
As Desmond incisively puts it, "When it is said that we must think
beyond or without metaphysics, one fears this 'other' thinking is
secretly captive to presuppositions that shape an inarticulate metaphysics. In claiming to be beyond metaphysics, we become unknowing metaphysicians—an inarticulate sense of the meaning of being
informs our post-metaphysical, or non-metaphysical thinking."[12]

From the outset, then, we have good reasons to be suspicious
of the postmodern rhetoric of the "overcoming" of metaphysics—
not least of all the fact that Heidegger himself increasingly backed
away from suggesting that metaphysics could ever really be overcome (*überwunden*).[13] Furthermore, the postmodern questioning of
metaphysics is itself riddled with questions. Indeed, whether it be the

Heideggerian "deconstructor" or the Derridean "solicitor" of metaphysics, both stand in need of interrogation: Is your own philosophy not itself a form of metaphysics? Is it not built out of the very stones and ambitions of the metaphysical tradition you reject? And, unless you honestly mean to apply this term univocally, which is to say, indiscriminately, exactly what metaphysics are you talking about?

In order to venture an answer to this last question, let us begin with Heidegger's well-known definition of metaphysics, the validity of which is remarkably uncontested, indeed virtually taken for granted, in postmodern continental thought. For Heidegger, metaphysics is "onto-theology," by which he means that metaphysics poses the question of being ("what is the being of beings?") and then answers this question without further reflection by automatically positing a highest (self-caused) being as the cause of (their) being.[14] In other words, at the very moment metaphysics rises above the physical to pose the genuinely metaphysical and *ontological* question of the being of beings, it immediately returns to the realm of beings (for even the supreme being is a being) to procure its ready *ontic* answer. Consequently, Heidegger alleges, we have forgotten the ontological difference between being (*Sein*) and beings (*Seiendes*). Moreover, having forgotten this all-important difference, we never become real philosophers, because we never leave the ontic circle of beings to allow ourselves to be startled by the question of being, which "has actually been forgotten, [having] been completely covered by metaphysics to the point that there is nothing to Being as such."[15] Such is the big "cover-up," which, according to Heidegger, has been going on willy-nilly since Plato defined being in terms of his Ideas, and which Heidegger, the chief investigator and prosecutor of metaphysics, seeks to expose.

This criticism is directly tied to another: when the question of being is no longer thought, all that remains is an ontic understanding of beings, which come to exist only as objects present to a subject who represents them and holds them in his or her conceptual gaze. According to Heidegger, beings then no longer appear from (the question of) being, or upon the background of nothingness (as disclosed, according to Heidegger's analysis, in anxiety), but only to the subject who is their master and whose ideational reason and categorical understanding provide the measure of their existence. In the famous words of Protagoras, which foreshadow the modern metaphysics of subjectivity (in Descartes's *cogito* and Kant's "Copernican revolution"), "man is the measure of all things."[16] Taken to its *logical* conclusion, however, it is not simply that beings must appear *relative* to the human being, but that thought is *constitutive* of being; indeed, that thought and being are one. In the radical formulation that comes down to us from Parmenides and has elicited any number of interpretations (including Heidegger's own), "τὸ γὰρ αὐτὸ νοεῖν ἐστίν τε καὶ εἶναι."[17] Thus, whereas Protagoras is the progenitor of all *transcendental* idealisms, Parmenides is the progenitor of all *absolute* idealisms. For here it is not simply that epistemology has precedence over ontology, determining in advance by thought what can be known of being (as is formally the case with all transcendental idealisms), but that the very question of being is so entirely subsumed under the question of subjectivity as to be a *function* of it.[18] As a result, on Heidegger's view, the *question* of being has been obliterated. The same can be said of the question of truth, which is no longer the truth of being in its free disclosure but the truth of a correspondence—the more masterable and comprehensible the better, because the truer and more certain—between subject and object. The age of metaphysics, which is ostensibly concerned with the question of being, thus turns out to be the age of the subject, who objectifies and establishes everything—even the being of beings—according to its own sovereign terms.

Having specified what Heidegger means by metaphysics, we can now summarize in no particular order the various forms of obfuscation that he takes it to effect. First, metaphysics forgets Being, allowing neither Being nor beings to appear *other* than as they appear to a reason-positing subject—a subject for whom nothing is without a cause and for whom even Being itself, in projection of its own grounding activity, is a *ratio.* Second, driven by a derivative notion of truth as conceptual certainty, metaphysics forgets truth (ἀλήθεια) as the un-forgetting of what is forgotten, as the un-concealment of Being in beings. Third, it forgets temporality as that through which Being is disclosed; for time is, according to the standard metaphysical model, nothing but a series of points of presence (analogues of

Being understood as static presence), and because only what is present and comprehensible is real, the past and the future are essentially meaningless; whereas, for Heidegger, authentic existence, as *temporal* existence, is a future-oriented existence that is mindful of past disclosure. Fourth, and by the same token, metaphysics causes us to forget what it means to live authentically within history (*Geschichte*) as the sending or destiny (*Geschick*) of being. And fifth, though Heidegger's real concern for theology is highly questionable (since he construes it as a merely ontic science that, as such, would have to be subaltern to philosophy), metaphysics causes us to forget God; for the "god" of metaphysics is not the God of faith, as encountered by Luther in existential anxiety, but a rationally posited "god" of the philosophers, indeed a conceptual idol, before which "man can neither fall to his knees in awe nor . . . play music and dance."[19]

Of course, the age of metaphysics is not without its benefits. For, according to Heidegger, it is precisely the (ostensibly) metaphysical reduction of ontology to epistemology, of being to beings, and of beings to objects that can be mastered, that has made modern technology possible.[20] At the same time, however, on Heidegger's view, metaphysics has stripped the world of wonder and given rise to the flattened and disenchanted "world picture" of the modern age, such that we now inhabit a world in which we are no longer at home. For the world of metaphysics, in which nothing is without a cause (according to the principle of sufficient reason),[21] not even God (who for Descartes is *causa sui*), is a conceptually predetermined world in which the *novitas mundi* (the sheer givenness of the world prior to all logic and conceptualization) and our own *given* place within this world fail to appear. In short, for Heidegger, "after metaphysics" all that is left of being is beings; all that is left of truth is a truth (or value) of our own assertion (which is the real cause of the nihilism that Nietzsche merely unmasked); and all that is left of the world is an increasingly uninhabitable world of our own making.

Such are the basic charges in Heidegger's indictment of the metaphysical tradition: metaphysics obscures and distorts nothing less than the way we think about being, time, truth, history, the world, our own existence, and even God. (Whether Heidegger actually believes in God is beside the point.) It is even, supposedly, the cause of nihilism, inasmuch as metaphysics makes truth a matter of our idea(s) of it, in short, a "value" that (since it is only ours to begin with) stands to be devalued, creating the empty space of "no values." Consequently, following Heidegger's diagnosis and prescriptive recommendations, if we are to remember what has been "covered up," resist the dangers of unchecked technology, endure the night of the (inevitable) death of the metaphysical God and the devaluation of all values, prepare ourselves for a new revelation of Being (which at present cannot even break through metaphysics' conceptual hold), rediscover our own (and our people's) historical destiny, and even serve the task of theology (by cleansing its temple of metaphysical idols), the task of philosophy consists precisely in a regressive "destruction," or, to be more precise, "dismantling," of the metaphysical tradition, not for its own sake, but for the sake of a positive goal: the recovery of an ostensibly more original kind of thinking that is mindful of the difference between being and beings, whose festal gathering the poet, as the "shepherd of Being" who "watches by night" (the night of Being's absence) and the guardian of the memory of what all others may have forgotten, resignedly but hopefully, in eschatological anticipation, awaits. As Heidegger programmatically put it in one of his last lectures: "Only the gradual *removal of these obscuring covers*—that is what is meant by 'dismantling'—procures for thinking a preliminary insight into what then reveals itself as the destiny of Being."[22]

Of course, it is precisely at this point, when metaphysics is set aside and there is nothing left for Heidegger to critique—when Heidegger's own philosophy, which lay conveniently concealed by his critique of the metaphysical tradition, begins to emerge from the shadows—that we are struck by the peculiarities of his own alternative gospel: of the *impersonal* gift of Being in beings; of the "hide and seek" of Being, which is nevertheless not an agent or personal; of the mythology of the "fourfold" of earth, sky, mortals, and immortals; of a "worlding world" *without* a cause; of the superseding of the Hebrew prophets by the German poets; of the pervasive borrowing, garbling, and redeploying of all manner of Christian tropes: from the "fallen existence" of *das man*, to the kenosis of Being in beings, to the inspired scriptures (of German poetry), to the dark night of Being's absence, to the prophetic expectation of Being's apocalypse, and so forth. All of which is arguably far more incredible than any gospel it is supposed to replace.

But even if, upon closer examination, one should find Heidegger's own philosophy wanting, and even if one might reasonably conclude that his philosophy (notwithstanding its avowed independence as a "pure" ontology from all supposedly "ontic" theological discourse) is a distortion of the Gospel of Christ, and even if this should give one pause before one commits oneself to his views, it cannot be denied that his indictment of the metaphysical tradition has swayed the minds, to varying degrees, of many notable Christian philosophers and theologians, who look to him as Dante looked to Virgil—as to an indispensable guide, who helps us to regain our consciousness of the difference between being and beings and thereby prepares us for the truth of being and/or revelation.[23] Of course, in the end it may turn out that Heidegger is more of a philosophical sorcerer than a Virgil,[24] and that his philosophy is more of a propaedeutic to nihilism than to a new age of Being. In the meantime, however, the spellbound reception of his critique of metaphysics by so many Christian intellectuals gives the impression that his (and the postmodern) case against metaphysics has long been won. How, then, in the interest of determining the future of Christian metaphysics—if indeed it has any—is one to respond?

The Forgetfulness of *Metaphysics*

As mentioned above and bears repeating, a preliminary response to these charges would have to point out two things that should be obvious but for the most part—and rather conveniently—go unsaid. *First*, the applicability of these charges depends upon a highly reductive account of what one means by metaphysics, as though every metaphysics from Plato to Hegel (notwithstanding the radical transformation of Greek metaphysics by any number of Christian thinkers from Gregory of Nyssa to Augustine to Maximus the Confessor to Thomas Aquinas) can be forced in Procrustean fashion into the same category.

In other words, there is little if any attempt to distinguish between metaphysics (whether Greek or modern) and Christian metaphysics. *Second*, the allegedly "postmetaphysical" philosophies of Heidegger and Derrida, no less than that of Nietzsche, are themselves, whether it be acknowledged or not, formally (and inescapably) metaphysical. What is really at issue, therefore, notwithstanding sensational proclamations of the "end of metaphysics," is not *whether* metaphysics has a future (since no philosophy worthy of the name can fail to have at least an implicit one) but *which* metaphysics has a future.

My concern in what follows, accordingly, is to defend not metaphysics per se but only one particular metaphysics, namely, *Christian* metaphysics, which turns out to be an analogical metaphysics. Instead of attempting to defend it against every particular charge, however, I will focus upon that charge from which the others more or less follow: namely, that metaphysics forgets and therefore fails to think the difference between being and beings, deadening our sensibilities to the wonder of being as such. In short, as Heidegger states the charge, because of metaphysics, Christian metaphysics included, "one can no longer be struck by the miracle of beings: that they are."[25] Accordingly, for Heidegger, whom Mary-Jane Rubenstein describes as a latter-day Theaetetus (the *Wunderkind* of Plato's eponymous dialogue), the task of philosophy consists in a recovery of the wonder of being that metaphysics, the everyday philosophy of inauthentic humanity, has supposedly forgotten.[26]

But, of course, the memory game can be played both ways. Heidegger has told us that metaphysics has forgotten something, namely, the truth of being. But what if Heidegger and his disciples, in their very allegations against metaphysics, are themselves suffering from amnesia? What if they themselves have (whether intentionally or unintentionally) forgotten or *misremembered* something? Following Cyril O'Regan's groundbreaking two-volume study of this particular pathology (on Hegel and Heidegger, respectively), I would argue that this is precisely the case.[27] More specifically, I would argue that what is generally forgotten in the charges of the forgetfulness *of* metaphysics (subjective genitive) is the forgetfulness of *metaphysics* (objective genitive). To be sure, like no other thinker since Augustine, Heidegger, the anti-Augustine,[28] places a premium on memory, making true thought a matter of true memory (in this case not a *memoria Dei* but an ostensibly more primordial memory of the difference between being and beings). But what if Heidegger's own memory cannot be trusted? What if his own memory has failed him? What if he has intentionally disregarded something (say, the God who has revealed himself in Christ), or even willfully misremembered something (say, about the Christian metaphysical tradition), with the effect that others, who have been captivated by his grand narrative and have trusted his own false memories, have come to suffer from a similar amnesia? If this is the case, then perhaps the Heidegger school is itself in need of a therapeutic mnemonic, and in need, moreover, of a deconstructive clearing away of all the false memories that have obscured the memory of God and the Gospel of Christ.[29]

To this end, let us first identify one of more obvious causes of Heideggerian memory loss, namely, the rigid uniformity of Heidegger's definition of metaphysics as "onto-theology,"[30] which is taken by many as a sufficient warrant to lump together and dismiss nearly every metaphysical thinker from Plato to William Desmond—with strikingly little sense of need to read these particular thinkers on their own terms, and even less regard for the many and often major revisions of the metaphysical tradition that were undertaken in light of revelation on the part of Augustine, Gregory of Nyssa, Pseudo-Dionysius, Maximus the Confessor, and Thomas Aquinas, among others. Unfortunately, under Heidegger's solvent influence, all these colors bleed into one. Thus, to name the most famous victim of Heidegger's Procrustean taxonomy, the sublime Plato, whose thought defies easy categorization, is reduced to a functional Platonism, for which the highest value is the "correctness" of representation, and a uniform caricature of just about everything that Heidegger opposes.[31] The more specific aspect of misremembering I wish to address, however, concerns the fundamental charge, aptly stated by Rubenstein, that metaphysics, including Christian metaphysics, entails the loss and foreclosure of wonder.

In fairness to Heidegger, one cannot deny that this charge finds some traction in various figures of the metaphysical tradition, most notoriously Leibniz, whose principle of sufficient reason, "nothing is without reason," Heidegger both impugns and rather ingeniously subverts.[32] But Heidegger, it should be noted, also has a selective memory, for Leibniz, though a Christian, is not the standard-bearer of the Christian metaphysical tradition. And, more generally, what Heidegger remembers (and highlights) comes at the expense of what he does not (and leaves obscure). Certainly, one must grant that all human thought is characterized to some extent by such neglect: we cannot think of one thing without failing to think another; like a camera lens, nothing comes into focus without other things being obscured. Such neglect becomes culpable, however, when certain things are intentionally forgotten or disregarded. And what is often forgotten here, or at least conveniently ignored, is that the same metaphysical tradition that Heidegger relentlessly criticizes *began* with wonder. As Plato says in the *Theaetetus*, "For truly, this experience of wonder is the mark of the philosopher. Indeed, philosophy has no other origin" (μάλα γὰρ φιλόσοφου τοῦτο τὸ πάθος, τὸ θαυμάζειν. Οὐ γὰρ ἄλλη ἀρχὴ φιλοσοφίας ἡ αὐτή).[33] And as Aristotle says in the *Metaphysics*, "It is on account of wonder that now and from the beginning human beings began to philosophize" (διὰ γὰρ τὸ θαυμάζειν οἱ ἄνθρωποι καὶ νῦν καὶ τὸ πρῶτον ἤρξαντο φιλοσοφεῖν).[34]

Needless to say, Heidegger was not unaware of these texts, which he briefly discusses in his 1937–38 winter semester lectures.[35] But for present purposes it is important to note that he downplays their significance and ultimately disqualifies them as indicators of real wonder. For, as Heidegger emphasizes, Plato is more concerned with the intelligible "whatness" of things and their essential archetypes, the Ideas, than their "thatness," their sheer, unfathomable existence.[36] Likewise, as Rubenstein rightly points out, while Aristotle may say that philosophy begins in wonder, in the way that one wonders about what one does not understand, for Aristotle this is merely the *beginning* of philosophy, not its aim. Indeed, for Aristotle it is precisely this sense of wonder, like that of an amazed child, that is gradually to be replaced by an educated understanding of the actual causes of things, in which the wisdom of *philosophia* consists.[37] In other words, the child at the zoo should grow up, embrace the Horatian maxim *nil admirari*, and become a zoologist.

At this point in our argument, therefore, given the Platonic stress on the intelligibility of the real and the Aristotelian stress on the scientific knowledge of the causes of things, we cannot free metaphysics from the standard Heideggerian charges. If it is free, it is free only on bail. Nor, on the face of it, does the Christian metaphysical tradition, which is so heavily influenced by Plato and Aristotle, seem to fare any better. As Rubenstein observes, for Albert the Great wonder was appropriate for beginning students and old women but not for mature philosophers.[38] And, far from being notably different in this regard, even Albert's student Thomas "entreats his readers to work their way out of as much *admiratio* as they can, that is, out of ignorance and into the knowledge of causes."[39] Thus, one might legitimately ask with Heidegger, if Thomas and Albert (the patron saint of science) understand the task of philosophy to be the gradual explanation of the causes of things, which cannot help but lead to the gradual replacement of philosophy by modern natural science, what room do they leave for wonder? Have they not paved the way for the *mathesis universalis* dreamed of by Descartes and Leibniz, and *eo ipso* for the obsolescence of genuine philosophical reflection?

The most obvious response, as Rubenstein points out, is to say that Albert and Thomas do not intend to eliminate wonder per se but merely to distinguish natural wonders, which science can or eventually will explain, from divine miracles, which by definition defy natural, scientific explanation. That is to say, they are merely trying to make room for what is *truly* miraculous: for the works of God and for God himself, the thaumaturge, who is most wondrous of all. All of which follows from scripture, which exhorts us not to bow down to the sun, moon, and stars (Deut. 4:19) and idolatrously confuse the Creator with the creature, but with all of creation to rise up and worship God who alone is exalted and worthy of praise (Ps. 148). Indeed, according to scripture's own terms, this is not understood to abolish wonder but, on the contrary, to deepen one's experience of it, as one is led from the wonders of creation back to their inexhaustible and infinitely more wonderful source. In the words of Bonaventure, "Whoever is not enlightened by such great splendor in created things is blind; whoever remains unheedful of such great outcries is deaf; whoever does not praise God in all these effects is dumb; whoever does not turn to the First Principle after so many signs is a fool."[40] It would be disingenuous, therefore, to insinuate that Christian metaphysics, especially of the Franciscan variety, is bereft of wonder. We thus come to the question: has Heidegger, then, forgotten something? Heidegger, let us recall, was a student of the Franciscan tradition: he wrote a habilitation on Scotus and was familiar with Bonaventure through his teacher Carl Braig.[41] In no way, therefore, was he ignorant of Bonaventure's work. Nor can he have been ignorant of Bonaventure's exemplar, Francis, who is popularly remembered as having lived after his conversion like an amazed child amidst the splendors of creation. So why is Heidegger so unwilling to admit that their experiences are genuine examples of wonder; and why in general does he refuse to allow that Christian aesthetic experience is capable of transporting us into the "beginning of genuine thinking"?[42]

In keeping with Heidegger's analysis of the various analogues of wonder (amazement, admiration, astonishment, and awe), one could conceivably argue that what we have in Christian wonder is merely an experience of the "wondrous," that is, of what is "striking, remarkable, an exception to the habitual," or an experience of astonishment, which Heidegger defines as being "struck by a determinate individual object of awe."[43] For Heidegger, however, none of this would qualify as wonder—*Erstaunen*—because wonder, as a basic and more original disposition, is a wonder at "beings as a whole, that they are and what they are, beings *as* beings, *ens qua ens*, τὸ ὄν ᾗ ὄν."[44] Certainly, one could object that Bonaventure is ultimately talking not about determinate objects but about the totality of creation, whose wonders elicit such praise. But even if this is granted, Christian wonder (and, for that matter, any instance of monotheistic wonder) still falls short of Heidegger's expectations simply because the marvels of creation are referred to a Creator; whereas, for Heidegger, the rose—and the entire universe?—is "without why."[45] In short, for Heidegger, there can be no question of wonder, or any question of "ontological difference" that might arise from it, if one is a Christian (or indeed a theist of any kind) and believes in a Creator. As he peremptorily puts it, "That beings must first be understood as created by God is adhered to as an unshakable conviction. By this ontical declaration a putting of the ontological question is condemned from the start to impossibility."[46] Creedal Christianity would thus seem ruled out from the start, along with any notion of Christian philosophy; for anyone who would begin with the notion or confession of a Creator, the "maker of heaven and earth," is apparently incapable of "original" thinking.

Whatever other reasons Heidegger may have had against the Christian doctrine of creation, his stated reasons are clear. He sees it, without much effort at disambiguation, as part of the problematic inheritance of Platonism.[47] For creation, as he portrays it, is an artifact on the model of demiurgic creation and, in any case, what corresponds to (divine) Ideas. As a result, he claims, the strange and striking question of being inevitably takes a back seat to the correctness of representation: before beings are anything else, before they are allowed to *appear* in their appearing, and before one can be struck by their gratuity, one is predisposed to understand them as created effects corresponding to divine ideas. The problem here is not simply that beings are immediately categorized, but that we tend to think of being from start to finish in terms of production: what "is" is what is produced; it is nothing more than the "actual of an actualizing."[48] Indeed, as Heidegger is wont to observe, even the cause of beings, the highest being, is either what is perfectly actualized (the Thomistic *actus purus*) or, in a deeper homage to the principle of causation, the cause of its own being (the *causa sui* of Descartes).[49] In any case, the result, Heidegger claims, is that we cannot even begin to think of anything, God included, in different terms.

Admittedly, resembling the form of a temptation, Heidegger's argument makes a strong, perhaps even convincing first impression, and its captivating power can be all the more irresistible when presented in the context of his grand narrative, which itself takes the form of a creed and goes something like this: under the regime of metaphysics, propped up by its principle of sufficient reason ("nothing is without a cause") and its *koinē* (the Christian doctrine of creation), we never come to experience the wonder of being; moreover, in our metaphysical (Platonic-Aristotelian, Jewish-Christian) captivity we are aliens to that original disposition adumbrated in great poetry as a favorable sign for our Being-forsaken times, and to which we must return if we are to have a new beginning, live authentically in the world, and prepare ourselves for Being's apocalypse.[50] As it is, bound to metaphysics and its popular idiom, Christianity, we remain in this present age of Being's withdrawal and absence, trapped within an ontic circle of understanding, since even the ground of being is another being; so trapped, in fact, that we don't even recognize the circle's boundary at which the question of being, as a real question, might appear. (We thus have here something akin to an anti-Platonic version of Plato's allegory of the cave.) Such is the basic narrative. The more of it one accepts, the more captive one becomes; and for this reason, engaging Heidegger, like a temptation, can be exhausting.

If one is able to free oneself from the spell and recover one's senses, however, one gets the distinct impression that in Heidegger's magic mirror Christian doctrine has been strangely distorted—with some things overemphasized, others minimized, and other things not appearing at all. Put differently, what we have here is either a case of bad memory or willful misrepresentation, which calls for a series of strong rebuttals. First, given Heidegger's tendency to conflate them, one must point out that Christianity is not identical to Platonism: the Ideas do not constitute a separate *ordo essentiarum* but are one with the divine mind. One must point out, furthermore, that we are no longer talking about creation out of preexistent material, as with the Greeks in general, but precisely about *creatio ex nihilo*, which is *toto caelo* different from mechanical or even artistic production. As Desmond puts it, "This origination would be *unlike* any artistry we could adequately conceptualize, since our artistry always operates in the context of the givenness of being. This other art is hyperbolic to our artistry."[51] Indeed, Heidegger has broken the strictest rules of analogical discourse in presenting the Christian doctrine of creation in univocal terms. Still more incisively, following Desmond, one would have to point out that the "ontological transition" here is "not from possibility to actuality, but from nothing to finite being via the creative bringing to be of this absolute origin."[52]

For Heidegger, however, none of these important qualifications matter: "For even if creation out of nothing is not identical with producing something out of a material that is found already on hand, nevertheless, this creating of the creation has the general ontological character of producing."[53] Apparently, Heidegger, who is otherwise capable of great subtlety, will tolerate none when it comes to Christianity; instead, he is content with a highly reductive caricature. With Desmond we might legitimately wonder why, and whether Heidegger is driven to such simplifications and distortions "by the need to omit the extraordinary challenge that the notion of creation presents, to philosophy in general, and Heidegger's thought in particular."[54] For his part, Heidegger can accuse Christian metaphysics of forgetting being: that is his mantra. A Christian, however, can also play the memory game and argue that Heidegger is himself suffering from amnesia: in particular, that his philosophy is marked by a (willful?) forgetfulness of the doctrine of creation—not to mention a complete disregard of the revelation given to the Jews—which, as Desmond suggests, is "not less fateful than the alleged forgetfulness of being."[55]

But while a thinker of Desmond's stature is understandably unimpressed, Heidegger's argument has nevertheless been entrancing enough to persuade many who are already prepared on other grounds (not necessarily of an intellectual sort) to believe it.[56] Similarly, any engagement with Heidegger, and any corresponding attempt to free Christian metaphysics from his charges, tends to involve a taxing process of reflective disentanglement. Further complicating this task, one must come to terms with the fact that prominent Christian intellectuals, most notably Jean-Luc Marion, tend to embrace Heidegger's critique of metaphysics as a foregone conclusion.[57] Certainly, there are differences between them: Marion finally takes leave of Heidegger precisely where he also takes leave of ontology. The fundamental conviction both share, however, which is of special concern here, is that metaphysics allegedly cannot think radical givenness, or the "es gibt," which is hidden in all that is. And this is why, for both of them, phenomenology, which allows things to appear in their appearing, to be *phenomena*, *before* any conceptual apparatus is applied to them, is preferable to metaphysics as first philosophy (even if Heidegger later had reasons to find his own phenomenological method lacking).[58] How, then, is one to respond to this last and possibly most serious charge?

Aside from noting the irony that Marion's anti-metaphysical polemic draws upon two major tropes of the metaphysical tradition (namely, the Platonic trope of the *Good beyond being* and the Schellingian trope of *God beyond being*, not to mention the Eckhartian trope of *God without being*),[59] contemporary theologians who take the task of *Fides et ratio* seriously would do well to respond with Desmond: "I do not subscribe to the view that Heidegger has a corner on being, and that to think God we must do so without being (Marion). . . . To have being without God seems as unsatisfactory as to have God without being."[60] One might wish that such straightforward wisdom had a wider audience and that theology might take more cues from Desmond—the better Virgil—than it currently takes from Heidegger. Still, the shared criticism of Heidegger and Marion presents a special difficulty, especially given the centrality of the notion of gift to Christianity—from the gift of creation to the gift of redemption. The all-important question, therefore, is whether Heidegger and Marion (beyond the need to recall their own indebtedness to the metaphysical tradition they so readily disavow) may have forgotten or misremembered something; or, to put it more positively, whether the Christian metaphysical tradition may have its own resources for appreciating the *novitas mundi* and the gratuity of existence prior to all essential determinations.

THE REAL DISTINCTION

To get to the heart of the matter, we need to recall the core ontological distinction of the scholastic tradition between essence and existence, commonly known and understood in Thomism as the *distinctio realis*.[61] For multiple reasons, I would argue that any defense of the Christian metaphysical tradition against Heideggerian charges turns upon it. For, however one parses it, this distinction cannot be conjured away, no matter how many times one declares the "end of metaphysics" or repeats the incantation "onto-theology," because it is a distinction at the heart of thought itself. Not even Heidegger can avoid it, which is why he wrestles with it, and why his own philosophy ineluctably

trades on variations and newly minted meanings of its basic terms—
from the early existential analytic of *Dasein* to the late cryptic inti-
mations of the *Wesen* (read "presencing in unconcealment") of *Seyn*.
Indeed, if there is a turn—a *Kehre*—within Heidegger's thought, one
could view it as occurring *within* the dynamic "space" of the real distinction: whereas his early work moves away from every essentialism
toward a phenomenology of existence (*essentia* → *existentia*), the later
work turns back to the question of essence but now reinterpreted as
the *Wesen des Seins* (*existentia* → *essentia*).[62] One could even attempt to
summarize the whole of Heidegger's philosophy as an attempt to think
the *essencing in unconcealment of Being to ex-isting being*. In which
case, and really in any case, what do we have here if not a strange permutation of the venerable scholastic distinction, which remains like a
palimpsest throughout the Heideggerian corpus, even when Heidegger
claims to be beyond it?[63] For, to give but one example, when Heidegger
speaks of wonder at "beings as a whole, *that* they are and *what* they
are," what is he restating, *in his own definition of wonder*, if not the
same real distinction and its two irreducible questions: the question of
the *what* of beings (their *essentia*) and the question of the *that* of beings
(their *existentia*)? All of which goes to say that this *metaphysical* distinction, however one parses it, is properly basic, even for Heidegger,
and that one forgets it (in the name of the supposed "end" of metaphysics) at the risk of thoughtlessness.[64]

But as soon as we remember this metaphysical distinction as
something no philosophy or fundamental theology can afford to
neglect,[65] we must also remember that Heidegger considered it inadequate to the question of being it is supposed to answer. Let us attempt
to summarize his reasons. First, he believed that it does not really
address the question of existence because being is always already
essentially predetermined and therefore covered up by metaphysical
concepts, especially that of actuality (*actualitas* being itself a Latin
corruption of Aristotle's more meaningful *energeia*); in short, on
his reading, metaphysics is essentially essentialistic (most obviously,
in Plato, who reduces being to the ideal). Second, he believed that
the distinction between essence and existence is a purely ontic distinction, which makes us oblivious to the all-important "ontological

difference" between being and beings. All of which he takes to justify his "dismantling" of the metaphysical tradition, in order to get at the question that may have been asked more than two millennia ago by the pre-Socratics but now lies beneath two millennia of metaphysical rubbish, which, alas, one has to work through if one wants to get "back" to a "new beginning."

With regard to the first claim, what is perhaps most striking is the presumption that the scholastics (with the possible exception of Eckhart) were incapable of thinking the very question of existence they posed: either because they could not (ultimately) think existence apart from essence, believing not without reason that nothing (i.e., the absence of every form or determination) is unintelligible, and that one cannot *think* existence without therefore also asking *what* it is that exists; or simply because they believed that whatever exists must have a cause, since nothing comes from nothing (*ex nihilo nihil fit*). Heidegger may be right that this has become metaphysical common sense, which he deplores. But this does not automatically exclude the question of *why* anything should exist, the grand metaphysical question that even the great rationalist Leibniz himself raised: *why is there something rather than nothing?* On the contrary, following Desmond, this question is the *fundamental* metaphysical question, presupposing a fundamental disposition of "deep openness to the ontological enigma of the 'that it is' of beings." As he memorably puts it: "This is the elemental wonder of metaphysical astonishment: astonishment at the sheer being there of the world, its givenness as given into being, not the 'what' of beings, but 'the that of being at all.' This is at the end of determinate science and more akin to religious reverence or aesthetic appreciation. Perhaps it is even a kind of unknowing love."[66] Granted, for his part, Leibniz does not linger over his own question but immediately provides his ready rational answer, *nothing is without a cause*, dispensing with the question of being, of existence, the moment it is raised. And Heidegger laments—not without reason—that something similar is true of modern philosophy in general, which he traces back to Suárez.

In the interest of determining the future of Christian metaphysics, we thus need to refine our response to Heidegger. Specifically, we need to address his legitimate concern that the Suarezian *distinctio rationis* paves the way for the modern reduction of ontology to epistemology and thereby for the whole of modern philosophy up to Nietzsche as a metaphysics of subjectivity. For here existence is nothing but the actualization of a given possibility, *which already exists,* having been "previously produced by God." [67] Indeed, this is why, quoting Aristotle, Suárez can say that "adding being to a thing does not add anything to it," but merely denotes the transition from one state to another, that is, from potentiality to actuality.[68] As Heidegger, commenting on this passage, pointedly observes, "Existence adds nothing. This is exactly the Kantian thesis. *Existentia nihil addit rei seu essentiae actuali.* Existence adds nothing to the actual what."[69] It is not without reason, therefore, that Heidegger can claim that metaphysics has trivialized the question of being, which is always already *essentially* predetermined by metaphysical concepts, especially that of actuality.

But again, pace Heidegger (and Rubenstein), if one follows Thomas (or Desmond) instead of Suárez, there is nothing about Christian metaphysics that forecloses the question of existence or the experience of wonder that it should elicit. On the contrary, the Thomistic *distinctio realis underscores* this question, and does so in a way that is far more radical and pressing than it ever would have been for the Greeks, who maintained the eternity of the world. Thus, notwithstanding his valorization of the pre-Socratics, Heidegger's interest in this question is *indebted* to the very Christian tradition, which, he alleges, has forgotten it. For what is implied by this teaching (for which existence *cannot* be included in the essence of any thing) is precisely the radical and unmasterable *difference* between essence and existence, between the sheer *fact* of being and our own conceptions of it. Indeed, countering all the metaphysical absolutisms from Parmenides to Hegel to Nietzsche, which threaten to close this creaturely gap in a usurpation of the divine, the point of the real distinction is precisely to *hold open* this difference and abide within this difference as the space of creaturely being *and* thought, neither of which is reducible to the other. Thus, whatever one makes of the Suarezian *distinctio rationis,* in no way on the Thomistic view can the question of existence be subsumed under the question of essence; nor, on the Thomistic view, can it be explained in terms of a Scotistic *distinctio modalis*, which would reduce the question of existence to a mode of the creature's *preexisting* essence. For this would again reduce the question of being to the question of being as possible being (i.e., essential being) or actual being (i.e., existing being), when what is at issue is precisely the question of there being anything, even anything possible, at all.

Far, then, from being essentially essentialistic (as Heidegger and his school tend to claim), a metaphysics based upon the real distinction militates equally against every essentialism, which is heedless of the gratuity of existence, and every existentialism, which is heedless of the creature's divine determination and destiny. Certainly, given its ontological constitution (its inhabiting the span of the real distinction), it is possible for thought to ascend to a rarefied essentialism, an abstract logic, which automatically comprises being within itself and forgets the wonder of existence. This is Heidegger's concern, and nowhere is this more evident than in Hegel, the modern-day heir of Parmenides, whom Schelling impugned precisely on this account.[70] Equally, in Promethean rebellion against all empyrean determinations, which are perceived as oppressive and as a form of imprisonment, thought can recoil with Nietzsche into the raw existential ground of possibilities proper to a lonely subject, who, left to his or her own possibilities (Nietzsche's *Wille zur Macht*, Heidegger's *je seine Möglichkeit*), is the sole arbiter, creator, and god of any meaning or value. In short, by dint of its creaturely constitution, creaturely thought can ascend to identity and sameness (with Parmenides) or descend into the flux of difference (with Heraclitus); it can ascend to an absolute determinism and fatalism (resignedly away from the freedom of historical existence) or descend into nihilism (in rebellious flight from the determinacy of essence). Or, in the ultimate example of creaturely defiance, which can tolerate no transcendence, thought can attempt to overcome creaturely difference entirely by collapsing one to the other: essence into brute existence, divine identity into chthonic difference, eternalizing and divinizing the becoming of difference as such (as one sees paradigmatically in Nietzsche and his French disciple Deleuze). In this case, however, the very difference that is so triumphantly affirmed is ironically denied; for with the collapse of any real difference (not just between creaturely essence and existence, but ultimately between the divine and the human, the absolute and the relative, the transcendent and the immanent) all is rendered univocally meaningless. Such are the basic poles and parameters of creaturely thought. In and of themselves, however, each represents an extreme, a *termination* of the natural *movement* of creaturely thought—as does, above all, the titanic attempt to obliterate any memory of the creaturely difference between essence and existence, the immanent and the transcendent, which is characteristic of postmodern atheism. In short, it represents a deadening absolutization of one side of the real distinction, a failure to think *as a creature* and abide *as a creature* within the metaxological space of what Przywara calls the "analogy of being" and Desmond calls the "being of the between."[71]

What, though, of Heidegger's charge that the real distinction is at the end of the day a superficial, ontic distinction that does not get at the question of ontological difference? As he rhetorically puts it, "But doesn't a quite different, more far-reaching distinction underlie the difference of *hoti estin* [that something is] and *ti estin* [what something is]?"[72] Indeed it does, and Heidegger is right to press this question. For, according to the Thomistic tradition, the real distinction is precisely not reducible to itself but points to a *greater difference* of which it is merely an analogue: an *ontological difference* between the real distinction, as a *creaturely* distinction, and the divine, which is both intimated *in* this distinction and infinitely *transcends* this distinction. In other words, the real, ontic distinction between essence and existence is not immanently self-contained but (to adopt Desmond's idiom) porous, being intersected by a still profounder, ontological difference between the creature, whose being is inherently in becoming (*in fieri*), and God, who simply *IS* (*Ipsum Esse*).

Admittedly, Heidegger will contend that here we have simply reintroduced another ontic distinction. But, of course, Heidegger can make such a charge only because he divorces God from Being and elevates the latter over the former, idolatrously treating God as an entity, as an ontic being, which appears like other beings on the ultimate horizon of

Being and, invariably, as ontologically *inferior* to it. A Christian, therefore, can rest content in giving theology priority over the usurpations of
Heideggerian philosophy, which, under cover of the language of ontological difference and the illusion of profundity it provides, willfully
forgets the *real* ontological difference between God and creation—a
difference that compels one not only to childlike wonder (in light of
the real ontic distinction between essence and existence) but also, and
more profoundly, to reverence (in light of the real ontological difference
between God and creation). This is the second and more radical difference that is forgotten in the forgetfulness of *metaphysics.*

Trinitarian Redux: A Metaphysical Postlude

I hope now to have shown that Christian metaphysics has its own
resources for responding to Heidegger's concerns (it certainly has
them in the *more original* philosophy of William Desmond) and that
it also has its own resources for seeing the comparative shortcomings
of Heidegger's philosophy. It is not, in any event, that one must go
beyond metaphysics, as the latest titles would have us believe; no real
thinker can fail to think metaphysically. Rather, one must simply get
metaphysics right: one must perceive the question of existence as a
question; one must perceive the question of essence as a question; and
one must perceive their correlation in created being as an even more
inscrutable question, which points beyond itself to something beyond
all human thought and being. Only then, in fact, do we begin to think
meta-physically, when the real distinction, which lies at the foundation of all creaturely being and thought, itself becomes a question—a
mystery—pointing to an answer that it cannot itself provide. This is
what Erich Przywara means by *analogical* metaphysics, a metaphysics that opens upward—*anō*—from within the dialectics of creaturely
thought and being to what lies beyond all creaturely thought and
being. This is what William Desmond means by the *porosity* of the
between, which cannot contain itself but points beyond itself to an
inscrutable, agapeic origin. This is that primal space that is made for

what exceeds it, and which leaves one frustrated and unsatisfied with all philosophical attempts, however refined, to deny it—and to deny metaphysics.

This is not simply because we cannot help but think meta-physically—which should be considered a gift, an endowment of our created nature, and an indelible sign of our origin—but because *Being itself*, as revealed by Christ, *is fundamentally meta-physical*. It is meta-physical above all in the trinitarian nature of the origin: in the procession and circumincession of the *hypostases*, each of which possesses the divine nature by transcending itself. It is metaphysical by analogy in that created being, which is made to image the divine, cannot be fulfilled—cannot fully *be* what it is—without transcending itself, like the Son of God, in agapeic service to its agapeic source. In the meta-physical words of the firstborn of creation, who, more than Heidegger, understands what it means to be: "Whoever would save his life will lose it, but whoever loses his life for my sake will find it" (Matt. 16:25). To put this paradoxical saying into the metaphysical idiom that it implies: the way to eternal life, following Christ *beyond* one's nature and thus to the *realization* of one's nature, consists in an analogous meta-physical procession (Phil. 3:13), whereby one is progressively divinized (2 Pet. 1:4) and, through conformity to Christ, united to God the Father, who before all ages is eternally, meta-physically *beyond himself* in his Son (who mirrors the meta-physics of the Father in the meta-physics of the incarnation). And what, then, to complete the trinitarian taxis, is the work of the Spirit if not to bring creation to its meta-physical fulfillment *beyond itself* in the saints, that is, in a blazing, manifold rendering of Christ, who did not cling to his divine nature but precisely left it behind (Phil. 2:6)? Indeed, were not all the saints, who together with their head constitute the *totus Christus*, in some sense metaphysicians? Was not Abraham when he left his *origin* and all that he had in *Ur* of the Chaldees a type of the Metaphysician to come? We may forget the metaphysical implications of these and other scriptures, including the meta-physics of *Ex-odos*, but it may be hoped that we not forget that metaphysics is another word—and perhaps the most sublime of philosophical words—for love.

Notes

1. Mark A. Wrathall, ed., *Religion after Metaphysics* (Cambridge: Cambridge University Press, 2003); John Panteleimon Manoussakis, *God after Metaphysics* (Bloomington: Indiana University Press, 2007); and Kevin Hector, *Theology without Metaphysics* (Cambridge: Cambridge University Press, 2011).

2. Augustine, *Confessions*, trans. Henry Chadwick (Oxford: Oxford University Press, 1998), 172.

3. For an example of the more reflective posture, following Heidegger, see Jean-Luc Marion, "The 'End of Metaphysics' as a Possibility," in Wrathall, *Religion after Metaphysics*, 166–89.

4. Dominique Janicaud and Jean François Mattéi, *Heidegger: From Metaphysics to Thought* (Albany: SUNY Press, 1995), 1: "No sooner was *eon emmenai* uncovered in Parmenides' poem than the sophists denied the veracity of any discourse on being." The archaic *eon emmenai*, which is notoriously difficult to translate since it appears to be the tautology "being is," though Heidegger prefers to read it more in terms of "being in its presencing," comes from the cryptic B6 fragment of Parmenides's poem, χρὴ τὸ λέγειν, τὸ νοεῖν τ᾽· ἐὸν ἔμμεναι· ἔστι γὰρ εἶναι, μηδὲν δ᾽οὐκ ἔστιν, which one could possibly translate as follows: "It is necessarily the case that whatever is spoken or thought about is in being. For what is is, and what is not possible is not."

5. See Kevin Hector, *Theology without Metaphysics: God, Language, and the Spirit of Recognition* (Cambridge: Cambridge University Press, 2012), 16–27.

6. This is so, especially since metaphysics has now been associated with violence and the "perpetuation of unjust social arrangements." See Hector, *Theology without Metaphysics*, 268. This is a curious development in light of Levinas's ethical philosophy. See *Totality and Infinity*, trans. Alphonso Lingis (Pittsburgh, PA: Dusquene University Press, 1969), 33–52. It is curious in that for one thinker metaphysics is thought to justify the reduction of the other to the same; for another, it is an explicitly ethical figure that resists violence and safeguards the otherness of the other. Clearly, the word *metaphysics* can be employed in very different ways.

7. *BB*, xvi.

8. See the introduction to Erich Przywara, *Analogia Entis: Metaphysics: Original Structure and Universal Rhythm*, trans. John Betz and David B. Hart (Grand Rapids, MI: Eerdmans, 2014), 83–115.

9. Martin Heidegger, *Nietzsche*, vols. 3 and 4, trans. David Farrell Krell (San Francisco: Harper and Row, 1987), 8 f. Conveniently, this designation serves to displace Nietzsche's pretensions to originality and to highlight the greater originality of Heidegger himself, who from his master perspective on the history of thought can now claim the distinction of being the first postmetaphysical thinker (mimicking the same megalomania that one finds in Hegel's claims to absolute knowledge).

10. See Jacques Derrida, *Positions*, trans. and annot. Alan Bass (Chicago: University of Chicago Press, 1981), 14.

11. As Przywara argued in the 1930s, what we have in Heidegger is not the absence of metaphysics but a "magical metaphysics." See Erich Przywara, "Katholische Metaphysik," *Stimmen der Zeit* 125 (1933): 228, where he contrasts Heidegger's "magical metaphysics" of Being qua Nothing with the "mystical metaphysics" of Catholicism.

12. *GB*, 9. The case of Heidegger is instructive here, for even as he turns away from metaphysics, one could argue that his philosophy turns on a pref- erential *metaphysical* option for potentiality—more precisely, for the *nihil* of pure potentiality—over actuality; that his "ontological difference" between being and beings (a difference that is supposedly beyond the ken of meta- physics) is at least analogous to the difference between the two terms of this ancient metaphysical pairing; and that, as Przywara pointed out, the rhythm in Heidegger between being's manifestation and greater concealment remains analogous to the familiar rhythm between positive and negative theologies of the Christian metaphysical tradition. See Erich Przywara, *In und Gegen: Stellungnahmen zur Zeit* (Nürnberg: Glock und Lutz, 1955), 58 f.

13. See Martin Heidegger, "Overcoming Metaphysics," in *The End of Philosophy*, trans. Joan Stambaugh (Chicago: University of Chicago Press, 2003), 85: "Metaphysics cannot be abolished like an opinion. One can by no means leave it behind as a doctrine no longer believed in and represented." Indeed, as he put it in his late lecture "Time and Being," "Our task is to cease all overcoming, and leave metaphysics to itself" (*Time and Being*, trans. Joan Stambaugh [Chicago: University of Chicago Press, 2002], 24). This does not mean, however, that Heidegger was not in his own mind "beyond meta- physics" or that he did not consider his own philosophy "postmetaphysical." On the contrary, for him metaphysics continues to represent an inferior, ontic level of thinking that he himself, the thinker of ontological difference, has transcended. What he means is that metaphysics cannot be overcome in that it endures as a possible way of thinking; and that even the thinker, who might be tempted by it, even one as great as Heidegger, must "deal with it" in the way

that one deals with an illness or passion that can be "dealt with" (*verwunden*) but not entirely "overcome" (*überwunden*).

14. Martin Heidegger, "The Ontological Constitution of Metaphysics," in *Identity and Difference*, trans. Joan Stambaugh (Chicago: University of Chicago Press, 2002), 54.

15. Santiago Zabala, *The Remains of Being: Hermeneutic Ontology after Metaphysics* (New York: Columbia University Press, 2009), 23.

16. This, notwithstanding Heidegger's novel attempt to read him differently and save him from the obvious connotations of his maxim. See Heidegger, *Nietzsche*, vol. 4, 95: "'Measure' has the sense of the measuredness of unconcealment." For further discussion, see Jacques Taminaux, *Heidegger and the Project of Fundamental Ontology* (Albany: SUNY Press, 1991), 165.

17. To be sure, as with Protagoras's maxim, Heidegger attempts to uncover the more original meaning of Parmenides's poem; the way in which Parmenides has tended to be received and interpreted, however, is nevertheless the kind of thinking that Heidegger abjures. See Martin Heidegger, *Parmenides*, trans. André Schuwer (Bloomington: Indiana University Press, 1998). See George R. Vick, "Heidegger's Linguistic Rehabilitation of Parmenides' 'Being,'" *American Philosophical Quarterly* 8 (1971): 139–50. For a concise introduction to the scholarly debate about Parmenides, especially the third fragment, which is at issue here, see E. D. Phillips, "Parmenides on Thought and Being," *Philosophical Review* 64 (1955): 546–60.

18. In this regard arguably no modern philosophers illustrate more perfectly what Heidegger means by metaphysics as a metaphysics of subjectivity and a regime of representation than did Berkeley, when he declared *esse est percipi*, or Hegel, when he declared in the preface to the *Philosophy of Right*, "What is rational is what is real; and what is real is rational."

19. Heidegger, "The Ontological Constitution of Metaphysics," 72.

20. This is also why for the Heideggerian school metaphysics cannot be disassociated from power, indeed, why metaphysics precisely funds it, and why Nietzsche was the consummate, unabashed metaphysician in defining truth as the will to power. See Miguel de Beistegui, "Questioning Politics, or Beyond Power," in *The Movement of Nihilism: Heidegger's Thinking after Nietzsche*, ed. Laurence Paul Hemming, Kostas Amiridis, and Bogdan Costea (London: Continuum, 2014), 60 f. This connection is explicit in Kant, who regularly speaks of a priori knowledge as being that which is fully in our power (*Gewalt*). See *Critique of Pure Reason*, B 871; *Critique of Judgment*, §91.

21. Martin Heidegger, *The Principle of Reason*, trans. Reginald Lilly (Bloomington: Indiana University Press, 1996).

22. Heidegger, *On Time and Being*, trans. Joan Stambaugh (Chicago: University of Chicago Press, 2002), 9. My emphasis.

23. Among German Catholics, some of the more prominent, who could be said to constitute the "Catholic Heidegger school," included (notwithstanding the fact that some of them eventually fell out with or were ill treated by Heidegger) Gustav Siewerth, Max Müller, Bernhard Welte, and Karl Rahner. See Thomas O'Meara, O.P., "Johannes B. Lotz, S.J., and Martin Heidegger in Conversation," *American Catholic Philosophical Quarterly* 84 (2010): 125–31. Among living philosophers, Jean-Luc Marion is undoubtedly the most prominent, though his own philosophy marks a decided advance beyond Heidegger from the primacy of Being to the primacy of love. Among contemporary theologians, see Laurence Paul Hemming, *Heidegger's Atheism: The Refusal of a Theological Voice* (Notre Dame, IN: University of Notre Dame Press, 2002). Indeed, it would be no exaggeration to say that Heidegger's philosophy has become to many a *praeambulum fidei* in the way that was once the case with Plato, Aristotle, and (among many Protestant theologians of the nineteenth and twentieth centuries) Kant. There is, of course, this ironic difference: whereas faith was once happily served by metaphysics (from Augustine to Thomas), it is now ostensibly served by anti- or post-metaphysical polemic, either the critical chastening of metaphysics in Kant, who famously purported thereby to make room for faith, or by the overcoming of metaphysics in Heidegger, who, curiously enough, could claim to be doing the same thing as Kant—though neither of them had any serious interest in the claims of Christianity, since both held philosophy, and not theology, to be the master discourse.

24. See Desmond's nuanced reading of Heidegger in *AOO*, 209–63.

25. Martin Heidegger, *Basic Questions of Philosophy*, trans. Richard Rojcewicz and André Schuwer (Bloomington: Indiana University Press, 1994), 169. Mary-Jane Rubenstein admirably captures the spirit of Heidegger's critique in *Strange Wonder: The Closure of Metaphysics and the Opening of Awe* (New York: Columbia University Press, 2008), 17: "Metaphysics *thinks* it thinks being, but really only thinks in terms of beings. Even when it proclaims itself to be 'ontological' metaphysics is merely 'ontic.' Attentive only to what is representable, metaphysics is incapable of thinking the unrepresentable event that sets representation in motion" (emphasis original).

26. Rubenstein, *Strange Wonder*, 17. As Rubenstein summarily puts it, echoing Heidegger, "To [escape the 'closure of metaphysics' and] attune itself to unconcealment . . . thinking will have to go back—and forward—to something like wonder" (28).

27. See Cyril J. O'Regan, *The Anatomy of Misremembering: Von Balthasar's Response to Philosophical Modernity*, vol. 1 (New York: Herder and Herder, 2014). Here it is not simply a matter of what Hegel or Heidegger may have "gotten wrong" about Christianity (in Hegel) or the Christian metaphysical tradition (in Heidegger), as though their memories had simply failed them, but of their counterfeit replication and creative misreading of it: "Heidegger, then, neither remembers scrupulously nor fairly, and tends to offer an alternative to Christian discourse, practice, and forms of life which involve a considerable amount of garbling" (25).

28. See Cyril O'Regan, "Answering Back: Augustine's Critique of Heidegger," in *Human Destinies: Philosophical Essays in Memory of Gerald Hanratty*, ed. Fran O'Rourke (Notre Dame, IN: University of Notre Dame Press, 2012), 134–84.

29. Of course, just as memory is layered, misremembering is layered, especially when the misremembering is intentional: when true memories are suppressed and covered over by false memories. In this case, complicating matters, beyond the duplicity with oneself, repeated misremembering can gradually cause one to forget the difference between the true and the false: at which point the false memory has become the true. (By analogy, one could say that an evil person is not initially evil but that he at first lives in tension with himself, with his psyche divided, still knowing the difference between good and evil; at a certain point, however, as evil progressively takes over, evil become indistinguishable from the good: indeed, evil has become good. For this reason, too, the devil's lie to Eve was an ironic one: it is the sinless, above all, who know the difference between good and evil, the latter of which they find instinctively abhorrent, whereas sin gradually leads to the psychic collapse of any difference between them.) As such, the task of recollection, whether on the part of or on behalf of the amnesiac, requires discernment—an ability to distinguish between true and false memories—and, ideally, if one's memory is to be healed, attention to the passions that may have caused one to misremember and to *want* to misremember in the first place. What is it, for instance, that makes Christ so forgettable to Heidegger? If Nietzsche was at some level, even as the self-declared "Anti-Christ," a Christ-haunted man, what is it that makes Heidegger so blithely indifferent to him? Was Nietzsche perhaps more of a residual Christian? Needless to say, such reasons for misremembering are beyond the scope of the present inquiry and, for that matter, any scholastic inquiry—if, indeed, the heart of man, as Augustine says, is an abyss (*In Ps.* 42 [41], 13). What is under consideration here therefore is merely the fact of misremembering and the visible, objective mechanisms that, functioning like ideologies, perpetuate it.

30. Heidegger, "The Ontological Constitution of Metaphysics," 54.

31. See Martin Heidegger, "Plato's Doctrine of Truth," in *Pathmarks*, ed. William McNeil (Cambridge: Cambridge University Press, 1998), 155–82. See also Drew Hyland's essay in *Heidegger and the Greeks: Interpretive Essays* (Indianapolis: Indiana University Press, 2006), 20 f.: "The Good, like *chora*, like *eros*, undercuts 'Platonism' [i.e., a caricature of Plato] from the beginning."

32. Martin Heidegger, *The Principle of Reason*, trans. Reginald Lilly (Bloomington: Indiana University Press, 1996). The subversion of this principle, which is a perfect example of Heideggerian and proto-Derridean deconstruction, plays on the different meanings of the German word *Satz* (which can mean both principle and leap) and (according to the second meaning, unintended by Leibniz himself) implies an ironic departure from this same principle as the foundation of all real thought.

33. *Theaetetus*, 155d.

34. *Metaphysics*, 982b.

35. For Heidegger's discussion of wonder and its various analogues, see *Basic Questions of Philosophy*, 133–56.

36. Cf. Etienne Gilson, *Being and Some Philosophers*, 2nd ed. (Toronto: PIMS, 1952), 20: "Even though Plato does not seem to worry about the fact that Ideas are, he cannot help but worry about the fact that each of them is that which it is."

37. See Rubenstein, *Strange Wonder*, 12.

38. See Rubenstein, *Strange Wonder*, 13: "Wonder is the movement of the man who does not know on his way to finding out, to get at the bottom of that at which he wonders and to determine its cause." The reference to Albert's *Opera Omnia* could not, however, be verified.

39. Rubenstein, *Strange Wonder*, 13.

40. Bonaventure, *The Journey of the Mind to God*, trans. Philotheus Boehner (Indianapolis, IN: Hackett, 1993), 10.

41. Braig's work *On Being: An Outline of Ontology* (Freiburg: Herder, 1896), which exercised a considerable influence on Heidegger, begins with an epigraph from Bonaventure's *Itinerarium Mentis in Deum*, ch. 5, §§3–4. See Sonya Sikka, *Forms of Transcendence: Heidegger and Medieval Mystical Theology* (Albany: SUNY Press, 1997), 43–107. For an extensive analysis of Heidegger's relation to scholasticism and a penetrating analysis of his thought as a whole, see Sean J. McGrath, *The Early Heidegger and Medieval Philosophy: Phenomenology for the Godforsaken* (Washington, DC: Catholic University of America Press, 2006).

42. Heidegger, *Basic Questions of Philosophy*, 136.

43. Ibid., 141, 143.

44. Ibid., 46.

45. Heidegger, *The Principle of Reason*, 35 f.

46. Martin Heidegger, *The Basic Problems of Phenomenology*, trans. Albert Hofstadter (Bloomington: Indiana University Press, 1982), 100.

47. Whether or not Heidegger had any general animus toward Christianity, like Nietzsche his critique of it follows directly from his attitude toward Plato: if Nietzsche was the anti-Plato—and by extension the "anti-Christ"—primarily on account of his defense of Thrasymachus and his corresponding deconstruction of the doctrine of the Good, Heidegger was the anti-Plato (and by extension tended to disparage Christianity) essentially on account of his animus toward Plato's doctrine of truth (as *recta ratio* and correct representation) and the Platonic doctrine of demiurgic creation. See Heidegger, *Basic Questions of Philosophy*, 102, 122.

48. Heidegger, *Basic Problems of Phenomenology*, 104. Heidegger grants that this tendency runs deep, so deep in fact as to be reflected in the German language, for which what is real is none other than *das Wirkliche*, i.e., that which is caused, *gewirkt*. See 87: "Being is *actualitas*. Something exists if it is *actu*, ergo, on the basis of an *agere*, a *Wirken*, a working, operating or effecting (*energein*). Existence (*existere*) in this broadest sense . . . means *Gewirktheit*, enactedness, effectedness, or again, the *Wirklichkeit*, actuality, that lies in the enactedness (*actualitas, energeia, entelecheia*)." For him, it is nevertheless a way of thinking from which we need to be displaced—through art and poetry—if we are to return to a more authentic, primordial way of being in the world.

49. According to Heidegger, there is a direct connection here between scholasticism and the *mathesis universalis* of modern philosophy and science (whereby Heidegger turns out to be an unwitting ally in Christianity's self-defense against the charges of antiscientific irrationalism that have been unabated since Galileo).

50. As is well known, Heidegger found an example of this more original disposition and the promise of this new beginning in the poetry of Hölderlin: "Hölderlin still thinks metaphysically. But his poetry is different." See Martin Heidegger, *Hölderlins Hymne "Andenken,"* in *Gesamtausgabe*, vol. 52 (Frankfurt: Vittorio Klostermann, 1992), 120. As he plaintively puts it in his reading of Hölderlin's hymn, regardless of how much *eisegesis* may be involved here: "How can one . . . come to see with a free state of mind and an open eye that something can be without it doing something or

being caused, that we can be with an other without this other being caused by another" (100).

51. *BB*, 137.

52. *AOO*, 251.

53. Heidegger, *Basic Problems of Phenomenology*, 118.

54. *AOO*, 248.

55. *AOO*, 248.

56. I mean here the kind of reasons discussed by Pascal and Newman in their penetrating analyses of religious belief *and unbelief.*

57. Just as for Heidegger metaphysics is inadequate to the task of philosophy, for Marion it is inadequate to the task of theology, being unable to think God, who, in the late Schelling's terms, is not subject to being but precisely the "Lord of being," i.e., free with regard to his own existence, and only as such free to be and give himself to us. Only thus, it seems, does Marion believe that we are able to wrest God free from the counterfeit double of the Cartesian *causa sui*, who is metaphysically bound to be the cause of his own being.

58. See Jean-Luc Marion, *Being Given: Toward a Phenomenology of Givenness*, trans. Jeffrey L. Kosky (Stanford, CA: Stanford University Press, 2002).

59. See Meister Eckhart, *Predigten, Traktate*, ed. Franz Pfeiffer (Leipzig: G. J. Göschen, 1857), 659: "Spräche man von Gott er ist, das wäre hinzugelegt."

60. *BB*, 8.

61. Although the Christian metaphysical tradition is by no means unanimous here—in light of Scotus's *distinctio modalis* and Suárez's *distinctio rationis cum fundamento in re*—I limit myself to the Thomist tradition, as represented, among others, by Giles of Rome (though an Augustinian) and Capreolus, who defended the *distinctio realis* precisely in order to uphold the gratuity of creation, for which existence is *not* included in its essence. While the distinction is discussed in various places in Thomas's corpus, the locus classicus for this discussion is still Thomas's *De ente et essentia.*

62. Obviously, this is a rather crass generalization, given how thoroughly Heidegger ends up reinterpreting *essentia* as the *Wesen* of *Seyn*. My point here, however, is merely to show that the real distinction figures throughout Heidegger's writings. This is most obvious when he speaks in his early writings of the *Wesen* of *Dasein*, i.e., the *essence of [human] existence*, but it is also evident after his so-called turn: as he gradually shifts his emphasis from a pure existentialism that would have beings unencumbered by essential determinations (so that one can appreciate *Dasein* in its "thrownness" and beings

in their givenness) to a curiously mystical doctrine of the essence—*Wesen*—of being (*Seyn*) as the horizon of beings (*Seiendes*). Granted, the language of *essentia* has undergone a radical transformation that no scholastic would recognize. But the *terms* of the real distinction have not gone away; they have simply been refigured, making Heidegger's philosophy, which is supposed to be an "overcoming" of metaphysics, in reality a strange permutation of it.

63. See Heidegger, *The End of Philosophy*, introd. and 1–19.

64. As even Heidegger points out, "The Scholastic way of posing the question is still to be regarded more highly than the unsurpassable ignorance about these problems in contemporary philosophy." See Heidegger, *The Basic Problems of Phenomenology*, 90.

65. For an incisive analysis of how philosophy is inexorably located within the play of this distinction between essence and existence, such that, to put it in contemporary terms, analytic philosophy is a parody of essentialism, whereas continental philosophy is a parody of existentialism, see Przywara, *Analogia Entis*, esp. 317–47.

66. *IST*, 13.

67. Suárez, *Disputationes Metaphysicae*, Disp. 31, 6, in *Opera Omnia*, ed. Berton, vol. 26. Quoted in Heidegger, *The Basic Problems of Phenomenology*, 97.

68. Heidegger, *The Basic Problems of Phenomenology*, 97.

69. Ibid.

70. One has perhaps insufficiently attended to the influence of the late Schelling (the real father of modern existentialism) on Heidegger. See Schelling, *Grundlegung der positiven Philosophie: Münchner Vorlesung WS 1832/33 und SS 1833*, ed. Horst Fuhrmans, vol. 1 (Turin: Bottega d'Erasmo, 1972), 82: "Plato says: 'The pathos of philosophy is wonder.' But the need for wonder is something common to humanity, which is why people praise artists and poets. A deduction, a purely *logical* necessity, on the other hand, tends to produce the *contrary* feeling" (emphasis original).

71. In his *Analogia Entis*, Przywara, borrowing Aristotle's idiom (*Nicomachean Ethics* 1131b) calls this metaxological space "analogical" (τὸ γὰρ ἀνάλογον μέσον). See *Analogia Entis*, 206.

72. Heidegger, *The End of Philosophy*, 8.

CHAPTER 3

On the Cause of Metaphysical Indeterminacy and the Origin of Being

COREY BENJAMIN TUTEWILER

The vast majority of William Desmond's corpus was penned when the postmodern turn against metaphysics was in vogue. Although his efforts to sustain constructive metaphysical thought once set him apart as "an outsider in continental philosophy," he has more recently come to be seen as being in "a certain proximity to the rumblings of the philosophical Zeitgeist."[1] Especially in present-day France, we witness an unabashed return to the perennial questions of the nature of being and its origin. This essay extends an application of Desmond's metaxological metaphysics to the thought of the speculative materialist Quentin Meillassoux.

Meillassoux has been described "as the most rapidly prominent French philosopher in the Anglophone world since Jacques Derrida in the 1960s."[2] His first book, *After Finitude: An Essay on the Necessity of Contingency* (originally published in 2006), marks the beginning of an undertaking to reconcile thought with the absolute.[3] The

French philosopher Alain Badiou (a former teacher of Meillassoux's) comments on the revolutionary nature of this work: "It would be no exaggeration to say that Quentin Meillassoux has opened up a new path in the history of philosophy, hitherto conceived as the history of what it is to know; a path that circumvents Kant's canonical distinction between 'dogmatism,' 'skepticism,' and 'critique.' "[4]

In what follows, I address the question of the sets of relations between mind, being, and the origin of being. I argue that there is a significant complementarity between Meillassoux and Desmond, since both have sufficiently overcome what I consider to be a major limitation of much modern and postmodern thought: namely, inadequate accounts of *metaphysical indeterminacy*, which I define below. Where this complementarity between Meillassoux and Desmond ends, however, my focus moves to how metaxological metaphysics (Desmond) surpasses speculative materialism (Meillassoux) in explanatory power, inasmuch as it is truer to the human condition.

Regarding the theological relevance of this essay, two points can be made. First, the essay is motivated by the language barrier that separates Christian theologians from contemporary continental materialists. Desmond's thought is uniquely equipped to mediate the barrier between these disparate academic communities. Indeed, he is no stranger to the between. Taken together, his sensitivity to the history of Christian thought and his prolonged engagement with the work of Hegel have birthed a philosophical vocabulary that might speak to both audiences. Second, for Meillassoux, the movement beyond modern and postmodern thought is concomitant with a movement toward a unique form of godlessness. Desmond, by contrast, paints a compelling picture of how it can be understood otherwise.

THE CAUSE OF METAPHYSICAL INDETERMINACY

By "metaphysical indeterminacy," I refer to the perceived lack that is "present" when the mind does not have complete and determinate knowledge of being. This essay endeavors to offer an account for this lack. Although a historical survey would show that many philosophers have treated it as a rational problem that is, in one way or another, caused by the finitude of human reason, I contend the issue is more complex.

The manner in which metaphysical indeterminacy is understood is of enormous methodological significance for any metaphysics.[5] Indeed, proper method does not necessarily beget a right orientation toward metaphysical indeterminacy; rather, presuppositions about metaphysical indeterminacy govern the way one proceeds toward an understanding of the nature of being. The way one interprets this lack of complete knowledge affects one's metaphysical method; any ascent toward the truth of being assumes a configuration of, and compensation for, the difference between mind and being. For this reason, metaphysicians should not restrict their consideration to questions *in* metaphysics (questions concerning being simply) but ought also to entertain questions *on* metaphysics (questions that concern the given senses in which mind and being are related in the first place—that is, prior to efforts of conceptualization).[6] Desmond helps to clarify this by pointing out that thinking *in* metaphysics addresses traditional metaphysical questions. In *Being and the Between* he sets these questions in systematic context, investigating origin, creation, things, intelligibilities, selves, communities, being true, and being good. He understands thinking *on* metaphysics as a phenomenology (of sorts) of the preconceptual relationship between mind and being. Thinking *on* metaphysics enables a mindfulness of the various senses in which mind and being are immediately related and provides a conceptual backdrop for the questions *in* metaphysics.

The question of mind's relation to being, then, has a twofold answer. There is, first, a *given, immediate, and preconceptual* relationship between mind and being; and, second, there is a relationship *to be established*—a relationship given coinciding with a relationship sought. Further, these relationships are inextricably intertwined, since the former conditions the manner in which the metaphysician can appropriately undertake the latter. The latter can also be seen as the fulfillment or perfection of the former.

Let me very briefly define how metaphysical indeterminacy has functioned (often uncritically) in philosophies of the past. I begin with the modern stress on the univocal sense of being and the postmodern stress on the equivocal sense of being.[7] This essay speaks to broad and overarching characteristics predominant in both positions rather than addressing individual voices in detail.

Most thinkers working within the Enlightenment tradition treat metaphysical indeterminacy as a *remediable* difference between mind and being. In other words, for the modern thinker this lack of complete knowledge is only a temporary lack—a gap that recedes as reason progresses (if used properly).[8] Just as the mathematician's miscalculation is merely a recognizable and rectifiable error, metaphysical indeterminacy is considered a reparable error on the part of the metaphysician.[9] Thus, "if we regulate the mind properly, then it can dissolve all perplexities, perplexities themselves made determinate as clearly formulated problems."[10] Indeterminacy is the "indefinite that must then be made determinate."[11]

Postmodern philosophy is largely a reactive denunciation of the expectations of modern philosophy. For the postmodern, metaphysical indeterminacy is an *irremediable* difference between mind and being. Reason, no matter how it is used, cannot overcome this perceived lack. Postmodern philosophers agree with the modern view that metaphysical determinacy is a lack rooted in human finitude. The postmodern, however, rejects constructive metaphysics entirely: this failure of mind is a necessity with which we must learn to come to terms. This lack, then, expresses the impossibility of the metaphysical dream: mind cannot come to terms with being in a pure and determinate manner.

Although an exhaustive analysis of the way both of these positions fail to account for the nature of being can be given, I am presently more interested in expressing this failure in terms of metaphysical indeterminacy.[12] To begin, the modern and postmodern, as defined above, both presuppose that being is a determinate totality, and both are likewise constrained by an inordinate anticipation of completion in metaphysical science. Although this is more obvious for the modern, it is nevertheless arguably the case for the postmodern as well.[13] As some have noted, despite the postmodern hostility to metaphysical totality, it often betrays its own concerns and perpetuates the very same problems that are at work in the modern.[14]

An examination of the postmodern critique of modern metaphysics and epistemology will clarify this. The postmodern insists that the modern drive toward totality and completion is met with an *impotence* of reason, an inability to realize the metaphysical and epistemological ends it seeks. The modern anticipates completion in metaphysical science, but the postmodern rejects this on the basis of the contingency and finitude of human beings. Postmodern thought embraces this impotence. But in this very embrace, postmodern thought reveals that the metaphysical and epistemological expectations of modern thought are operative in its philosophical orientation. In *Ethics and the Between*, Desmond describes this postmodern assumption of impotence as the "self-laceration" of the human. Postmodernism, he writes, is

> an accentuation of the modern, an aggravation of the powers of self-determining, but now grown skeptical and bitter about themselves: wanting still to be absolute, insisting on themselves always, secretly now, overtly now; and yet knowing that these cannot be absolute. . . . The self-determining human lacerates itself, as it still clings to itself; preaches about the other, while still shouting about its right to be in control; vacillates between knowing in its heart of hearts that the tale is told and the impotence to let go of its own power. The laceration brings us to no self, no God; and we are in the between with a bewilderment we hysterically call creative freedom, all the while without wise counsel about our bewilderment and our hysteria.[15]

This is not to say that the postmodern is wrong to call attention to modern philosophy's inability to realize its expectations, but what is centrally problematic about the modern is not altogether reducible to this impotence. The issue lies deeper within the underlying presuppositions that provided the conditions for it. Therefore, one will not satisfactorily overcome the modern by calling attention to its impotence if one nevertheless retains its basic presuppositions. That is, *one must relinquish the very underlying conditions that motivate this inordinate goal in the first place.*

AN ALTERNATIVE UNDERSTANDING
OF METAPHYSICAL INDETERMINACY

The modern and the postmodern alike understand metaphysical inde-terminacy as a failure of reason or mind. According to Meillassoux and Desmond, neither tradition discerns that it is actually the *nondeter-minate nature of being* that gives rise to metaphysical indeterminacy. Against the modern and postmodern, metaphysical indeterminacy is not to be understood principally as an epistemological problem but an ontological problem. In order to surpass the aporias of modern and postmodern thought, therefore, it is necessary to abandon the notion of being as a determinate, proportionate totality.

In this alternative to the modern and postmodern positions, we find a significant preliminary consensus between the metaphysical commitments of Meillassoux and Desmond: they agree that in order to move beyond the modern and postmodern one must understand that metaphysical indeterminacy is not principally caused by the finitude of human reason but is somehow grounded in the very nature of being itself. To help clarify the meaning of this, Desmond identifies four instances in which being's recalcitrance to totalization and determi-nate intelligibility is especially apparent on a phenomenal level, which he calls "hyperboles of being"—"signs in immanence of that which exceeds exhaustive immanent determination or self-determination."[16]

The first hyperbole pertains to the astonishing fact that being exists at all. Why being, why not nothing? According to Desmond, this question is unique since it is "not about coming to be in the sense of determination, but about coming to be as *that it is at all*—that beings are in being at all rather than nothing."[17] Such a question provokes an astonishment that beings exist at all, for they contain no immanent reason for their existence. The question, moreover, intimates a strange sense in which being is, at its very core, *without why, irreducibly gra-tuitous* from even the highest summit of human knowing.[18] Meillas-soux makes a similar observation: "there is no reason for anything to be or to remain thus and so rather than otherwise."[19]

The remaining hyperboles turn from the astonishing "that it is" of being to something of "what it is."[20] Desmond refers to the second as the "aesthetics of happening"—the "self-showing" of a universe "marked by radiance beyond fixation, by singularity, dynamic form, and ordered, open wholeness."[21] The "surd thereness" and radical contingency of the first hyperbole becomes the singularity of aesthetically experienced being: "that it is" becomes "it is *this*."[22] Further, the universe's immanent power of novelty and creativity, which births a beautiful and harmonious order of things, is an undeniable happening. But nothing about the universe itself guarantees this happening. It is without immanent reason, for "the intelligibility of finite intelligibility" is not "itself intelligible in finite terms."[23]

The third hyperbole pertains to the "erotics of selving."[24] Desmond uses the term *erotic* to signify a being that is driven toward completion, wholeness, and fulfillment. "This hyperbole of self-being" reveals that human beings are marked by a certain "indeterminacy which allows of the freedom of self-becoming, as well as the potential for greater chaos."[25] Given "the equivocity of aesthetic happening," it is a wonder that human beings can identify themselves as a kind of unity.[26] It is an even greater wonder that human beings have a say in how the determination of this unity unfolds. The capacity for desiring, knowing, loving, and self-determination are "all human exceedings beyond finite determinability."[27]

The fourth and final hyperbole pertains to the "agapeics of community": "that things are communicative in their being, that they are together, this is astonishing."[28] Erotic selving does not tell the full story of how things are in the universe, for there is a "metaxological relativity of community beyond immanent self-mediating totality."[29] In a sense, the agapeics of community reveals an imperative to continually think together the extremities of pluralism and wholeness without reducing one to the other. On the one hand, beings are not monads, as though the universe is a collection of isolated self-determining entities. On the other hand, the individuality and singularity of beings are not absorbed into a totality or whole, "for community is a cum-unity: a 'being with' of unities, a togetherness of integrities of being, not just one whole."[30] Experience reveals a *something more* that cannot find full expression in terms of pluralism, absorbing monism, or some intricate interplay between the two: the community of beings. This community is hyperbolic, without rational guarantee or necessity—a happening *without reason.*

The modern and postmodern presuppositions about metaphysical indeterminacy render them unequipped to reflect upon these hyperboles of being, since they exceed purely immanent determination. The modern will look for an answer in the wrong places, and the postmodern will discourage looking for an answer in these wrong places. But neither seeks out a transformation of metaphysical presuppositions that will allow insight into these hyperbolic dimensions of reality. In discerning that metaphysical indeterminacy is somehow caused by the nature of being itself, Meillassoux and Desmond each attempt to offer such an account.

Speculative Materialism: Correlationism, Facticity, and Hyper-Chaos

Meillassoux's *After Finitude* begins with a revelation that he argues has the power to break apart the foundations of contemporary philosophy. On the one hand, empirical science has demonstrated a capacity to make judgments about the universe in itself, the truth of which is independent of our relation to it. Specifically, science's ability to date (albeit in the form of revisable hypotheses) the advent of the universe, the advent of life, and the eventual termination of life on our planet demonstrates its ability to know being prior to, and independent of, its manifestation to consciousness.[31] On the other hand, Meillassoux argues that contemporary philosophy (both continental and analytic) is unequipped to accommodate these scientific claims. Since Kant, he asserts, philosophy has predominantly viewed being as inaccessible to thought. Hence, "up until Kant, one of the principal problems of philosophy was to think substance, while ever since Kant, it has consisted in trying to think the correlation [between mind and being]."[32] Meillassoux identifies this line of thought as "correlationism," by which "we mean the idea according to which we only ever have access to the correlation between thinking and being, and never to either term considered apart from the other. We will henceforth call correlationism any current of thought which maintains the unsurpassable character of the correlation so defined. Consequently, it becomes possible to say that every philosophy which disavows naïve realism has become a variant of correlationism."[33] "Science itself," therefore, "enjoins us to discover the source of its own absoluteness," and *After Finitude* responds to this call.[34] It is an attempt to overcome the epistemological limits of correlationism by rethinking thought's relationship to the absolute.[35]

After exposing contemporary philosophy's inability to accommodate the "absolute reach" of mathematics and science, Meillassoux turns to the question of what form his argument should take.[36] In order for philosophy to accommodate this absolute reach it must ground the latter in some kind of absolute necessity. Descartes provides an exemplary model of this line of argumentation, inasmuch as he grounds the reliability of our commonsense apprehension of the external world upon a proof of the existence of a supremely good and trustworthy God. In similar fashion, Meillassoux claims that a "derivative absolute" must be founded upon some sort of "primary absolute."[37]

However, Descartes's reliance upon the validity of the ontological argument and its precritical character renders his thesis indefensible in Meillassoux's eyes.[38] Nevertheless, it is the content of Descartes's argument that fails, not its form. In order to provide explanatory capacity for a derivative absolute, philosophy must establish as a ground some absolute necessity—but this necessity need not take the "form of [an] absolutely necessary *entity*."[39]

Meillassoux turns to the question of being's origin, with reference to Wittgenstein and Heidegger, as the key to the solution. For Wittgenstein, he quotes, "it is not how things are in the world that is mystical, but *that* it exists."[40] Similarly, Heidegger holds that the human mind cannot account for the sheer givenness of beings. "Of all beings," Heidegger says, "only the human being, called upon by the voice of Being, experiences the wonder of all wonders: *that* beings are."[41] Meillassoux refers to this instance of metaphysical indeterminacy—this lack or absence of knowledge in reference to the origin of being—as "facticity."[42] In the cases of Wittgenstein and Heidegger, "the fact that beings are, or the fact that there is a logical world, is precisely what cannot be encompassed by the sovereignty of logic and metaphysical reason, and this because of the facticity of the 'there is'; a facticity which can certainly be thought—since it is not grasped through a transcendent revelation, but merely through a grasp of the 'internal limits' of this world—but thought solely on account of our inability to gain access to the absolute ground of what is."[43] Many understand facticity as that which prevents human beings from a relation to the absolute. Meillassoux finds it necessary to reevaluate this limitation, however, because the absolute reach of science presses us to discover the philosophical source of its absoluteness.

For Meillassoux, the answer to overcoming the apparent limitation of facticity demands a "change in outlook."[44] "We must," he writes, "grasp in facticity not the inaccessibility of the absolute [as was the case for Wittgenstein, Heidegger, and most philosophers since Kant] but the unveiling of the in-itself and the eternal property of what is, as opposed to the mark of the perennial deficiency in the thought of what is."[45] Whereas twentieth-century philosophers have understood facticity as a sign of reason's inability to access the absolute ground of being, the speculative materialist holds that facticity expresses the incomplete character of reality itself. In order for us to surpass the impasse of correlationism, Meillassoux states, we must *put back into the thing itself what we mistakenly took to be an incapacity in thought.* In other words, instead of construing the absence of reason inherent in everything as a limit that thought encounters in its search for the ultimate reason, we must understand that this absence of reason *is*, and can *only* be the *ultimate* property of the entity. . . . We must grasp how the ultimate absence of reason . . . is an absolute ontological property, and not the mark of the finitude of our knowledge."[46] Speculative materialism, then, can be understood as a rejection and reversal of the Aristotelian claim that the cause of difficulty in the science of being "is not in things but in us."[47] Being is marked by a constitutive lack—more exactly, a lack of reason or why for its very being at all. Meillassoux's position, therefore, also denies Leibniz's principle of sufficient reason, resulting in what he terms "the principle of unreason."[48]

This principle of unreason, which states that there is no necessary reason for any entity or event to be and be otherwise than it is, has a radical ontological consequence. If there is no ultimate reason for the existence of being, then nothing prevents the possibility that "everything could actually collapse: from trees to stars, from stars to laws, from physical laws to logical laws."[49] In this Meillassoux has discovered the ground he sought: the absolute necessity that will ground the absolute reach of science and mathematics is the absolute necessity of contingency—not merely the contingency of particular entities and events within the universe, but in addition that of the laws and universals that govern them. The truth of being's radical contingency satisfies the criteria for an absolute truth of philosophy; its truth is in no way dependent upon its being thought. Meillassoux coins this absolute "hyper-Chaos," the condition of a universe without reason for its being.[50]

Certainly more could be said on Meillassoux's discussion of this matter. This heavily abbreviated summary of the first half of *After Finitude* presents a mere sliver of his overall argument and sets aside several responses to anticipated objections. We have nevertheless reached a satisfactory account of how the speculative materialist understands metaphysical indeterminacy and its relation to the origin of being. Metaphysical indeterminacy is not caused by the finitude of the mind but by the nature of being itself. Being has no reason to be or to be otherwise than it is, and we can know this. Our astonishment and ignorance of the reason anything exists at all must be transformed into a radical certainty that nothing guarantees the existence or persistence of things and their way of being.

If Meillassoux's conclusions are seductive it is because they cannot be directly refuted by metaphysical argumentation grounded in a phenomenological account of human experience. For instance, Desmond holds that the original ground of being must be understood as consonant with the "irreducible plurality" of the universe.[51] The original ground must have sufficient explanatory power to account for the aforementioned "hyperboles of being," as they exceed exhaustive immanent determination.

As we have seen, however, such an argument has absolutely no bearing on Meillassoux's conclusions, given his claim that a hyper-Chaotic universe is infinitely capable of producing any phenomenal order whatsoever, and without any reason for doing so. Given the phenomenal order of things (including the saturated, hyperbolic nature of phenomena), the speculative materialist's answer to the question of "from whence" is quite simply "from nothing."[52] There is no reason for the hyperboles; they just are. The speculative materialist could find herself in any phenomenal reality, indeed any possible universe whatsoever besides her own, and the conclusions would hold just as well. As Meillassoux observes in his unpublished dissertation, "In principle, an utterly chaotic world in which all laws are subject to the power of time might be phenomenally *indiscernible* from a world subject to laws that are actually necessary."[53] For this reason, the conclusions of speculative materialism are wholly impervious to critique based on metaphysical argumentation grounded in an appeal to phenomenal experience.

SPECULATIVE COURAGE AND THE *PASSIO ESSENDI*

However forceful Meillassoux's conclusions, two critical responses come to mind. First, although phenomenological argumentation cannot refute Meillassoux's conclusions, it has good reason to call into question the presuppositions that lead to their development. *After Finitude* assumes an unquestioned cognitional theory and theory of objectivity, both of which belong to an antiquated philosophical past. To be specific, his understanding of the mind-being relationship reassumes its pre-phenomenological (more specifically, modern) articulation, and the question as to how mind relates to being itself is reinstated as a genuine philosophical problem for reflection. However, phenomenology's basic claim that consciousness is always consciousness of being arguably does not receive due merit in *After Finitude*. The absolute severance between subject and object is, as the phenomenologist argues, a later construction of the mind—one which presupposes a prior community of mind and being.[54] To put the matter in Meillassoux's language, I find no compelling reason to assume that a precondition for knowledge of the absolute, or being itself, is that it must be known absolutely, apart from the operations of the intellect.[55] The problem of the absolute reach of science and mathematics, it seems, is quite simply not a problem after the phenomenological turn of the twentieth century.[56]

Second, and more important, I argue that speculative material-ism lacks *speculative courage*. It might seem strange to say this since Meillassoux does indeed venture a return to the absolute. It is not my intention to deny this. There are two kinds of speculative cour-age, however. The first is "fidelity to a noble calling, solicited to say something about what is most ultimate for thought,"[57] despite the postmodern denunciation of the perennial questions of metaphysics. Consider the words of Hegel: "The human being . . . should and must deem himself worthy of the highest. . . . The initially hidden and con-cealed essence of the world has no power to withstand the courage of knowledge."[58] Speculative materialism certainly displays this courage in its venture to reinstate thought's relationship to what is most ulti-mate for thought.

There is another kind of speculative courage, though, one that asks more of the philosopher. If she seriously seeks knowledge of what is most ultimate for thought, she obviously ought to be willing to sacrifice everything that stands in the way. Indeed, this readiness to sacrifice is central to a healthier, more modest sense of the term *objec-tivity*, if by this we understand nothing more than a fidelity, birthed of wonder before being, to the pure desire to understand. But as the philosopher nears the threshold of what is most ultimate for thought, she may find this fidelity demands the courage to call into question the absolute sovereignty of reason itself. Indeed, what if it is the phi-losopher who stands in her own way? It is ironic that objectivity would then require of the philosopher that she become a question unto herself and renounce reason *as sovereign*. Speculative courage and adherence to objectivity would then reveal that she ought to do away with the desire to know being *absolutely*, to do away with rea-son as sovereign and supreme over the truth of being.

As Desmond appositely asks, "What is the courage of the philoso-pher? . . . What then are the sources of strengthening of philosophi-cal courage itself? If they do not merely come from philosophical thinking itself, from where or what do they come?"[59] This question of origin brings the mind to reflect upon its own possibilizing source.

Desmond continues: "Before being courageous there is a being en-couraged. The 'en' refers us to the immanence of the source of the courage within oneself; but the source, as communicated or offered from attendant powers, is not to be called 'mine,' or one's own."[60] This second, higher courage is a willing subjection to the consequences of reason's givenness prior to self-determination.

Desmond does not stand alone here. Kierkegaard, too, understood well this higher expression of speculative courage, as is evidenced in his discussions on patience. He defined patience as "the courage that freely takes upon itself the suffering that cannot be avoided."[61] But what does it mean to speak of unavoidable suffering, and what good or nobility is there in the act of consenting to that which cannot be avoided? At the heart of Kierkegaard's philosophical anthropology is the notion that human beings are not origins unto themselves.[62] In agreement with Kierkegaard, Desmond writes, "We do not first choose our being or freedom; both are first given to us; and being given, we begin to give ourselves to ourselves."[63] The unavoidable suf-fering of which Kierkegaard speaks concerns our radical contingency: we did not first give ourselves to be.[64] Yet we find ourselves given to be, and only subsequent to this do we choose to consent or reject our given being. For Kierkegaard, rejection is despair, and patience is the courage that freely undergoes unavoidable suffering. For Desmond, such consent is to what he terms the *passio essendi*—the suffering of being.[65] In our freedom, in our striving to be (*conatus essendi*), we can consent to our *passio essendi*, but we can just as well rebel against it. As Nietzsche stated, to consent is to "become what you are."[66] To rebel, however, is to be like a baby that turns against its own mother in the womb.[67]

One may wonder what any of this has to do with the sover-eignty of reason. Aquinas, following Aristotle, provides us with a clue: "The thing known is in the knower according to the mode of the knower. Hence the knowledge of every knower is ruled accord-ing to its own nature."[68] Knowledge of being is mediated according to what it means to be human, but if being human entails a suffer-ing of being at the most elemental level, *then there is no ontological basis for the absolute sovereignty of reason.*[69] To be human is to be "pathological"; the human being is "a *pathos* with *logos*"—a suffering with the capacity to reason.[70] There is no way for the *logos* to overcome this elemental *pathos*, for "it cannot give a univocal *ratio* of this *passio essendi*."[71]

How might one then account for the hyperboles of being? Desmond would argue that the foregoing analysis of the *passio essendi* implies that it may be rash to view the cause of metaphysical indeterminacy as a mere indigence at the heart of being. He insists that the origin of being is not determinate, but this is not to say that it is merely nondeterminate. Rather, the loss of the sovereignty of reason ushers in an opening through which we can acknowledge being beyond determinacy. It is for this reason that Desmond speaks of being as *overdeterminate*. The *over* in overdeterminacy stresses that there is *more* to being than what can be understood determinately. "It refers us to the inexhaustibility of a dynamic plenitude, not the static completion of a totally determinate being."[72] The overdeterminacy of being establishes an "affirmative sense" of metaphysical indeterminacy.[73] The perceived lack expressed by metaphysical indeterminacy is not solely rooted in the mind (modern and postmodern) or being itself (speculative materialism). The "lack" of metaphysical indeterminacy is rather an affirmative difference between being and transcendent being, between creation and origin.

COMPLEMENTARITY AND OUT-NARRATION: FROM HYPER-CHAOS TO OVERDETERMINACY

To a far greater extent than the modern and postmodern traditions, however, Meillassoux's thought is on the brink of a liberating power that, if only it were to attain a higher realization, could open the mind to an otherness of being beyond all determinate thought. His account of origin obviates the modern obligation to give a sufficient reason for how and why being *is*. At the same time, he does not sidestep this obligation by perpetuating the shortcomings of the postmodern insistence on being's indefinite and unintelligible nature. He exceeds both these traditions by turning to the origin of being itself as the cause of metaphysical indeterminacy. For this reason, Meillassoux and Desmond can *here* be understood as complementary to one another. Both hold that a mindfulness of being's origin results in a blindness that is not fully explicable in terms of human finitude. However, whereas Meillassoux finds that the answer is that there is nothing to be seen here, Desmond insists that there is rather *too much* to be seen in the origin's excessive brilliance. Therefore, I believe Meillassoux's conclusions affirm those of Desmond *to an extent*. That is, from the standpoint of sovereign reason there is no reason to be, and the origin of being is this radical contingency or hyper-Chaos. Desmond's metaphysics "out-narrates" speculative materialism, however, by offering the key to a fuller realization of its latent potencies. I will now explore this complementarity and out-narration through an analysis of sufficient reason, the contingency of creation, and the origin of being.

First, Meillassoux's rejection of the principle of sufficient reason with respect to the origin of being can be likened to that of Schopenhauer, for whom "sufficient reason is grounded on no rational ground, but derived from the ultimate."[74] Against those who attempt to argue for the validity of sufficient reason on univocally determinate grounds, Desmond is in agreement with Meillassoux on "the level at which the question has to be put."[75] Meillassoux correctly recognizes that the ground of univocal intelligibility "is not itself another instance of univocal intelligibility": from the standpoint of the univocal, there is "no rational ground."[76] Any answer to the question of the ground of sufficient reason must appeal to an absolute as other to determinate intelligibility.

Although, as Desmond says, "the ultimate ground of intelligibility may not be itself intelligible in a manner that yields completely to our efforts to conceptualize it," this does not require the judgment that the principle of sufficient reason is simply ungrounded, "absurd, or devoid of intelligible relation to the intelligibilities available to us in the milieu of finite creation."[77] But to say that sufficient reason has a ground is not to say it is determinately grounded by the origin of being. If we are going to speak of the ground of sufficient reason as a cause, the term "should be used with diffidence in relation to the origin."[78] That which gave determinacy to be cannot itself be made determinate in the same way.

Second, in saying that the universe is radically contingent we admit that it does not possess within itself the conditions for its own possibility or the ground of its own being.[79] As a result, beings could have been otherwise. There is no necessity that secures *how they exist* or *that they exist at all.*[80] For this reason, the "that it is" of being appears as an "unintelligible surd" from the standpoint of determinate intelligibility.[81] Meillassoux and Desmond are in agreement that the fact of this unintelligible surd "is perfectly intelligible given the nature of what is at issue."[82] This absence of reason is driven not by an epistemic poverty but by the very lack of the universe's necessity.

Is this all there is to be said on the issue? Sovereign reason's answer is "yes." If there is no reason according to this sovereignty, there is no reason to be had. Alternatively, in its openness to being in excess of determinacy, metaxological metaphysics is prepared to offer a more comprehensive "hermeneutics of contingency."[83] Being does not need to "be seen as just an unintelligible surd, mocking the inclusion in a system of necessary categories. It might be seen as the excess of a gift of being, given to be in the finitude of the between."[84] As a gift born of generosity, there is no compulsion on the part of God to give; creation is not a necessary act. Moreover, being "is not originally given in the expectation of a return on the gift. . . . God gives for nothing."[85] This *nothing* manifests itself in being as the lack of necessary reason governing the creative act of the origin. The unintelligible surd of being's brute thereness, then, can open into a broader horizon through an understanding of the creative act as beyond both *compulsion* and *expectation of a return.*

I want to close with a consideration of the origin of being. Particularly, my concern is the meaning of a transition from the origin of being as hyper-Chaos to an overdeterminate origin. Meillassoux's articulation of origin is, once again, reminiscent of Schopenhauer's, for whom "there is an (ab)surd or primal nonrationality about the ultimate origin."[86] Desmond expresses some sympathy for this view, inasmuch as it is understood as ontologically prior to both determinate being and reason. Meillassoux's refusal to characterize the origin of being as *an entity* is another judgment Desmond would assuredly endorse.[87] For the overdeterminate origin of being is "the God who is no-thing."[88] Most significantly, Meillassoux's decision to prefix his origin with the term *hyper-* seems indicative of an unwitting movement toward an articulation of being as overdeterminate. For this origin is not simply *chaos*, since this would imply that it could be understood immanently as mere indeterminate or indefinite being. It is *primordially* chaotic with respect to determinate being, although it is better conceived as an origin of primordial darkness rather than light.

I perceive something dubious about hyper-Chaos, however. The nature of its ontological status does not receive due attention in *After Finitude*. It is somewhat clear that Meillassoux does not intend for it to be thought of as substantial being. What differentiates speculative materialism from traditional metaphysics, according to Meillassoux, is that the latter posits an absolute entity as the ground of being, whereas the former attempts to "uncover an absolute necessity that does not reinstate any form of absolutely necessary entity."[89] For this reason, I believe hyper-Chaos is defined better as an ontological consequence correlated to his principle of unreason; it is an expression for reality conditioned by the absolute necessity of contingency. In accordance with this view, it is perhaps more appropriate to employ the term adjectivally: being is "hyper-Chaotic." But this presents arguably irresolvable issues that go unacknowledged. How can Meillassoux speak attributively of that which is not substantial but is simply a condition of reality? More to the point, how can that which lacks agency be identified as causal and capable of producing novelty? Desmond's answer is to turn to the origin of being as overdeterminate—the source that *gives* determinate being to be. There is nothing for sovereign reason to see here, but this no-thing is "Being itself and yet beyond Being."[90] It is "original power to be," not merely for itself, but also for what is other to itself.[91] Its creation is a gratuitous gift, an opening for otherness to be and, in its radical contingency, to be free. To turn from hyper-Chaos to the overdeterminate origin is to turn from the darkness of lack to the excessively luminous light of lights, the Good of being itself.

I am quite positive that a closing reflection on the foregoing course of thought should say something about the *passio essendi* and its implications for how we ought to situate ourselves as mindful beings. In an important respect, the consideration of speculative courage and *passio essendi* is the most decisive point in this essay. It is decidedly polarizing. For some, this suffering involves an outright renunciation of reason, as though the sovereignty of reason is that which provides the mind with the capacity to relate to what is absolute. But what philosophical basis is there for this sovereignty? Its basis seems to be the univocal mind's affinity for a kind of certainty that is given in our relationship with determinate being.

Determinate being is not exhaustive, however. Recall the hyperboles and their indomitable resistance to the determinate categories of mind. As Desmond reveals, these are not merely negative—a negation of determinacy. There is something about being in excess of determinate intelligibility. The language of *uncertainty*, although helpful for the frustration of totalizing determinacy, falls short before this excess of being. First, this is because it communicates a lack. The "un-" denotes an absence of a quality or state, not something *more*. Second, uncertainty is usually understood as having a merely epistemic significance. But the difference between mind and being cannot be accounted for entirely in terms of mind. The difference of being and mind is first ontological. In order to overcome these two objections, I am tempted to take after Desmond and speak of an *over-certainty*.

This is not a new idea. Aristotle taught that there are two senses of certainty: the intelligibility *of being* and intelligibility *for mind*. They are inversely proportionate to one another. There is the mind's ability to know something determinately and in a, more or less, assured fashion. There is also a sense of certainty that speaks to the integrity, simplicity, and *power to be* of being itself. As the mind ascends toward greater certainty *in being*, the certainty of determinate intelligibility is shaken and subdued; as mind retreats to being as certain *for it*, it becomes proportionately relative to being that is less certain in itself. This troubles the assumption that reason's sovereignty is what possibilizes a relation to what is absolute. Indeed, it seems that only in giving up the sovereignty of reason, and giving in to *passio essendi*, does one become released to think the absolute, as being beyond determinacy, a certainty of being.

Notes

1. Christopher Ben Simpson, "Between Metaphysics and God: An Interview with William Desmond," *Radical Orthodoxy: Theology, Philosophy, Politics* 1, nos. 1–2 (2012): 363.

2. Graham Harman, *Quentin Meillassoux: Philosophy in the Making* (Edinburgh: Edinburgh University Press, 2011), 159.

3. Quentin Meillassoux, *After Finitude: An Essay on the Nature of Contingency*, trans. Ray Brassier (New York: Continuum, 2009).

4. Ibid., vii.

5. "Our understanding of being in the between calls for the acknowledgement of indeterminacy." *BB*, xiv.

6. I am referring directly to a distinction made by William Desmond in his *Being and the Between*, but he is certainly not alone in doing so. The same distinction between *the question of being* and *the question of mind's preconceptual relationship to being* is found in Alain Badiou's *Being and Event*, which he refers to as ontology and meta-ontology, respectively. Indeed, Badiou's meta-ontology establishes the criteria for *what* we can know about being as well as *how* this knowing occurs. See Alain Badiou, *Being and Event* (New York: Continuum, 2007).

7. "Much of traditional metaphysics, I think, is defined by an oscillation between univocity and equivocity." *BB*, 47.

8. *BB*, 16.

9. *BB*, 49.

10. *BB*, 59.

11. *BB*, 179.

12. Desmond argues at length that the failure of the modern and postmodern positions is seen most clearly when one recognizes that neither of them can ultimately do away with the other, thus issuing a final word on the matter. See *BB*, 47–130.

13. On the modern, Desmond writes, "We find an insatiable quest for completeness, and this most especially with respect to Kant's architectonic ambitions. This insatiable will to completeness was to become even more feverish in the idealisms following Kant. Think of the revealing fact that Kant repeatedly contrasts the 'random groping' of all previous metaphysics with his own claim to put philosophy successfully on 'the secure path of science.' The results are said to be marked by completeness, unity, absolute necessity, and apodictic certainty." *BB*, 24.

14. See Christopher Ben Simpson's metaxological critique of John D. Caputo's postmodernity as hypermodernity. Christopher Ben Simpson, *Religion, Metaphysics, and the Postmodern: William Desmond and John D. Caputo* (Bloomington: Indiana University Press, 2009), 61–64.

15. *EB*, 169–70.

16. *GB*, 4.

17. *BB*, 225. All emphases in quoted passages are in the original unless indicated otherwise.

18. *GB*, 243.

19. Meillassoux, *After Finitude*, 53, 60.

20. *GB*, 134.

21. *GB*, 134.

22. *GB*, 128, 135.

23. *GB*, 138.

24. *GB*, 141–50.

25. *GB*, 141–42.

26. *GB*, 141–42.

27. *GB*, 142.

28. *GB*, 151.

29. *GB*, 151.

30. *GB*, 152.

31. Meillassoux, *After Finitude*, 14.

32. Ibid., 6.

33. Ibid., 5.

34. Ibid., 28.

35. In addition, he clarifies his use of absolute: "a being whose severance (the original meaning of *absolutus*) and whose separateness from thought is such that it presents itself to us as non-relative to us, and hence as capable of existing whether we exist or not." Ibid.

36. By "absolute reach," Meillassoux means "that any aspect of a body that can be thought mathematically . . . can exist absolutely outside [the thinker]." Ibid., 30.

37. Ibid.

38. With reference to the latter, Meillassoux writes, "But even if we were to grant that this necessity is not merely sophistical, it still would not have proven the existence of an absolute, because the necessity it affirms is merely a necessity *for us*. But we have no grounds for maintaining that this necessity, which is for us, is also a necessity in itself—we can reiterate the argument

from hyperbolic doubt and maintain that we cannot know for sure that our minds are not originally deluded, leading us to believe in the truth of an argument which is actually inconsequential." Ibid, 30–31.

39. Ibid., 34. Emphasis mine.

40. Ibid., 42.

41. Ibid.

42. Ibid., 41.

43. Ibid., 42.

44. Ibid., 53.

45. Ibid., 52.

46. Ibid., 53.

47. Aristotle continues, "For just as the eyes of owls are to the light of day, so is our soul's intellective power to those things which are by nature most evident of all." Aristotle, *Metaphysics*, 993b7–11.

48. "From this perspective, the failure of the principle of reason follows, quite simply, from the *falsity* (and even from the absolute falsity) of such a principle—for the truth is that there is no reason for anything to be or to remain thus and so rather than otherwise, and this applies as much to the laws that govern the world as to the things of the world." Meillassoux, *After Finitude*, 53; see also 60.

49. Ibid., 53.

50. "Our absolute, in effect, is nothing other than an extreme form of chaos, a hyper-Chaos, for which nothing is or would seem to be, impossible, not even unthinkable." Ibid., 64.

51. *BB*, 226.

52. "This indicates in the most striking fashion that if we think advent in its truth, it is an advent ex nihilo and thus without any reason at all, and for that very reason it is without limit. In revealing the contingency of laws, reason itself teaches that becoming is ultimately without reason." Harman, *Quentin Meillassoux*, 176.

53. Ibid., 178.

54. *BB*, 4.

55. "One must guard against the dubious and unwarranted transition from knowledge of the absolute to absolute knowledge—the triumphalist dogmatism that mistakes truth about the divine as a truth that *is* divine and so unassailable." Simpson, *Religion, Metaphysics, and the Postmodern*, 133–34.

56. "This suggests that there is no purely external relation between the knower and the known whereby the known could be approached without any mediation by the knower." *BB*, 79.

57. *IST*, xiii.

58. *IST*, 238.

59. *IST*, 259.

60. *IST*, 248.

61. Søren Kierkegaard, *Upbuilding Discourses in Various Spirits*, trans. Howard V. Hong and Edna H. Hong (Princeton, NJ: Princeton University Press, 2009), 118–19.

62. "The human self is such a derived established relation that relates itself to itself and in relating itself to itself relates itself to another." Søren Kierkegaard, *Sickness unto Death: A Christian Psychological Exposition for Upbuilding and Awakening*, trans. Howard V. Hong and Edna H. Hong (Princeton, NJ: Princeton University Press, 1983), 13–14.

63. *EB*, 368.

64. "Suffering here does not necessarily mean *pain*: we can *suffer joy*, be 'surprised by joy,' as Wordsworth put it. The delight in the 'to be' as good is such a suffering of ontological joy." *IST*, 246.

65. *EB*, 368–72.

66. Friedrich Nietzsche, *The Anti-Christ, Ecce Homo, Twilight of the Idols, and Other Writings*, trans. Judith Norman (New York: Cambridge University Press, 2010), 69 ff.

67. *EB*, 370.

68. Thomas Aquinas, *Summa Theologiae*, I, q. 12, a. 4.

69. "Yet reason's equivocity is the equivocity of the human being itself: its *conatus essendi* can seek to overcome its *passio essendi* and *assert itself hyperbolically* as absolutely self-determining. From a metaxological perspective, this is untrue to selving and reasoning, since it sends into recess what the *passio essendi* communicates: the being given to itself of thinking, and the excess of the enigmatic origin in the immanence of thought itself." *GB*, 143.

70. *EB*, 367.

71. *EB*, 367.

72. *PU*, 207.

73. *PU*, 207.

74. *BB*, 354.

75. *BB*, 354.

76. *BB*, 354–55.

77. *BB*, 333–34.

78. *BB*, 357.

79. *BB*, 336.

80. *GB*, 250.

81. *PU*, 184.

82. *GB*, 165.

83. *BB*, 229.

84. *PU*, 184.

85. *PU*, 231.

86. *AOO*, 133.

87. "This is precisely what we obtain by absolutizing facticity—we do not maintain that a determinate entity exists, but that it is absolutely necessary that every entity might not exist." Meillassoux, *After Finitude*, 60.

88. *GB*, 179; see also 196, 285–86, 290.

89. Meillassoux, *After Finitude*, 34.

90. *GB*, 287.

91. *GB*, 283.

CHAPTER 4

The Positivity of Philosophy

William Desmond's Contribution to Theology

D. C. SCHINDLER

The question of how properly to interpret the relationship between philosophy and theology is more than merely "academic." On the one hand, if philosophy is the paradigm of reason and reason defines the essence of man,[1] and, on the other hand, if theology is the study of God's personal self-revelation in history—claims I take for granted in this essay—then to ask after this relationship is in fact to ask in a basic way about the essential encounter between God and man. It is of course not only in the reflection on this question that the encounter takes place; but it is nevertheless the case that one cannot address this question without interpreting and in some sense deciding the basic nature of man's relation to God in creation and redemption. And because there is nothing that stands outside of this relation, this is not the sort of questioning that can be undertaken from some neutral space. Instead, the questioning will inescapably be a kind of answer to what has already presented itself, and so the gradual revelation of a response to a claim, to a call that has moved one before one has moved oneself.

From the very outset, reflection on the relationship presents a series of fraught dilemmas, of which I can mention two of the most fundamental.[2] First, there has to be a radical openness to the transcendent that defines the very essence of reason, or else God's self-revelation will be an utterly foreign sound, beyond the spectrum of reason's receptive capacities. In this case, man will be essentially deaf to God's call. On the other hand, if revelation does *not* exceed this spectrum, it would seem to imply that God's capacity to reveal himself is *measured* by reason's natural aptitude. In this case, philosophy would simply take the place of theology. Second, as a work of redemption, God's self-gift in his self-revelation in Christ has to be understood as a full and over-full response to man's need for healing and love, and as an answer to his most profound and urgent questions regarding the meaning of life, of history, and of the cosmos as a whole. On the other hand, if it is indeed a definite and unsurpassable answer, it would seem of necessity to put an end to questioning, at least of the profound sort, and to leave for reason only the work of ordering what is already known, or perhaps the apparently more creative but finally unsatisfying work of interpretation. In this case, theology has rendered philosophy obsolete. The dilemmas appear to force us in the end to choose *between* philosophy and theology, for each would seem to need to be false to the other in order to be true to itself.

These dilemmas are not able to be solved in a definitive way, any more than philosophy itself or man's reception of the Word of God (*theo-logos*) can be simply "solved," and so put to rest. Instead, navigating through the dilemmas in a manner that remains true, that does justice, *both* to philosophy and to theology is a task that—again, like philosophy and receiving the Word of God—must be "reenacted" in every age and indeed in a certain respect by every human being. In our own age, this task has become especially difficult, above all because of what might be called a radical impoverishment of philosophy, due—as I hope to suggest—to a loss of a sense for what Gabriel Marcel dubbed the "ontological mystery,"[3] and the undermining of the confidence of reason that results from this loss. Evidence of this impoverishment is abundant. Among philosophers, one finds, on the one hand, a tendency (primarily among those in the analytic tradition) toward rationalism, which shrinks, as it were, the scope of reasoning—a defender might say it is a "focusing" of reason—in order to have more control, and so more clarity and certainty, ultimately to the point of rendering philosophy a matter of rational self-preoccupation. To philosophize in this case is to think about arguments, to clarify language. "We might not be able to say *what is*, but let us establish the criteria that would allow us to determine whether we are saying it with precision and logical necessity." On the other hand, one finds a tendency (principally among those in the continental tradition) toward irrationalism, a suspicion regarding reason that leads to its replacement by will or emotion or feeling, or more broadly by history, culture, or political interests. There is typically an attempt to save this tendency from its drift into the trivial, into the bourgeois, and ultimately into nihilism, through an appeal to the ethical. One thinks here of Nietzsche's sarcastic remark that, having gotten rid of God, the English salve their conscience by clinging all the more resolutely to morality.[4] In the end, however, an ethics that has nothing to do with *truth* will eventually, after the infinite passion for the impossible has been spent (!), show itself to be trivial, bourgeois, and nihilistic. Those who do not fit into either of these two groups are usually placed in a third—and, in the contemporary academic scene, much smaller—category "history of philosophy." However different these various tendencies may seem, they in fact share a profound unity: What is missing in all three groups is *precisely philosophy* itself, that is, the love of wisdom. This is a love of the *whole truth*, which involves the *whole person*, body and (rational) soul.

If philosophy becomes impoverished in this way, and so preserves reason, if at all, then only in a conceptually restricted form, theology too is transformed. When reason is reduced, philosophy tends to become a faint image of some other discipline, against which it cannot seriously compete. Today it is typically no longer philosophy that therefore stands as theology's "handmaiden," as was the case in the premodern age, but either (for moderns) some form of science—sociology, history, linguistics, critical methods, and so forth—or (for postmoderns) *politics*. But when politics, rather than philosophy (as love of truth first for its own sake), is theology's handmaiden, the servant will inevitably come to rule her mistress; theology will turn into just another version of the political. What is most astounding in gatherings of academic theologians is not only how much ideology there is, but how self-conscious that ideology has become. What is missing here, again, is a sense of responsibility, finally, to the absolute truth of God—and the contemplative prayer and quiet adoration this responsibility implies.

While one might generally think that philosophy and theology, however they might interact in different contexts, are essentially independent disciplines, these brief observations regarding typical deficiencies in the contemporary age already suggest that the health of each depends in a certain asymmetrical sense on the health of the other. If philosophy separates from theology, it does so by surrendering its aspiration to the ultimate, and this leads to a definition of reason in instrumentalist terms. If theology separates from (genuine) philosophy, it tends to lose its essentially receptive and contemplative relation to the *truth* of revelation and becomes preoccupied above all with forms of praxis.

In the rest of this brief essay, I want to propose that the recovery of a genuinely metaphysical philosophy that William Desmond *presents* (rather than just *describes*) brings us beyond the difficulties that beset contemporary thought, and so helps us to navigate the dilemmas mentioned at the outset in a way that is especially fruitful in our age. To put the argument in a nutshell: Desmond recovers the ancient aspiration of reason for the ultimate but interprets this aspiration in the light of reason's origination in being. This original rootedness in the mystery of being implies an openness to what is other that is, as it were, *inside of* the most intimate "self" of reason, so that transcendence in relation to God is not something that occurs at the *end* of reason, as a result of its self-driven striving, but in some sense is present from the beginning and accompanies reason all along its way. Desmond's way of thinking thus allows a profound *intimacy* in the relation between philosophy and theology, and so an openness to the other that lies at the center of each. We will see that such a conception of philosophy allows us to make our way beyond the dilemmas presented at the outset. Desmond's notion of reason, which stands, so to speak, always on the edge of paradox, thus offers an alternative to the impoverishment of both philosophy and theology in the modern academy.

I approach this discussion by presenting the positivity of being and the positivity of reason and then raising the question of the positivity of religion. We will see, at the end, that a reflection on the encounter between philosophy and religion, considered specifically as *theology* (and so founded in faith), compels us to ask whether philosophy can and should consider, not just the possibility of God's self-revelation in history, but its actuality. Can one philosophize inside of the actual assent of Christian faith? I close with a response to this question that is suggested by Desmond's own notion of reason and being. Needless to say, what follows here is not an attempt to offer a general exposition of Desmond's very rich philosophy, with an explanation and elaboration of its basic terms and ideas, but rather a particular interpretation of that philosophy specifically with a view to theological engagement.

THE POSITIVITY OF BEING

One of the most distinctive features of Desmond's thinking is his somewhat unfashionable embrace of metaphysics, an embrace that is all the more striking for its not coming explicitly from within the tradition of Thomism. The mystery of being is arguably the key to Desmond's thought, and it is crucial to understand this properly in order to understand anything else.[5] For Desmond, being is not an object that would somehow stand over against the knower as subject.[6] Instead, it is far more "intimate" than that: one finds oneself always already "in" being, and one finds being always already "in" one's thinking. This is one of the meanings of the *metaxu*, the "between," in Desmond's metaxological thinking, which acknowledges that we do not start our reasoning—pace Hegel![7]—at some absolute point outside of being so as to enter into it on reason's own terms. Instead, we find ourselves having always already begun "in the midst" (*meta*) of being and therefore of beings. For this reason, a connection with reality, an understanding of being, is not something that has to be achieved, as it generally is taken to be in post-Cartesian thought, but is already "given" from the start. We cannot help but be profoundly familiar with the meaning of being. At the same time, however, we are not *only* familiar with this meaning: just as there is no point *prior* to being on which reason can take a stand, so too there is no point *after* it, outside, from which reason could gather up that meaning in a single statement or notion. Being cannot be circumscribed within a concept, because it has no boundaries to separate it from anything else. By definition, as it were, there cannot *be* anything outside of *being*. The metaxological character of thinking is inescapable, even if this fact has not always been noticed.

This recognition of the mystery of being is crucial for understanding key features of Desmond's thought and how they relate to one another. Moreover, as we shall see, it is also a key to the profound contribution he is able to make to specifically theological thinking. Being cannot be defined: on the one hand, this is due to its radically "intimate" character. Only what is general can be defined, but being is more interior to me than I am to myself.[8] Desmond uses the word *hyperbolic* to describe the essentially "excessive" character of being.[9] In this case, however paradoxical this may seem, being exceeds my own self in intimacy; it presents what Desmond strikingly calls a kind of "idiotic" character—after *idiotēs*, the individual or the private. Being is more primordial than my thinking, and this primordiality, which renders being something unable to be fully retrieved in concepts, gives reality a note of the "surd." This note turns up in a variety of decisive human experiences of grief, joy, perplexity, surprise, and so forth.[10] On the other hand, being is hyperbolic in the direction of transcendence. It cannot be defined because it has no outer limit; being is also more external to me than my outermost exteriority. For this reason, it can never be closed in a totality, a self-justifying system. Desmond helpfully insists on the "overdetermined" nature of being, which is a characterization that bears some similarity to the Thomistic view of the "supra-formal" character of *esse* that distinguishes it from the formal determinacy of the essential order. The hyperbolic character, the always more, the out beyond, is an intrinsic and essential feature of being. The Ignatian insight into the nature of the divine turns out to describe well Desmond's notion of being: *non coerceri maximo, contineri tamen a minimo.*[11] Being includes the most extreme intimacy of the idiotic *and* the most extreme otherness of what Desmond refers to as the "agapeic," which is a radically positive affirmation of radical otherness.

To say that being cannot be defined does not at all mean that it is irrational in the sense of being foreign to thinking or opposed to rational reflection. Quite the contrary, being is profoundly familiar. To say that it is irrational would imply that reason is itself somehow outside of being, prior to its immersion in and emergence from being, so that to dwell in being would be to enter into some wholly foreign territory. But there is no place outside of being, even if being always remains beyond. The essentially hyperbolic character of being nevertheless has implications for what it means to *be* rational, to understand being. The extremes I mentioned are all extremes precisely *of being*; they are, for all their apparent opposition, inseparable from one another, to such an extent that we need to see that they *inform* one another. Thus, the intimacy of being, its immanence in the self or its familiarity, nevertheless always remains what Desmond calls an "*intimate strangeness,*"[12] for *what* is intimate to me is precisely what I will never get to the end of, never have finished with. By the same token, the otherness of agapeic community, which includes an ethical responsibility to and for the "other," as Levinas has shown, is never a strict *alien* (*aliud*), a foreign intrusion or imposition on the self. The other is not essentially *alienating* but most fundamentally *in-viting*. Because the self relates to itself from the beginning always already in relation to the other, by virtue of the intimate strangeness of being, the direct and sometimes disorienting encounter with the other is never in principle a violent contradiction to the self but rather a perhaps unexpected revelation of the truth of the self, no matter how apparently violent it may seem. The incredibly rich internal fruitfulness of being exceeds both the unity of univocity and the diversity of equivocity, and has, as it were, infinite room for anything in between: from the surprise of aesthetic happening to the striving of erotic self-achieving self-transcendence. One of the most remarkable features of

Desmond's philosophy is his capacity to describe a seemingly endless diversity of phenomena without "bracketing out" their metaphysical depth, and thus to do so with an attentiveness to unities and relations that would otherwise remain hidden.

As I mentioned earlier, a basic strategy in late modern and post-modern thought has been to keep reason open to what is other qua other by limiting reason, and one of the main expressions of this strategy has been the rejection of metaphysics.[13] But if Desmond is right in his interpretation of the intimate strangeness of being, then in fact there *can* be no rejection of metaphysics; one is always already involved in being from the beginning.[14] As Gilson famously put it, metaphysics always buries its own undertakers. Desmond has clearly shown that the putative rejection of metaphysics is inescapably itself a metaphysics, insofar as it is a taking of a position with respect to the "to be," in which one is always already involved, and therefore an interpretation of what it means "to be." This means that it is not only professional philosophers who do metaphysics, but every human being is a meta-physician, one way or the other. Recognizing this allows us to see why the mindfulness that properly defines philosophy is not an activity cut off from normal living but a deepening of human *being* simply; more-over, it allows us to see that *even theologians* have a responsibility to the meaning of being that cannot be evaded even if their starting point lies in some sense beyond philosophy. The question can therefore never be whether one affirms or denies metaphysics; the question can only be whether or not the metaphysics to which one commits oneself willy-nilly is adequate to the full mystery of being. The rejection of metaphysics turns out, (perhaps) in spite of its pretensions to humility, to be a self-assertive presumption, because it implies that reason exists, begins its activity, somehow prior to any relation to being. But a metaphysics that is ignorant of itself as such cannot but mindlessly impose itself insofar as it disallows a priori the fundamental sort of questioning that could relativize it and call its particular interpretation into question. Desmond's alternative to this self-ignorant presump-tion is a metaxological metaphysics, the two terms of which are joined together in the *meta*, a word that means both "in the middle" and "beyond." For Desmond, it is the one *because* it is the other: because our thinking finds itself only ever in the *midst* of being and so as *preceded* by what is other, it is of its essence opened from the beginning and all along the way to what transcends it. Desmond speaks of this thinking as a "mindfulness";[15] the term captures the concreteness of a being present to what one experiences *hic et nunc*, the respect of memory and so the past, and the responsiveness to and for what is yet to come.

I have used the expression "positivity of being" to describe Desmond's metaxological metaphysics. The expression is meant to set in relief the *givenness* of being in the full sense of that word. On the one hand, being is the always prior; it is not the object of a self-sufficient reason but awakens reason to itself, and so reason finds being *already there* prior to its activity. On the other hand, because this givenness is so radical, it bespeaks a nonintrusive otherness, and so a kind of ultimate generosity. A constant theme in Desmond's philosophy is the goodness of being, which outstrips, without simply eliminating, the possibility of evil. Being is a gift; we are *given* to be.

THE POSITIVITY OF REASON

The significance of this last point stands out most sharply if we contrast Desmond with Hegel, who appears to represent a sort of archnemesis to his philosophy. Hegel surpasses all modern philosophers for being able to receive the immediate as full of philosophical significance rather than as a surd: history is not just a series of empirical facts, but has a genuinely philosophical depth. For Hegel, the immediacy of the given is meant to be affirmed but only because it is simultaneously overcome. Hegelian philosophy comes to its perfection by *recovering* immediacy, by mediating it through what is other to it. In this sense, Hegel moves decisively beyond Cartesian solipsism by affirming that the other is essential to reason. But it is so, for Hegel, in a negative rather than a positive sense. The positive *precisely as such* is not, for Hegel, intelligible, but it becomes intelligible only in the form of the negation of the negation. To use Desmond's language, the negation of the negation is a sort of "counterfeit double" of the positive.[16] It seems in a sense to be the same thing, to serve the same purpose or function, but in fact it seems so only given a radical reversal. Hegel's dialectic appears to cover much of the same ground as Desmond's metaxological metaphysics insofar as it (at least apparently) rejects both a monolithic univocity and a nominalistic equivocity, and attempts instead to mediate between them, to interpret each only in terms of a reciprocal dependence on the other. But in fact for all of its aspiration to comprehensiveness, Hegel's dialectical concept of reason has no room for the absolute uniqueness of the idiotic or the unforeseeable miracle of the agapeic. Hegel's notion of reason is essentially negative, because it develops *only* as a result of inward need, a lack in relation to its own self-identity. For Desmond, by contrast, the movement occurs more basically in the mode of fruitfulness,[17] a reflection of an original superabundance rather than the hunger of a lack. Because of the positivity of being, reason, too, is positive; it "reflects" being in having an essentially generous form.

One of the most decisive responses that Desmond makes to modern thought, which will bear directly on what his thought can contribute to theology, is his notion of the *passio essendi*. Desmond insists that this *passio* is more fundamental than Spinoza's *conatus essendi*, the desire to be. In a recent interview, in response to the suggestion that his insistence on the rich positivity of being bears some resemblance to Spinoza's idea, he explained: "I've tried to talk about the *passio essendi* as more primordial than *conatus essendi*. Our endeavor to be is subtended by our being given to be. Our self-affirming will to be emerges out of a more primal being given to be."[18] Reason does not first set itself in motion, in order thus to achieve itself, but is rather at its core moved by what is other than it (even if this "being moved" is not a dead passivity). Reason is therefore primordially receptive in its structure, and its most basic act is affirmation and assent, even if it goes on at a later moment to doubt or take a critical distance. Reason first "lets be." Desmond refers to the *sabbatical* character of genuine thinking, its fundamental disposition of rest, leisure, celebration, a full silence.[19] On this point, Desmond's view of reason appears to converge with the classical view presented by Josef Pieper.[20] While this appearance is essentially true, he adds something decisive. Somewhat differently

from Pieper, Desmond says that reason is not only essentially contemplative, but if we considered it more attentively we would have
to use the poetic language of Wordsworth to characterize it: reason
in its ultimate act is not just a gazing *at*, first of all, but a "beholding
from."[21] Reason is *given* to behold, its gazing is always responsive and
so always respectful of what prefers to be held "in reserve."

Because reason is radically responsive, it is defined in itself and
in all its activities by its relation to what transcends it, by its other.
Let us recall that this understanding of reason is a result of the specifically *metaphysical* conception of reason that Desmond is offering.
Now, because of what we might call the otherness that is "built in" to
reason, from the ground up and from inside out, reason does not in
any sense at all need to be limited or otherwise curtailed in order to
make room for the other. In other words, it does not need to be con-
tradicted according to its innate impulse or nature. Instead, making
room for the other is precisely what reason does "naturally." If there
is an almost inevitable tendency for reason to close itself off, to force
things into clarity, to lord it over what is other, to grasp aggressively
and possessively, and to marginalize mystery, this tendency has to be
understood not as an *expression* of its nature but rather as a betrayal
of that nature. To correct this tendency, then, no violence is necessary, no "artificial" setting of limits. (As Kant famously stated, "I have
sought to eliminate knowledge in order to make room for faith.")[22]
Reason will inevitably respond to violence with violence in turn. For
Desmond, we avoid the degeneration into nothing but the posing and
positioning of the will to power only by recalling reason to its natural
aspiration to truth.

We should note how different Desmond's proposal is here from
the usual postmodern approach—for example, that of Gianni Vattimo,
who considers the desire for truth to be inevitably an expression of
fascism.[23] Vattimo therefore seeks to *replace* truth with love, whereas
Desmond understands these to be inseparable from each other. There
is in the aspiration to truth a true *coincidence* of closure and openness,
a coming to internal satisfaction *precisely* in the excessus beyond any
strictly immanent bonds. At the heart of reason, interpreted as the
correlate of the hyperbolic overdetermination of being, is a kind of

space, which is the *positive* openness of a generous and receptive self-gift rather than the negative emptiness of a hungry void. As Desmond puts it, "What looks empty is an expectancy of mindfulness that does not have the measure of itself, since it is just the readiness of thought to be in communication with what exceeds the measures of its own thought."[24] Because this readiness is native to reason, reason becomes more open to the other beyond itself the more it is true to itself, the more it is strengthened in its natural impulses. Rationalism is properly overcome, not by setting limits to reason, but in a certain sense by *removing them*, that is, by keeping reason from prematurely setting limits *to itself* and thereby closing itself off from the other.

Now, Desmond's insight into the "readiness of thought" with respect to what exceeds it allows him to discover analogies of faith within the proper operation of reason itself. These analogies are precisely what make this conception of reason fruitful within theology, because they allow us to see a *continuity* between reason's activity in philosophy and its elevated activity in the light of faith, even within a genuine discontinuity. It is only such an analogy that permits a notion of theology as a liberating completion of philosophy rather than a rival discipline. Desmond elaborates many such analogies in his writing; I will mention just two in the present context. First, there is something like a "vocation" in philosophy. According to Desmond, thinking does not authorize itself but, as we have seen, comes into play always in response to what has preceded it. In this respect, to think philosophically is to heed a call. Genuine philosophical thought, because of the originality and ultimacy of its aim, requires that this response not be superficial and episodic but a commitment of the *whole* of oneself, and an ongoing fidelity to this commitment. Desmond refers to this faithful commitment as "consecrated thinking," a reasoning that devotes itself to what lies beyond it.[25] Second, Desmond elaborates—in sharp contrast once again to typical postmodern currents—the importance of *confidence* in thinking. Correcting our tendency to interpret this word most immediately as the *self*-assertion of *self*-confidence, Desmond points out that there is an essential reference to the "other" embedded in the word. As he explains, "We notice the reference to *fides* in confidence—there is a *con-fides*, a faith with. One might say there is a companionship of faith, companionship marked by fidelity. Confidence thus enfolds within itself relationality to something beyond self."[26] This confidence is thus another expression of the positivity, the *givenness*, of being. Prior to any act of reason, any will to think this or that or even to begin thinking at all, there is a *givenness* to think, an offering of the intelligibility of what is intelligible and a corresponding antecedent *willingness* to understand. We are *en-trust-ed*, first, with the truth of things, and it is just this that allows us to trust that things can be known in truth. The source of our trust precedes us. This point cannot be overemphasized if we are to make sense of Desmond's descriptions of the proper activity of reason and see that they are not mere metaphors. *Because* this source precedes us, our confidence in thinking is not a mere self-confidence (which is in fact an oxymoron of sorts) but a faith-with; a radical heteronomy precedes the autonomy of our reason and will and in fact first makes them possible. It is for this reason that our thinking bears such profound foreshadowings of the personal act of supernatural faith.

Before turning to inquire directly into the relation of faith proper to metaxological thinking, it is helpful to make one last observation with regard to the positivity of reason. Desmond's conception of reason entails a revaluation of sorts of the nature and role of *wonder* in philosophical thought, and that revaluation opens up yet another fruitful resonance in relation to theology. It should be obvious, given the importance of the mystery of being and the positive presence of the other in thinking, that wonder would have a decisive position in Desmond's philosophy. But there is a dimension of his appreciation of wonder that goes beyond the obvious, and will prove to be crucial in the consideration of theology. Desmond does more than recall our attention to the wonder that sets philosophical thinking in motion, as the classical tradition has it, but insists that wonder is *also* found *at the end*. Wonder, for Desmond, is not just the spur to thinking, but represents a sort of culmination of thinking, a privileged mode of mindfulness. It can be such, once again, precisely because of the inexhaustible positivity of being: "But if there is something before and beyond determination and self-determination, namely, the overdetermination of given being, there is the ever fresh source of the originating and the outliving wonder. It gives birth, it will be reborn. It never died, for it was always being reborn, though we do our worst to abort it, while claiming our choice to be for life."[27] Thinking *culminates* in wonder precisely because the self-giving and unmasterable other codetermines thinking from its very roots. Thinking therefore does not have to strive—through erotic dialectic—to close every distance, and leave behind the "*love* of wisdom," as Hegel notoriously put it, but can embrace the distance and the "reserve" it implies, *precisely as* a perfection and completion. Affirming a perfection inside the distance of wonder, however, does not mean that reason is finished simply in its being astonished and seeks no more intimacy, more profound knowledge, of its object, but only that this seeking will take the essentially *generous* form of agapeic love, a willingness to be surprised by its other, and the gift of genuine (and *rational*) intimacy.

THE POSITIVITY OF RELIGION

Having sketched out, however briefly and inadequately, some of the basic features of Desmond's sense of being and the shape of the thinking that arises from within this boundless mystery, we may finally turn back to the dilemmas presented at the outset in order to see how Desmond's thought navigates deftly—with "finesse"![28]—through them, and therefore offers a philosophy that can fructify and be fructified in turn inside of a relationship with theology. On the one hand, we see that the transcendent, for Desmond, is never wholly alien to reason, even while its nonalien character does not attenuate its genuine transcendence. An abiding theme in Desmond's thought is the desire for God that lies so deep within reason it may be said in fact to define its essence. But this desire, it should be noted again, is not a mere lack. This point is crucial, and a misunderstanding here would have far more problematic implications than it might initially appear. If the desire were a mere lack, a mere "negativity," it would be an impetus (*conatus essendi*) simply to fill the hole. But this would make the desire in itself an imperfection, which means it would be eliminated to the extent that reason reaches completion; it would necessarily measure the transcendent other by reason's need. The gratuity of God's self-revelation, which defines theology, would in this case be eliminated. For Desmond, the desire is, from the beginning, not an expression of mere need but more basically of abundance (which does not mean that the desire, as we tend to live it in our fallenness, does not inevitably include elements of neediness). It is primordially and ultimately a gift, of which reason is both object and subject. All this has its roots in what I have called the *positivity* of being.

Let us call this desire *love*, and thus invoke with it aspects typically ascribed on the one hand to *eros* and on the other to *agape*, without needing to separate these aspects out from each other in the present context. A love of being entails, precisely to be true to itself, a desire for and affirmation of its source. If we define reason as the love of being, we can see how the love of God may thus be said to be *intrinsic* to reason, that is, to arise from its very center, without this implying either what the tradition has condemned as "ontologism" or, on the other hand, what Heidegger and his followers have condemned as onto-theology.[29] It is crucial to see that it is *precisely* metaphysics that enables Desmond to avoid these. Being, for Desmond, is itself "hyperbolic." In its positive givenness, and so perfect immanence within thinking, which allows reason precisely to think whatever it thinks, being at the same time is no fixed and delimited object but an openness to the ever greater. There is a simultaneity in reason's relation to being of closure and openness, which makes the erotic/agapeic love *of the other* an internal perfection of the self (and not the result of a mere lack). The movement to the other is therefore not (merely) from potency to act, from imperfection to perfection, but from overdeterminacy to a greater overdeterminacy, from perfection to perfection—"grace upon grace." In this regard, the radical transcendence in relation to God is analogously anticipated in reason's normal activity, interpreted metaphysically. The love of being itself opens up into love of God in a way that does not simply project an immanent measure which would define in advance the possibilities of God's self-disclosure. Instead, the love of being, because of being's absolute priority, its *givenness*, is a capacity to receive measure from above. Understood from the perspective of the love of being, faith would not represent a "heteronomy" that simply reverses reason's autonomy, or more precisely, its essential heteronomy would not be in principle opposed to, but would instead recapitulate and elevate, reason's proper activity, because reason's autonomy always already has a heteronomous structure. Desmond's metaxological metaphysics thus implies an *intrinsic* openness of philosophy—specifically *as metaphysics*—to theology, without any preemptive setting of conditions of possibility.[30] We thus have a response to the first dilemma.

Above, we saw that wonder, for Desmond, is not only the beginning of philosophy, but is also reborn, so to speak, at its end. It should be clear how this point relates to the simultaneity of closure and openness in the love of being and the love of God. But we ought to see more specifically the relevance of this point to theology. Here we come to the second dilemma presented at the outset, which indicated the need to see theology as offering a fulfillment of philosophy but without making philosophy thereby obsolete. If wonder—and all the desire, questioning, reflection, distance, and so forth it implies—is not simply a function of imperfection but belongs to the fulfillment of reason, we can see how it is the case that theology can satisfy philosophy without, so to speak, shutting it off. Concretely speaking, a metaxological philosophy, as handmaiden to theology, would help prevent theology from drifting into fideism, fundamentalism, biblical or doctrinal positivism, and ideology insofar as it would remind theology that the task of coming to understand is never simply left behind, and truth is not something that can be grasped in a closed fist. The data of revelation, and the theological thinking that has been generated by it, is never something simply to be *used* for some extratheological project (such as shoring up morals or driving political action), however laudable. The *listening* to the Word of God, *theo-logos*, is *itself* the point: theology is *supremely* "sabbatical." Whatever we have understood opens us first of all to the possibility of deeper understanding. God's self-disclosure is *not* the overcoming of mystery, as Hegel thought,[31] but is precisely a deeper and more immediate, because more directly personal, *gift* of that mystery. Through the analogies of philosophy, metaxologically understood, we come to see the task of theology as the devotion of the whole person in abiding fidelity to the boundless truth of God.

But this last point leaves us with a fundamental question with respect to the approach to philosophy that Desmond offers. If God's self-revelation does not eliminate wonder, and the questions that belong to the heart of philosophy, if it does not render philosophy in principle obsolete, then we have to ask whether it is necessary to make the explicit assent of faith an ever open possibility, rather than an actuality, as Desmond seems to do, in order to preserve the distinct integrity of philosophy and its difference from theology. In concrete terms, is philosophy simply *about* saying yes, and what it means to do so, or might it not at some point fall *to philosophy itself* to say yes? To put the question in yet another way, is it possible that insisting on being *between* could in given circumstances imply an indecisiveness that becomes principled, an indecisiveness that could undermine the very positivity of being and reason that constitutes the metaxological character of philosophy? Clearly, what it would mean to philosophize in explicit Christian faith in a manner distinct from theology is an extremely difficult matter, and we cannot of course work out the details here.[32] In any event, we do have some examples in the modern era, that is, after the two disciplines were clearly distinguished from each other, in whose company it would be easy to imagine putting Desmond himself: Maurice Blondel, who famously ended his first major work with a "yes" ("C'est!"), and whose late work was explicitly accomplished inside of faith;[33] Gabriel Marcel, who often pointed—in the distance, no doubt, but no less directly—to the Catholic mysteries, such as the Eucharist, that inspired his philosophical reflection;[34] and perhaps most clearly Ferdinand Ulrich, who, as Hans Urs von Balthasar said, stands "eye to eye" with the innermost Christian mysteries without ever departing from the strictly metaphysical realm.[35] The list could go on extensively, but the point is simply that, if what is actual is ipso facto possible, it is possible to think inside of an explicit assent of faith without ceasing to be a philosopher.

My suggestion is that if this were not a possibility, then the relationship between philosophy and theology that I have argued is essential to the health of *both* would finally break down: if the explicit assent of faith marked the *end* of philosophy and the *beginning* of theology, we would be left in the end having to choose between the two. We would thus fall back inside the terms of the dilemmas. Desmond's metaxological mindfulness, with its rootedness in the positivity of being, would seem to offer especially abundant resources for avoiding this collapse. Typically, philosophy of religion points in the end in a vague way to "the divine," or speaks of religion "in general," in order to avoid, presumably, positing the authority for reason of a particular tradition. It is not false, of course, or in itself problematic, to speak about "religion" or "the divine." But if thinking ends there and defines itself in these terms, closing off the possibility of an *actual* historical revelation of God that would make a particular tradition authoritative, it does indeed become problematic. It is not accidental that this sort of thinking conceives philosophy as simply *preparing the way* for theology, and reason opening up to the possibility of faith, whether or not it defers this possibility, finally, into eternity. The final stress in this sort of philosophy of religion lies on the negative: the ultimate darkness or incomprehensibility of God. Hegel, as it turns out, clearly saw the dangers of this sort of irrationalism. He is one of the few canonical figures in philosophy who understood the profound philosophical implications of what is referred to as the *positivity* of religion: above all, the specific dogma, but also the positive institution of the church, the positivity of tradition, magisterium, authority, and so forth. The problem of course is that, as we saw, he rejects the philosophical intelligibility of the positive qua positive and so recuperates its positivity through the dialectical negating of the negative, which is simply its "counterfeit double." But this is precisely why Hegel absorbs religion into philosophy.

One of Desmond's great accomplishments has been to recover a certain priority of religion *over* philosophy, eye to eye with Hegel. The transcendence of religion (and art)[36] in relation to philosophy is, as Desmond has shown, part of the *perfection* of philosophy itself. It would seem that this conception of reality and reason would be able to include the specifically positive features of religion, beginning with the positive fact of God's self-revelation in Jesus Christ, as superabundantly fruitful for the mindfulness precisely of philosophy. The conventional separation of philosophy and theology attempts to preserve the distinction by insisting that a thinking which begins from within the positive claim of faith is ipso facto *theological* in the strict sense, and no longer philosophical. But this insistence takes for granted precisely what Desmond disputes, namely, that philosophical thinking is most properly *not* the response to an other but follows its own lights, as it were. As we have seen, Desmond interprets thinking as heeding a call and so being accompanied by its "other" from the beginning to the end of its operation. For him, therefore, reason becomes more perfectly rational in this "con-fidence." This *con-fides* would seem to make reason inwardly apt, beyond this trusting response to what has entrusted itself, to accept *fides sensu stricto*. To see this is to recognize how Desmond's metaxological notion of being and reason can offer a genuinely new way of thinking about the relationship between philosophy and theology, and indeed the possibility of a fruitful collaboration between them in the service of Christian faith.

NOTES

1. Cf. Aquinas, *Commentary on the Metaphysics*, 1.1.2: The intellect is that "a quo homo est id quod est."

2. There are subtler variations of the two arms of each dilemma, which would be fruitful to trace out and reflect on, but reasons of space require a certain simplification.

3. See Gabriel Marcel, "On the Ontological Mystery," in *The Philosophy of Existentialism* (New York: Citadel Press, 1984), 9–46.

4. Friedrich Nietzsche, *Göttzen-Dämmerung*, Kritische Studienausgabe, vol. 6, ed. Giorgio Colli and Mazzino Montinari (Berlin: De Gruyter, 1988), 113.

5. Cf. *ISB*, xv. On the *positive* sense of mystery, which pervades Desmond's writings, see, e.g., *BB*, 205.

6. See *BB*, 4.

7. See G. W. F. Hegel, *The Science of Logic* (Atlantic Highlands, NJ: Humanities Press, 1969), 67–78, where Hegel explains why philosophy must begin with a pure (i.e., empty) concept of being. For a profound critique of this starting point, see Ferdinand Ulrich, "Über die spekulative Natur des philosophischen Anfangs," in *Innerlichkeit und Erziehung*, ed. Franz Pöggeler (Freiburg: Herder, 1964), 27–72.

8. Augustine, *Confessions*, bk. 3, ch. 6, §11.

9. On the important notion of "hyperbole" in Desmond, see Christopher Ben Simpson, *Religion, Metaphysics, and the Postmodern: William Desmond and John D. Caputo* (Bloomington: Indiana University Press, 2009), 132–34. See also William Desmond, "Hyperbolic Thought: On Creation and Nothing," in *Framing a Vision of the World: Essays in Philosophy, Science, and Religion*, ed. André Cloots and Santiago Sia (Leuven: Leuven University Press, 1999), 23–43.

10. See, e.g., the great wealth of description Desmond offers of ways we open up to God (again) in a godless age: *GB*, 31–45.

11. See Friedrich Hölderlin's reflection on this statement, which is known as Ignatius's "Grabschrift," in his *Hyperion: Sämtliche Werke*, vol. 3, ed. Friedrich Beissner (Stuttgart: Cotta, 1958), 163.

12. Significantly, Desmond used this phrase to describe a collection of essays spanning fifteen years of his reflection: *ISB*. Emphasis mine.

13. On this, see especially the introduction to *ISB*, xiii–xxxii.

14. *ISB*, xxv–xxvi.

15. See, e.g., *BB*, 151–61.

16. Cf. *HG*. This notion is to my mind one of Desmond's most fruitful.

17. Desmond explains that a reaching out beyond the self can occur, not (only) because of some need, but also from the superabundant "joy of being itself." *GB*, 40. The importance of this point cannot be overstated, and represents a significant contribution to traditional (and indeed contemporary) reflections on the nature of desire.

18. *The William Desmond Reader*, ed. Christopher Ben Simpson (Albany: SUNY Press, 2012), 242.

19. We might compare Desmond's notion to Joseph Ratzinger's reflection on what he calls the "sabbath structure of creation": *"In the Beginning . . . ,"* trans. Boniface Ramsey (San Francisco: Ignatius Press, 1995), 30–32.

20. Josef Pieper, *Leisure, the Basis of Culture* (San Francisco: Ignatius Press, 2009).

21. *BB*, 9–11 (original emphasis); *ISB*, 266–67. Note that Pieper would not likely disagree with the observations Desmond makes here, but it is nevertheless certainly not a dimension Pieper himself highlights.

22. Kant, *Critique of Pure Reason*, preface, Bxxx.

23. See, e.g., Gianni Vattimo, *A Farewell to Truth*, trans. William McCuaig (New York: Columbia University Press, 2011).

24. *IST*, 333.

25. See William Desmond, "Consecrated Thought: Between the Priest and the Philosopher," *Louvain Studies* 30 (2005): 92–106.

26. *ISB*, 217.

27. *ISB*, 293–94.

28. Desmond often refers to Pascal's notion of *l'esprit de finesse*, which tends to be forgotten in the modern world dominated by *l'esprit de géometrie*.

29. These two notions are, of course, not the same, though there may be a distant kinship between them.

30. We might contrast this with Jean-Luc Marion, who believes one has to reject metaphysics in order to avoid preset conditions of possibility; this judgment reveals only that Marion does not have a specifically "metaxological" notion of being.

31. See G. W. F. Hegel, *Lectures on the Philosophy of Religion*, vol. 1, ed. Peter Hodgson (Berkeley: University of California Press, 1996), 184 fn. 85.

32. For a more thorough argument, see D. C. Schindler, *The Catholicity of Reason* (Grand Rapids, MI: Eerdmans, 2013), 305–33.

33. Maurice Blondel, *L'Action*, trans. Oliva Blanchette (Notre Dame, IN: University of Notre Dame Press, 1984), 446.

34. See, e.g., Marcel, "The Ontological Mystery," 44.

35. See the cover of Ferdinand Ulrich, *Homo Abyssus: Das Wagnis der Seinsfrage*, 2nd ed. (Freiburg: Johannes Verlag Einsiedeln, 1998).

36. Whereas Hegel famously subordinates art and religion to philosophy, as lesser incarnations, so to speak, of Absolute Spirit, Desmond argues for art and religion as genuinely transcendent "others" of philosophical thinking in positive relation to which philosophy has its proper integrity; see *PO*.

CHAPTER 5

Way(s) to God

William Desmond's Theological Philosophy

JOSEPH K. GORDON AND D. STEPHEN LONG

One of the great merits of William Desmond's philosophy is his ability to welcome and affirm the legitimacy of the question of God anew out of the rubble of ascendant modern and postmodern philosophies that have hitherto forbidden it. Desmond's unique and constructive approach to thinking about transcendence allows for a fresh recasting of traditional approaches to the question of God. His philosophy troubles any rigid distinction between secular and religious categories, between reason and faith or philosophy and theology. As he himself puts it:

> We can plot a border between territories and insist that faith and reason only travel to the other's country under proper visa. Then they will enter illegally, without certification or passport. There are no univocal borders in mind and spirit which bar trespass or illegal entry; there is a porosity more elemental than all

passports and academic policing. . . . Where is the pure faith relative to which thought is excluded? Where is there pure reason that entirely excludes all trust?[1]

In Desmond's hands, philosophical reason manifests and draws on faith while theology contributes to, corrects, and perfects philosophy. Any settled, satisfied division of labor between the two disciplines is unsettled. As will be shown, however, he does not collapse philosophy into theology; he refuses to cordon theology off into some sphere of pure faith relegating to philosophy rationality qua rationality. The distinction between philosophy and theology cannot be equated to the distinction between reason and faith. Reason assumes faith. Faith entails reason.

Desmond's philosophical theology—or better put, theological philosophy—frequently returns to the question of God but never directly, for God is not an object in the world among other objects. We cannot begin with God; we must begin with our existence in the "between" of being. Desmond recognizes the difficulty of the task of seeking God from this starting point. He regularly refers to his visits with the philosopher Paul Weiss, who would ask him, "How do you get from being to God?"[2] He does not allow a fear of onto-theology to prevent him from finding a way.

Desmond's theological philosophy, his traditional and yet revised teaching on God, is not easily presented. In order to do so, our essay unfolds in two stages. The first sets forth what Desmond is for. It presents Desmond's teaching on God, beginning with his take on the ontological argument and his articulation of the relationship between "ways" and "ethos." That beginning point moves us into metaxology and his fourfold way. Only after we have some sense of what Desmond is for can we then express his concerns about modern teachings on God that too often understand God as an erotic sovereignty rather than agapeic communication, an understanding often indebted to Hegel. Desmond worries that many theologians working in Hegel's shadow have not quite gotten beyond Hegel; they have perhaps not grasped the gravity of their capitulations to Hegel's malformed understanding of transcendence.[3] Desmond's convincing provocation of the "postulatory finitism(s)" of contemporary philosophy emerges from his comprehensive attempts to wrestle with the "sublationary infinitism" of Hegel, and so our second section offers an account of his extensive engagement with Hegel. As Desmond puts it in a recent interview, he "[tries] to develop a post-Hegelian systematic form of thinking that takes due notice of what is at issue in his system."[4] He does not reject Hegel outright. Hegel is too close to being right for him to set up a simple opposition. Yet as his compatriot philosopher Cyril O'Regan also argues, Desmond affirms that Hegel is a "seducer" whose approximation to Christian theology makes him more dangerous than even the revisionary Schleiermacher.[5] Hegel produces a "counterfeit double" of the perfectly simple Triune God.[6] Desmond's philosophy of God provides a way that finally gets beyond Hegel. Once we have established what Desmond affirms and how he is able to do the work he has done through engaging and finally moving beyond Hegel, we can offer some suggestions regarding future theological uses of Desmond's work. In our conclusion we gesture toward fruitful encounters Desmond's theological philosophy could have with some key voices in contemporary theology.

DESMOND'S THEOLOGICAL PHILOSOPHY

The "Ontological Argument" and Its Ethos and Ways

Desmond frequently returns to and comments on Anselm's "ontological argument" and its historical reception by subsequent philosophers and theologians.[7] What is the ontological argument? Is it a logical argument grounded in a "neutral" use of reason that sought to demonstrate God's existence to anyone? If so, "Enlightenment reason" found it lacking and concluded that God's existence cannot be demonstrated. Not to be dissuaded, theology was tempted by a "fideism" that also found it lacking, asserting that knowledge of God comes by faith alone and retreating into its own "fideistic self-legitimation."[8] Desmond argues that both positions have something in common: both agree that there is no "neutral" use of reason that can demonstrate God's existence. Enlightenment rationalism asked for such a neutral rationality. Fideism rejected the possibility of any such neutral rationality. Desmond rejects both.

Given his rejection, one might expect Desmond to find solace among the modern neoscholastics who affirm a neutral, metaphysical reason and argue it can prove God's existence. But as he often does, Desmond surprises his readers by refusing this all-too-trodden path and by finding a different path beyond modern sureties. Desmond agrees with Enlightenment rationalism and fideism that there is no "neutral reason" and that interpreting proofs for God's existence in these terms is a mistake, but he draws vastly different conclusions. The difficulty with Enlightenment rationalism, fideism, and, we might add, neoscholastic neutral metaphysics is their common "univocalization of being." Each of them fails to be mindful of the "ontological context" out of which Anselm's and Aquinas's "ways" to God emerge. Neutral rationality requires of the "proofs" an abstraction from their original contexts that renders them intelligible. Desmond states that "we do an injustice to the 'proofs' if we abstract them from the ontological context in which they are formulated; we have to acknowledge a complex interplay of ways and ethos."[9]

What is meant by "ways and ethos"? An ethos is our ontological givenness whether it comes to us in terms of our being or from a summons to goodness. There is for Desmond a primal ethos in which we are already "coming to be" before we are "becoming." The primal ethos can be reconfigured into a second ethos that often neglects that "coming to be" for the sake of our "becoming." The ontological argument is one "way" to God; it is a way that begins from an understanding of the "primal ethos" that is open to transcendence. Desmond argues that modern understandings of the ontological argument often occlude an authentic sense of transcendence by a secondary ethos that has reconfigured that primal ethos. The modern tendency to the "univocalization of being" is a reconfiguration of the primal ethos that does not have to be, but once it is, and once it becomes mindless of the primal ethos, it blocks off or is forgetful of potential "ways" to God.

Desmond's point can be best understood, not by offering definitions of *ethos* and *ways*, but by comparing his interpretation of Kant's and Anselm's versions of the ontological proofs. Kant's version, he states, is "formulated within the metaphysical ethos of the modern world-view."[10] For that reason, it has an "extraordinary thin notion of existence." Existence is not "redolent with the fullness of being" or founded upon "agapeic astonishment"; instead it is emptied of such fullness and is reduced to an autonomous subject who posits based on a limited understanding of experience.[11] Once this secondary ethos takes hold, God primarily becomes a "fixed being outside the world."[12] Any way to God founded upon this secondary ethos will seek a way from creation to such a fixed being, but this univocal way always fails, ending in equivocity. From univocity emerges equivocity, and the way to God is caught within an unbridgeable dualism.

Such a way is not all bad. Kant's criticism of the ontological way, given this ethos, will rightly acknowledge that there is no way from a concept of God to the reality of God. Kant opposes all conceptual idolatries of immanence that move too readily from our concept to God's reality. Yet why should this ethos condition our ways to God? Desmond does not think it should. Instead, he provides a therapy of "unclogging" that pushes the secondary ethos back toward its primal ethos, questioning the former's adequacy to the latter.[13] What is missing in Kant? He states, "We find no sense of the context of prayer that informs Anselm's version of the proof: no inkling that the idea of 'that which none greater can be conceived' is logically thought through by Anselm, but within the ethos of religious meditation. None of this nurturing matrix is present in thinking about, so to say, an *orphan concept* of God."[14]

Desmond continues this critique in his *God and the Between*. Kant's ontological argument is an inheritance from Wolff that was an "orphan concept" because it failed to be mindful of "prayer and meditation." Desmond argues forcefully and compellingly that prayer and meditation arise spontaneously and authentically from agapeic astonishment in the primal ethos.[15]

Desmond revisits the ontological way (no longer proof) throughout his work, acknowledging that his account of it is nontraditional. It is not a conceptual logic locked in subjectivity but "a relation to a community." He explains, "I mean that the power of the ontological way is just *its dwelling on a consummate relation, or an ultimate togetherness:* the ultimate togetherness of God with the mindfulness that comes to wakefulness in human selving. It is the being of the human to be communicative but its communicative being finds itself in an inescapable community with ultimate communicative being."[16]

Anselm is not an analytic philosopher providing an irrefutable logical argument; he prays, and in his prayers he becomes astonished by what "importunes" him.[17] A way is opened, but it is not the univocal way of the modern ethos. No such univocal way to God could possibly exist; as Desmond notes, "There is no absolutely univocal way to God, for any such a way is itself a derivative from the interplay of ethos and ways."[18] We always find ourselves "between" a way and an ethos. The question upon which the discernment of ways to God turns is the following: What kind of self is the self which is doing the finding?

The Primal Ethos of Transcendence, Selving, and the Way(s) to God

Desmond's theological philosophy begins with the self, but it is not a self that already contains everything it needs for its way to God. It is not a self that looks within and finds a feeling of absolute dependence upon which theology can be established. It is an astonished self, perplexed at the recognition that it exists at all. This perplexity leads Desmond to differentiate three forms of transcendence; each is a relation of difference.[19] First transcendence (T1) is the "other being of nature." What is external to the self can never be reduced to the "categories" of the self; it exists as inexorably other. Second transcendence (T2) is "of the self-being of the human." We transcend ourselves interiorly. We are driven to be more than what we are through the exercise of our freedom. Third transcendence (T3) is the "difference of the divine." Without third transcendence, second transcendence becomes *conatus essendi*, the struggle or striving for being. With third transcendence, second transcendence is not understood as strife and struggle but as *passio essendi*.[20] Desmond explains this in one of his earlier works, *Art, Origins, Otherness*:

The between is given in this primal coming to be. The between then is the finite happening of being within which the togetherness of beings, and human being's togetherness with being, is made actual. And we come to ourselves there, we may think we are "projectors"—but this is not original enough, and it is conducive to false being, if we forget that there is a *passio essendi* before there is a *conatus essendi*. Our *passio essendi*, our receiving of being given to be is not a "throw," and our being gifted with *conatus essendi* is not our "projecting."[21]

A *conatus essendi* without a *passio essendi* would be a striving or projecting of human subjectivity as found in Nietzsche's "postulatory finitism." "Postulatory finitism" is a philosophical position in which the philosopher refuses to postulate the possibility of God on principle.[22] Mindfulness of the *passio essendi* which is antecedent to—and the very condition of the possibility of—the *conatus essendi* produces a self caught in astonishment and led to prayer. "Prayer," suggests Desmond, "is a form of astonished thought, sometimes so astonished it seems thought is laid asleep in reverence. Thought is prayer become perplexed at the mystery before it. What does perplexity find unavoidable? The thought of the being greater than which none can be conceived. Thus Anselm's definition of God."[23] God is not a logical concept for Anselm but an overdetermined source who gives rise to being, making it "coming to be" before it can "become." Anselm's argument arises from prayer, for it is a form of thought willing to be perplexed by the self in the between.

The Between

The "between" in Desmond's thought comes from Plato's use of *metaxu*; it designates how the *eidē*, the forms, relate to what is.[24] We are between the forms and their reality, but Desmond's metaxology is more than Plato's *metaxu*. Desmond's *metaxu* depends upon God creating out of nothing. There is nothing intrinsic to being that necessitates creation, and yet creation is. Mindful creatures reflect upon the fact that they already are before they can become. Being then is "porous." It is not fixed, determinate, or secure in itself. It comes from something other than itself before it can become what it might become. It exists in the between of this porosity.

What are we between in Desmond's thought? Perhaps Desmond's most succinct statement of the between is found in his essay "Wording the Between":

> We start in the midst of things, and we are open to things. We are open because we are already opened. Before we come to ourselves as more reflectively thoughtful, we already are in a porosity of being, and are ourselves as this porosity of being become mindful of itself. This ethos of being I call 'the between,' and for me metaphysics is not an abstraction from this but a more deeply mindful engagement with it. We are already enabled to be within the between.[25]

Although this succinct statement of the between is not difficult to understand, it resists a precise determination, which is central to the between. It resists any ontological determination where to be is to be determinate. Such an ontology, found in Kant, seeks to determine being by setting it within definite and univocal categories. The between resists categorization. It is more movement, "a milieu of passing and transiting," than it is determination.[26] The between cannot be isolated, but its "field of movement" can be identified. We are between a primal and a second ethos, a coming to be and a becoming, a *passio essendi* and a *conatus essendi*. The between is a "way."[27]

The Fourfold Way: Univocity, Equivocity, Dialectic, Metaxology

Desmond's theological philosophy, like his metaphysics, traces a fourfold way. This fourfold way assists philosophy "to rethink the perplexities of metaphysics."[28] The perplexities are many, but Desmond's work returns again and again to the perplexities of being, the good, and God. The fourfold way produces a "plurivocal" ontology that refuses to be content with "the univocal reductions of modernity, the equivocations of postmodernity, and the dialectical sovereigns of modern idealism."[29] The fourfold way begins with the "univocal sense" of being where there is a sameness of mind and being and a "search for determinate solutions to determinate problems."[30] It tends toward the mathematical, the instrumental, and the technological. It does not mind the primal ethos but addresses God as a problem to be solved whether in terms of Descartes's defense of the ontological proof or Kant's rejection of it.[31] Because it seeks determination, it finds perplexity to be a sign of failure. If understood solely from the univocal sense, God becomes little more than absolute power, the *ens realissimum*.[32]

The univocal sense of being, however, passes unavoidably into the equivocal. God, being, and goodness resist the categories of the univocal way. Their very positing in the univocal way, because they must always also be more than mere positing, produces the "perplexity" that defines the equivocal sense, which is the "unmediated difference of being and mind."[33] Because it is "unmediated," the god who emerges from the equivocal way could be a good that we do not know, or equally it could be a dark abyss, an evil at the origin, or the *khora* that does little more than trouble us, eternally escaping our gaze.[34] Unlike the univocal sense, the equivocal relishes perplexity. Whereas all perplexity is only something to be overcome in the univocal sense of being, resigned perplexity is the only answer in the equivocal sense. The dialectical sense moves beyond the equivocal and recognizes that the human ability to identify the equivocal already entails more than perplexity alone. Something has been mediated. The dialectical is the "mediated conjunction of mind and being."[35] It is, however, a self-mediation. As he writes in a recent essay, "In this mediation, the fixity of univocal identity gives way to more fluid differences, while these, in turn, are not merely dissolving moments of flux but mediating moments of a process of becoming. . . . There is here a mediated return to identity—not the first univocal identity but speculative identity."[36] God mediates God's self to us for the sake of what God lacks; dialectic produces an erotic sovereignty that cannot affirm the primal ethos of agapeic communication.

If we are attentive to the primal ethos, then the metaxological sense arises. Like the dialectical sense, it is a mediated sense but "not in terms of the self-mediation of the same." The metaxological is a "pluralized mediation . . . hospitable to the mediation of the other, or transcendent, out of its own otherness," which is better described as "intermediation" than "self-mediation."[37] Desmond presents God's intermediation in terms of ten "metaphysical cantos" that take up traditional teachings on God's existence, simplicity, eternity, omnipotence, omniscience, immutability, impassability, and unity. Although the results of his cantos are quite traditional, the context in which these results operate depends upon his metaxology. It is not so much the affirmation of God's traditional "attributes" that is decisive as it is *why* this way of speaking about God matters.

Desmond's unique articulation of these traditional affirmations is significant because it allows us to speak about God in God's absoluteness without being content with God as pure power, equivocal difference, or erotic sovereignty. That God is power, difference, and sovereign is undeniable, but such terms will lead to significant errors if the metaxological sense gets neglected, misremembered, or denied from a reconstructed secondary ethos. Why does a metaxological way to God matter? It reveals God's absolute power as an "enabling letting." Desmond writes:

> The scandal of absolute power is that it communicates itself in an enabling *letting*: it lets the finite being be as other, it lets it be power—and the letting forces nothing, constrains nothing, coerces nothing; it simply releases into the goodness of free power itself. The scandal of divine (over)all-power is that it is the ultimate patience: it is manifest in giving, in giving away from itself, not giving such that the recipient is forced to recognize the good of the giver, for the pure giving is for the good of the receiver, who may not comprehend he, she or it is the recipient.[38]

The significance of Desmond's theological philosophy is that it presents a traditional rendering of God in nontraditional terms which attends to legitimate concerns that have arisen in the wake of both modern and postmodern developments. He allows theologians to address many contemporary criticisms of that traditional teaching without the theological revisions for which those critics call. Such revisions, he suggests, would produce a counterfeit double of God that finally cannot sustain God's absolute power as an "enabling letting." Desmond diagnoses a significant problem among contemporary theologians.[39] In the wake of Hegel, God is frequently cast as an erotic sovereignty who may or may not be trustworthy. These new theologies may have valid criticisms, but their solutions frequently only exacerbate the problems they seek to address. For too often Hegel's "counterfeit double" stands in for the God of agapeic communication.

DESMOND'S ENGAGEMENT WITH HEGEL

Throughout his career Desmond has maintained a high degree of respect for Hegel. Desmond's assessments of Hegel are born of decades of thorough and careful engagement with Hegel's philosophy.[40] Hegel proves himself an especially important conversation partner in matters of religion. As Desmond writes in the conclusion to *Hegel's God*, "Hegel makes us reconsider the question of God and how he answers it. He also forces us to ask how we might differently pose the question and respond."[41] "One of the great attractions of Hegel," he admits in *Is There a Sabbath for Thought?*, "is just the seriousness with which he appears to take religion."[42] "On the surface," he emphasizes, "Hegel's thinking saturates us with God."[43] Even given his high respect for Hegel, he does not shy away from sharp criticisms of Hegel's deficiencies. As he candidly states in a recent interview, "I have been increasingly more critical of Hegel in thinking there is a systematic bias at work in his practice of dialectic."[44] Desmond's reading of Hegel is not solely exegetical.[45] He offers an erudite and frequently penetrating reading (or better readings) of the development(s) of Western philosophy throughout his works, but he has stated emphatically that he is not "primarily concerned with giving 'readings.' I am thinking about things."[46] Desmond reads Hegel as though Hegel was also thinking about things; he asks the question whether Hegel's thinking is adequate to what is actually the case. Hegel's speculative dialectic, in Desmond's judgment, lacks finesse for authentic philosophizing in the primal ethos of being. As he notes in another recent interview, the Hegelian sense of wholeness "finally collapsed differences in a manner that was not compatible with my own existential experience of 'being between.'"[47] This collapse is especially evident in matters of religion and God. Hegel only seems to take religion seriously. For Desmond, Hegel's emphasis on the value of religion cannot but be superficial.

Hegel's Ontological Argument: God as "Thinking Thinking Thinking" and the Distortion of Transcendence

Why does Desmond come to these conclusions? He argues that Hegel's radical recasting of God stems from his refusal to grant the legitimacy of thinking of transcendence as other to us. The way Hegel recasts the ontological argument illustrates his radical revision of divine transcendence. In the wake of Kant's deconstruction of Anselm's argument, Hegel provides a "speculative rehabilitation" of it.[48] While Kant dogmatically posits the impossibility of bridging the gap between the possibility and the actuality of the concept of God, Hegel bridges it through the speculative concept: "In the most fundamental sense of the concept or *Begriff* for Hegel, you cannot establish a gulf between possibility and actuality. The true concept is self-actualizing, and hence it is true only as being, only as being beyond a dualism of possibility and actuality: it actualizes itself. In a sense, the Hegelian concept performs the ontological argument on itself: it gives itself existence by thinking itself."[49]

For the ontological argument to be successful in Kant, one would have to be able to move from a conception of God through thought to the existence of God on the reserves of immanent human thought alone. This is impossible, however, because Kant restricts autonomous human thinking to the realm of determining possibility. External experiential evidence is required for verification of knowledge; one needs more than the subject's thought thinking *in ipse*.[50] But there is no gap between external evidence and internal thinking for Hegel's *Vernunft*.[51] In Hegel's understanding of human knowing, what for Kant is an unbridgeable dualism of subject (S) and object (O) in human consciousness is transcended and sublated in self-consciousness, S(S-O):

Self-consciousness refers us to a *knowing of the knowing* involved in consciousness of an object. As the latter is marked by the dyadic relation (S-O), so the former shows the triadic structure S(S-O). In being related to an object, I am in relation to myself as in relation to an object. The I of self-consciousness epitomizes the power of the more inclusive relativity, for not only can it relate to an other, it can include in itself its relation to an other. Hence in its self-relation, that other is not a radically alien other, but *its* other. There is the fact too that this inclusive relating is not static; and since in principle it can think anything, its inclusivity knows no absolute boundary but itself. It is the 'absolute self' that, in relating itself to an other, relates itself to itself as including that other within itself.[52]

Hegel's understanding of human self-conscious knowing sublates Kant's sharp dualism between thought and the external world of *Dingen an sich*. How does Hegel get from his understanding of human knowing to his counterfeit double of God?

It is important to note that Hegel's understanding of human self-consciousness, knowledge, and freedom is not entirely wrong. He does articulate something constitutive of the human experience and self-knowledge. As Hegel rightly notes, all limits regarding human knowing seem surpassable. One must know—or at least guess at—what is beyond a limit in order to plot that limit in the first place. "A limit, at most," Desmond writes, "is a provisional boundary that with further thought can be transcended.... [T]here seems something infinitely self-transcending about human thought. It is *capax infiniti*."[53] Though we could rightly object that it is too far a leap to identify the unrestricted scope of human questioning and thinking with some sort of absolute knowledge, Hegel would suggest that within the human subject's knowledge of herself we do not encounter this difficulty: "When knowing seeks to know itself, it is both the subject and the object. And while it might be mistaken about itself, it can also interrogate and test itself. So it seems it can be both the question, the judge, and the answer in one. There seems to be no need to appeal to an extrinsic standard, for it, the self-knowing, seems also to be the *immanent* standard."[54]

Hegel privileges this self-sufficient knowledge of self as the highest form of knowing and so shows himself to be "the epitome of the privilege given to self-determination in modernity."[55] Though Hegel differs from Kant decisively in many ways, the former's elevation of self-consciousness in its self-determination can be seen as an attempt to fulfill the program of Kant's challenge: *Sapere aude!* Hegel's description of the subject's self-conscious knowledge of herself in her self-determination radicalizes the program of Kantian autonomy. Thinking himself to have gotten beyond Kant's restrictive epistemological dualism, Hegel proceeds to project his understanding of dialectical self-consciousness onto the divine. Hegel scorns Kant's timidity regarding the possibility of affirming transcendence in his rebuttal of Kant's critique of the ontological argument. The ontological argument which Kant rejects is for Hegel the highest argument for God's existence. It shows God to be self-determining self-consciousness.[56] Hegel affects the apotheosis of dynamic autonomous self-consciousness as the highest form of knowing and so represents God as "thinking thinking thinking."[57] Hegel will go even further than this; his version of the ontological argument ostensibly takes us beyond mere representation: "It is no *model*—it is the *reality* of Godself. God is as self-creating; as thinking is as self-determining; as the transcendental ego is as self-positing."[58]

Hegel's God and Three Transcendences

Recall our discussion of Desmond's differentiation of three transcendences. Hegel's deification of human self-transcendence, or T2, necessarily denigrates the other two transcendences. Hegel cannot countenance the otherness of creation (T1) or the otherness of an absolute transcendence (T3), so in his *Vernunft* the objectivity of other contingent beings and of the possibilizing ground of said beings (T1 and T3, respectively) must be recast.[59] All must be speculatively dialectically reconfigured so it can be absorbed.

Because Hegel's own understanding of T2 distorts T1 and T3, his understanding of T2 itself requires critique. In his elevation of dialectical selving, Hegel seems to have forgotten the very contingency of such selving. That we are *capax infiniti* depends on the antecedent reality that we are at all. As we saw above, for Desmond the human *conatus essendi* depends on a prior *passio essendi*:

> The *passio essendi* [is] more primordial than the *conatus essendi*. Our endeavor to be is subtended by our being given to be. Our self-affirming will emerges out of a more primal being given to be. I even interpret *conatus* in the light of the co- of co-nature: conatus is a 'being born with.' We are birthed as ourselves but not by ourselves; we are marked by a 'with,' that from the origin binds us to what is more than we can produce through ourselves alone. In that sense, the conatus itself can't be just described in terms of a self-affirming will to be.[60]

A truer sense of the infinite inwardness of human subjectivity, Desmond argues, would recognize in it an "ineradicable recalcitrance to complete objectification," which would point it "beyond objectness and subjectness to transobjective and transsubjective transcendence (T3)."[61]

As we saw above, for Desmond the plurality of other contingent being (T1) makes it impossible for us to categorically domesticate it entirely. Even the finite always exceeds our determinations. Hegel reconceptualizes the other being of creation drastically. For him, God others god's self in "creation." Hegel's *Geist* thinks beyond the dualism of its own other of creation in self-consciousness of self as subject and as objectified other.[62] For Hegel "creation" is a "divine particularization";[63] it is a specific moment in God's "immanent self-determination."[64] For that reason, creation lacks otherness. Hegel's speculative dialectic is ultimately inadequate to account for the full force of the question of the coming to be of finite creation (the "that-it-isness" of it).[65] The "that it is at all" is what is finally at stake in the Christian doctrine of creation.[66] In fact, Desmond argues, the way Hegel reimagines creation is actually an erasure of creation: "an absolute that has to become itself to be itself cannot be an absolute to begin with, and hence cannot begin, or create, the new beginning we find in the finite between."[67]

Besides the insufficiency of Hegel's philosophy of God and creation to account for the irreducible otherness of finite being, his position on creation bears darker and more troubling implications. Hegel presents his philosophy of history as a theodicy.[68] For him this theodicy is "the rational history of God's reconciliation with *Godself.* His self-overreaching trinity, via its *Aufhebung* of the death and resurrection of Christ, does the evil on itself and undoes it, and so justifies the speculative-dialectical necessity of evil as necessary for God's own self-reconciliation."[69] Hegel's theology of creation ontologizes evil by making it a constitutively necessary moment within God's adventuring self-determination.[70]

As Desmond shows, Hegel shares in the modern rejection of a transcendent otherness which would impinge on human freedom and autonomy.[71] While many of his successors will inhabit positions of "postulatory finitism," Hegel proposes instead the "sublationary infinitism" of the *Begriff.*[72] He will not accept transcendence as an excess that is finally beyond the mediation of his speculative dialectic. In this, he inherits the distrust of transcendence in much modern thought and makes it his own. There is an invincible antinomy between the modern project of autonomy and transcendence as other.[73] Instead of Kantian timidity regarding the question of transcendence, Hegel boldly recasts transcendence. Hegel thinks he finds a way to get beyond transcendence as other in the immanent self-transcending power of the subject.

The counterfeit double God that Hegel envisions, however, is unworthy of worship or prayer.[74] It is no wonder that Hegel recasts transcendence as such; he always had a distaste for the submissive posture necessary for authentic worship and prayer.[75] Hegel recasts prayer as "auto-erotic." It is human participation "in coming back to itself through the other that is itself."[76] "In what true sense," Desmond asks, "can Hegel's God love, and in what sense could one *pray* to Hegel's God, once having made the speculative surpassing to philosophy as absolute knowing? The others will continue to pray to God, and love, but the Hegelian philosophers will know, and know beyond love and prayer."[77] For Desmond, philosophy must exhibit a poverty akin to prayerfulness if it is to have any chance of successfully thinking the between, the self, and God.

Hegel's apotheosis of dialectical selving is the projection of a truncated understanding of the *imago dei* onto God. Despite Hegel's affirmation of the superiority of Christianity, Hegel recasts everything constitutive of Christian thought and practice; everything is *aufgehoben* within his philosophy of *Geist*. Hegel thus creates a false double of God. Hegel succumbs to something like the fiery brook of Feuerbachian projection a couple of decades before Feuerbach formulated it.[78] More is needed than Hegel's omnicompetent and voracious dialectic. We have to get beyond that dialectic. Being true to being in our state of betweenness is necessary:

> This one form of inclusive self-mediating dialectic cannot 'cover' what God, creation, man each is; either in itself or in its relation to the others. Even if God is absolutely self-mediating, hence absolutely at home with self, there is more to be said, both with regard to creation, and the community of surplus good that saves, and especially with regard to what remains in reserve of God in relation to creation as other, and the free difference of the human.[79]

Desmond's constructive philosophical project, the product of decades of meticulous serious engagement with Hegel (among other philosophers), provides a way, at last, beyond Hegel's counterfeit double of God.

Concluding Thoughts: Prospective Encounters between Desmond and Theologians

In his magisterial *Kantian Reason and the Hegelian Spirit*, Gary Dorrien states, "Hegel . . . made the strongest bid that any thinker has ever made to be the Protestant Thomas Aquinas."[80] Dorrien, the best heir to the liberal Protestant tradition, recognizes how central Hegel is to that tradition. Nonetheless, he does not affirm Hegel without critique.

Hegel, he suggests, "wrongly left no room for apophatic theology, the intuition of God as the holy unknowable mystery of the world." Yet he acknowledges how thoroughly "Hegel's fluid, spiraling, relational panentheism changed the debate in theology about how God might relate to the world" and "paved the way for Troeltsch, Temple, White-head, Tillich and numerous Hegelians by offering an alternative to pantheism *and* the static being-God rejected by Nietzsche, Heidegger, and Levinas."[81] While Dorrien on the whole affirms the Hegelian moment in Protestant theology, Catholic neoscholastics recoil in horror. Steven A. Long counsels that beginning with Hegelian dialectics results in "checking Christian theology into the Graveyard Motel."[82] The problem with much contemporary Catholic theology is "hyper-trophic Hegelian relationality," which produces the "categoric error of superordinating relation to substance."[83] If we begin with relation rather than substance, we will lose the analogical interval necessary for theology. Only a metaphysics of pure nature can save us from the Hegelian infection. In this all too familiar and tired debate among, and within, Protestant and Catholic theologians and philosophers, Desmond's work offers a joyous and fresh way forward that resituates, without rejecting, traditional teaching on God. We need not choose between substance and relation as both Dorrien and Long suggest. Nor need we tarry any longer with the "completion" or "end" of metaphysics. We can begin "in the between" and find a metaphysics amenable to theology that avoids the criticisms found in Nietzsche, Heidegger, and Levinas.

Some theologies will not find Desmond's work congenial, especially those that have traded on the assumption that Western metaphysics has come to an end and a decisive break must now be made. Process theology will have little time for metaxology just as Desmond has little time for it. He offers an incisive criticism. Not only can process theology not distance itself from God as an erotic sovereign, but it does not take seriously the threat of an *"eros tur-ranos."*[84] Too much is at stake not to take such a god seriously. The commitment of process theologians to univocity prevents a careful consideration that their god is such a tyrant. Desmond does not mince words:

Whiteheadians insist that God cannot be an exception to the system of metaphysical principles. But if God is God and nothing but God is God, we are dealing with the *absolute exception*. To insist on metaphysical homogeneity to uphold integral intelligibility would have something unintelligible, if not obtuse about it. If it is God they are talking about, we do not know what they are talking about. For if it is God they are talking about, then they are not talking about God.[85]

Yet Desmond is able to offer us a way to God that takes up what process theologians, at their best, seek—a God who is not a tyrant but who generally provides for creatures in all their freedom and goodness. Desmond writes, "In originating creatures, God communicates but reserves power to allow power to be. God's power is *absolute* relative to the coming to be, but it is *cooperative* relative to the becoming of created beings."[86]

Desmond is more sparing in critiquing theologians who seek to pursue theology without metaphysics than those who adopt the revisionist process metaphysics. If Barth or some Barthians fall into that category, they might find a therapy for Barthian "hegeling" that does not react against God's involvement in history by positing a "substance metaphysics" that keeps God from such an engagement. What Barthian would not affirm Desmond's recognition that "if God is God and nothing but God is God, we are dealing with the *absolute exception*"? Yet Desmond also challenges any satisfaction with equivocation or dialectic that rejects the possibility of finding a way from the between to God. Like Barth, however, Anselm shows such a way through prayer.

Desmond also moves theology beyond well-worn debates about the end of metaphysics, and does so without romanticism or a hankering for the Middle Ages: "I reject what has followed from the alleged completion of metaphysics by a Hegel, or a Nietzsche, or Heidegger." He continues, "I do not simply reject, but hold that the fourfold offers us some basis to rethink the tradition of metaphysics. We must move beyond the paralysis and stultification generated by this rhetoric of the end of metaphysics."[87] Note his argument. He is not defending the "tradition of metaphysics" against those who would putatively liberate us from it; he is "rethinking" that tradition based on the "fourfold" way and showing us how engaging in the "end of metaphysics" is a waste of time and being.

This rethinking of the tradition of metaphysics also proves to be an interesting engagement between Desmond and Jean-Luc Marion's *God without Being*. On the one hand, Desmond cautions about an interpretation of Thomas in which "the name God is said to give in Exodus is seen as religiously converging with what metaphysics reasons out of God as Being."[88] This approach too easily leads to "univocity." On the other hand, reacting to univocity and its correlate onto-theology by saying that "God is without being" risks resting with equivocation.[89] We are not yet moving into the metaxological way. "God without being," suggests Desmond, "becomes being without God."[90] Such a theology loses the primal ethos of our being.

Desmond's teaching on God, found in his ten cantos, is refreshingly traditional in unexpected ways. His fourfold being raises questions that on first glance one might suspect of being nontraditional. For instance, he states, "An agapeic God makes it impossible to deny the divine involvement with time. But the question is the 'how' of that involvement, and of a 'how' that does justice to both a richer apprehension of the traditional sense of immutability and equally traditional sense of divine involvement."[91] He is not moving away from immutability and divine involvement, nor is he in any sense suggesting we must choose between them as univocation always demands. Instead, a "richer apprehension" shows how they depend upon each other. Much like von Balthasar, such a deepening of traditional teaching leads to dramatic encounters. Desmond dares to ask the question, "Can God ever be surprised?" He answers, "Any ventured answer must be diffident." But this does not prevent him from offering one: "But perhaps, in another sense, agapeic beminding is 'always' in a condition of surprise: joy in the giving to be, in the arising of the new, for all finite being is refreshed and freshly created, again and again."[92]

A conversation should take place between Desmond's agapeic communication and Sarah Coakley's affirmation of *erōs*. For Coakley, desire "is an ontological category belonging primarily to God, and only secondarily to humans as a token of their createdness 'in the image.' "[93] Such a claim could be seen as challenging Desmond, but for Coakley, like Desmond, God's desire knows no lack. Her theology also affirms the importance of prayer as a form of desire that entails a rich pneumatology regarding the incorporation of creatures into God's desire for us. Desmond's work, we think, would be amenable to Coakley's "théologie totale" and benefit from her pneumatological excess. Likewise her theology would find a common concern in his metaxology.

Desmond proves a rich conversation partner for contemporary theologians. If we neglect him, we will lose one of the more promising contemporary philosophical voices for theology. Unlike the inhabitants of so many philosophy departments, especially those in religious institutions, Desmond does not want to cordon us theologians off into our academic, ecclesial, or guild silos. With a joyful delight, he shows us what he has seen and invites us into conversation. Moreover, he understands that prayer and praise must have a place in philosophy and theology if they are not to be policed by a "postulatory finitism."

NOTES

1. *IST*, 98–99.

2. *GB*, 282.

3. "I'm afraid many of those who think they are beyond Hegel and dialectic," he states, "are not quite where they claim to be." Christopher Ben Simpson, "Between God and Metaphysics: An Interview with William Desmond," *Radical Orthodoxy: Theology, Philosophy, Politics* 1, nos. 1–2 (2012): 357–73, here 362.

4. Ibid., 359.

5. O'Regan finds von Balthasar recognizing the problem more than Barth: "Balthasar's concern is whether Hegelian thought does not constitute a deeper danger than the Enlightenment, since it more surreptitiously liquefies and ultimately liquidates Christianity." Cyril O'Regan, *The Anatomy of Misremembering: Von Balthasar's Response to Philosophical Modernity*, vol. 1: *Hegel* (New York: Herder & Herder, 2014), 33.

6. This is the carefully and thoroughly argued thesis of *HG*.

7. See William Desmond, "God, Ethos, Ways," *International Journal for Philosophy of Religion* 45 (1999): 13–30.

8. Ibid., 13.

9. Ibid., 14.

10. Ibid., 16.

11. Ibid., 17.

12. Ibid.

13. For more on "unclogging," see *GB*, 12–13.

14. Desmond, "God, Ethos, Ways," 18; original emphasis.

15. *GB*, 95.

16. *GB*, 152; original emphasis.

17. *Proslogion* 15.

18. *GB*, 4.

19. See *BB*, 231–32; *HG*, 2–4, 7, 25, 93–94; and *GB*, 22–23. We will return to Desmond's articulations of these transcendences in our examination of his treatment of Hegel below.

20. See *GB*, 23.

21. *AOO*, 261.

22. See *AOO*, 253 n. 41; for his application of this to Nietzsche, see *GB*, 2, 8. John Lennon's "Imagine" is perhaps the quintessential example of "postulatory finitism" in popular culture.

23. Desmond, "God, Ethos, Ways," 21.

24. *Symposium* 202b5. See *GB*, 57.

25. William Desmond, "Wording the Between," in *The William Desmond Reader*, ed. Christopher Ben Simpson (Albany: SUNY Press, 2012), 195–227, here 196.

26. "The between then is not a neutral space between fixed univocal points but a field of movement. It is a milieu of passing and transiting—a milieu of motion: of remotion and promotion, of submotion and supermotion. I speak of this between in terms of an *original porosity of being*, neither objective nor subjective, but enabling both, while being more than both. The porosity is a between space where there is no fixation of the difference of minding and things, where our mindfulness wakes to itself by being woken up by the communication of being in its emphatic otherness." Desmond, "Wording the Between," 201–2; original emphasis.

27. "We wish to think beyond the mind that instrumentalizes. The middle is not given to us as a mere means; it is the place of a way, a passage." *BB*, 46.

28. William Desmond, "Being, Determination, and Dialectic," in *Being and Dialectic: Metaphysics as a Cultural Presence*, ed. William Desmond and Joseph Grange (Albany: SUNY Press, 2000), 3–35, here 28.

29. Desmond, "Wording the Between," 197.

30. Desmond, "Being, Determination, and Dialectic," 28.

31. *GB*, 64, 68–71.

32. "It is especially important not to become fixated on overpowering univocity, so that absolute power does not become power as dominating force. God then becomes something like the *ens realissimum* who is also the supreme *efficient cause*, and in such a wise that our use of these notions does not distinguish between coming to be and becoming and the original of these that yet is more." *GB*, 316; original emphasis.

33. Desmond, "Being, Determination, and Dialectic," 28.

34. "That there is darkness in this world allows no escape from the perplexing thought that it is so because there is darkness in the origin." *GB*, 77.

35. Desmond, "Being, Determination, and Dialectic," 28. If projected onto the divine, the dynamism of self-mediation constitutive of human experience recasts the divine decisively. God mediates God's self to us for the sake of what God lacks; the dialectical way produces an erotic sovereignty that cannot affirm the primal ethos of agapeic communication.

36. *ISB*, 237–38.

37. Desmond, "Being, Determination, and Dialectic," 28.

38. *GB*, 320.

39. "[Hegel's] taking over of Christianity turns it to ends that are neither religious nor Christian. Theologically one must be concerned about the production of counterfeit doubles of a post-Hegelian sort." Simpson, "Between God and Metaphysics," 367.

40. In the interview with Chris Simpson, Desmond details the history of his engagement with Hegel's work and its reception among Hegel scholars: "One of the reasons I wrote *Art and the Absolute* (1986) was to try to give Hegel a sympathetic run for his money. . . . The book was liked by the Hegelians, though I now think I was sometimes ventriloquizing through Hegel—making him say things one would like him to say. The Hegelian confraternity liked *Art and the Absolute* since it seemed to offer a more open Hegel, and I was welcomed as a Hegelian sympathizer. Then in time I became a critical sympathizer, then a sympathetic critic, then a critic, and then with *Hegel's God* (2003) the door at the back of the church was pointed out to me and I took the message that for the pious Hegelians I was now anathema. So be

it." Simpson, "Between God and Metaphysics," 361–62. An examination of Hegel's own work would clearly take us far afield of our present concerns. Moreover, it would be impossible to offer an assessment of the relative merits of Desmond's reading of Hegel. What follows, then, represents a summary of Desmond's key critiques of Hegel's philosophy of God.

41. *HG*, 187.

42. *IST*, 117.

43. *HG*, ix.

44. Simpson, "Between God and Metaphysics," 362.

45. *HG*, 1–2.

46. Simpson, "Between God and Metaphysics," 359. See also *HG*, 10–11.

47. William Desmond and Richard Kearney, "Two Thinks at a Distance: An Interview with William Desmond by Richard Kearney on 9 January 2011," in Simpson, *The William Desmond Reader*, 229–44, here 229.

48. *HG*, 22.

49. *HG*, 22–23.

50. *HG*, 93–98.

51. *HG*, 95.

52. *HG*, 83 (original emphasis); see also *HG*, 79, 105. In this latter reference, Desmond describes Hegel's utilization of this triad (S(S-O)) to rethink the trinitarian theology. Desmond concludes that Hegel's trinity is a monistic whole; the absolute qualitative distinction between finite and infinite, between creation and God, is bridged in God's erotic self-othering and self-assimilation.

53. *HG*, 81.

54. *HG*, 82; original emphasis.

55. *ISB*, 240; *HG*, 5.

56. See *HG*, 93–99.

57. *HG*, 99 n. 10, 139.

58. *HG*, 96; original emphasis. Again, "Hegel would not say: this is a *model* taken from finite life which I apply to the divine; a finite metaphor of the absolute. He cannot do that, for such a strategy would necessarily entail a gap between finite and infinite. Rather he must say: this *is* the divine life, and no (mere) metaphor of it, no (mere) representation of it. It comprehends the energy of divine life itself. For a holistic God, otherness is no otherness at all" (*HG*, 106; original emphasis).

59. In his elevation of human self-consciousness "we can see the convergence between epistemology and morals, theory and practice: the diminution of the contribution of the given, and other-being (whether T1 or T3) in the

determination of intelligibility, goes with the elevation of the significance of the self's determining power (T2). The diminution and elevation are simply two sides of the same process by which the self stakes and consolidates its own claim to complete immanent self-determination." *HG*, 86.

60. Desmond and Kearney, "Two Thinks at a Distance," 242.

61. Ibid., 7.

62. See Desmond and Kearney, "Two Thinks at a Distance," 122–42.

63. Desmond and Kearney, "Two Thinks at a Distance," 123.

64. Ibid., 128.

65. Creation is thus "idiotic." On "idiocy," see *PU*, 55–101.

66. *HG*, 134.

67. *HG*, 134.

68. *HG*, 143–66.

69. *HG*,144; original emphasis.

70. David Hart offers an arresting description of the Hegelian sublation of evil which takes place in Hegel's understanding of God: "The collapse of the analogical interval between the immanent and economic in the Trinity, between timeless eternity and the transcendent and time in which eternity shows itself, has not made God our companion in pain, but simply the truth of our pain and our only pathetic hope of rescue; his intimacy with us has not been affirmed at all: only a truly transcendent and passionless God can be the fullness of love dwelling within our very being, nearer to us than our inmost parts. This 'Hegelian' God is not transcendent—truly infinite—in this way at all, but only sublime, a metaphysical whole that can comprise us or change us extrinsically, but not account for or transform us within our very being. And this is a fearful thought, especially if, like Moltmann, one seeks in the passions of the divine an explanation for the suffering of creatures: what a monstrous irony it would be if, in our eagerness to find a way of believing in God's love in the age of Auschwitz, we should in fact succeed only in describing a God who is the metaphysical ground of Auschwitz." David Bentley Hart, "No Shadow of Turning: On Divine Impassibility," *Pro Ecclesia* 11, no. 2 (2002): 192.

71. See *HG*, 19–26.

72. See *GB*, 8, 11, 235.

73. See *EB*, 32; *HG*, 4–5.

74. Adriaan Peperzak corroborates Desmond's judgment: "Driven by his desire to overcome all contradictions, he [Hegel] comprehended God as the unique and all-encompassing Spirit that is and comprehends itself as the *archē* and *telos* of the universe. The result was a God as wide as the universe, but not wider, and thus not more amazing or desirable." Adriaan Theodoor

Peperzak, *Philosophy between Faith and Theology: Addresses to Catholic Intellectuals* (Notre Dame, IN: University of Notre Dame Press, 2005), 191.

75. Desmond's biographical comments on Hegel's disdain for Schleiermacher's "feeling of absolute dependence" are illustrative: "Why did Hegel despise Schleiermacher? . . . We recall the contempt in his remark on Schleiermacher's view of religion as bound up with the feeling of dependence: and so, mocks Hegel, the dog would be the best Christian. . . . Hegel distains dependence. Even if there is some truth to his remarks, nevertheless there are dogs and there are dogs." *IST*, 122 n. 6.

76. *HG*, 61.

77. *HG*, 198; original emphasis.

78. Hegel died in 1831. Feuerbach's *Essence of Christianity* was published ten years later. In the early Hegel, Desmond suggests, "we find a theory of religion as projection *avant la letter*—and this is not only in a theoretical but in a practical sense. A *project for the future* is being insinuated. This will be an *epochal task* to reclaim heaven for earth, divinity for man. Hegel was a left-wing post-Hegelian, like Feuerbach and Marx, before he became a 'Hegelian.'" *HG*, 42 (original emphasis); see also *HG*, 74.

79. *HG*, 183.

80. Gary Dorrien, *Kantian Reason and the Hegelian Spirit: The Idealistic Logic of Modern Theology* (Malden, MA: Wiley-Blackwell, 2012), 160.

81. Ibid., 13; original emphasis.

82. Steven A. Long, *Natura Pura: On the Recovery of Nature in the Doctrine of Grace* (New York: Fordham University Press, 2010), 194.

83. Ibid.

84. *GB*, 25 n. 5.

85. *GB*, 245; original emphasis.

86. *GB*, 257; original emphasis.

87. *BB*, xvi.

88. *GB*, 283.

89. See *GB*, 283–84.

90. *GB*, 284.

91. *GB*, 298.

92. *GB*, 327.

93. Sarah Coakley, *God, Sexuality, and the Self: An Essay "On the Trinity"* (Cambridge: Cambridge University Press, 2013), 10.

CHAPTER 6

God Beyond and Between

Desmond, Przywara, and Catholic Metaphysics

PATRICK X. GARDNER

The prevailing myth of conflict between faith and reason has left a great many of us seeking refuge either in Athens or in Jerusalem. William Desmond distinguishes himself by seeking refuge in both, a stance so unconventional as to seem intellectually treasonous. In the eyes of believers claiming to be "without" or "beyond" metaphysics, he has far too much faith in reason. Yet in the eyes of rationalists claiming to be rid of religious fictions, he is too theologically garrulous—even insisting that the true philosopher, let alone the true theologian, is the one who prays. Desmond acknowledges, in other words, that reviving metaphysics means stripping philosophy of its arrogance while disabusing religion of its sacred irrationalities.[1] And in a modern setting like ours, these roads *between* Athens and Jerusalem can be lonely roads to walk.

Though perhaps not as lonely as we are tempted to think. The German Jesuit theologian Erich Przywara (1889–1972) stands out as a thinker after Desmond's own heart, a kindred spirit who moves in the space between faith and reason.[2] Like Desmond, Przywara sought to rescue metaphysics from a premature demise and place it once more in service to divine things. More noteworthy, however, is the resemblance that Desmond's reasoning bears to Przywara's in its very structure. Przywara is remembered as the great modernizer of the *analogia entis*, or analogy of being, a concept that he saw as the key to brokering lasting peace between faith and reason. What is perhaps less apparent is the extent to which his use of this concept anticipates distinctive features of Desmond's thought.

The significance of this affinity consists in its potential to resolve the question posed by theologians engaged with Desmond's work: how best to "theologize" Desmond and help him " 'come out of the closet' as a theologian as well."[3] Indeed, the parallels between these thinkers are so extensive that, barring terminological differences, Przywara's account of analogy could be considered a version of Desmond's metaxology *avant le lettre*. This suggests that the way in which Przywara relates analogy to theology can serve as a model for understanding how we might appropriate Desmond's thought theologically. More specifically, it offers a rationale for explaining why Desmond's thought constitutes a resource for Catholic theology in particular: a means of showing how his philosophy as a whole coincides with Catholic theology in ways that are not merely incidental, but derive from the structure of his metaphysics.

The best way to provide an explanation of this sort, I suggest, is to interpret Desmond through the lens of Przywara's *analogia entis*. In what follows, I begin by demonstrating how Desmond mirrors Przywara's understanding of the basic shape of being (defining it as a kind of "middle" or "between"). I then describe how Desmond follows Przywara in applying these principles to the relationship between God and creatures. Finally, I examine Przywara's reasons for claiming that the analogy of being amounts to a fundamental form (*Grundform*) or structuring principle (*Strukturprinzip*) of Catholic theology.[4] If the many parallels between Desmond's metaxology and Przywara's analogy prove to be valid, then Przywara's arguments about the Catholic *Grundform* suggest an intrinsic relation between Desmond's thought and the foundations of Catholic theology. It is possible then to "theologize" Desmond by bringing his metaphysics into more direct reflection on revealed doctrines, as it can be shown to enact not only a philosophy but also a kind of fundamental theology.[5]

CREATURELY METAPHYSICS

The first point on which Desmond and Przywara converge is their basic description of being and metaphysics. What is most distinctive of Desmond's thought, and considered his signature contribution to philosophy, is the notion of the between. By "the between" (*metaxu*), Desmond means the milieu or the condition of being as we experience it.[6] We never encounter being simply in terms of one extreme or another—presence or absence, subject or object, time or eternity, and so forth. Rather being always includes all of these and more, spanning the distance between them. It is never purely determinate, like the One of Parmenides, or indeterminate, like the flux of Heraclitus.[7] It is rather *over*determinate, "too much" in the sense that it incorporates the whole ontological spectrum and is never exhausted by either end of it. To inquire into "the being of the between" is therefore to inquire into what constitutes being's depth and complexity.

In addition, when we, as minds, engage in metaphysics, our thinking also has the character of being-between. "Mindfulness," Desmond writes, "comes in the middle, out of an enigmatic origin, in expectation of an uncertain end." We find ourselves in media res, never standing at an Archimedean point from which to survey the whole.[8] Indeed, for Desmond the "meta" in metaphysics signifies that our thinking is simultaneously "in the midst," always between pure subjectivity and pure objectivity, as well as "on the way," always moving beyond toward what is other than ourselves.[9] The between is then best described as a *community* of beings, minds, and different senses of being and mind, all entering into complex relations or mediations with one another.[10] And to philosophize well, our metaphysics must possess a certain finesse, attuned to these complex tensions and relations that together make up the between.[11] In the end metaphysics must be metaxological: a reasoning (*logos*) within and about the between (*metaxu*).[12]

A notion comparable to Desmond's between emerges in Przywara's writings from the 1920s and 1930s: that of being as a "dynamic middle."[13] The "middle" is the basic concept Przywara employs to present being as analogical in nature, that is, as an *analogia entis*. He draws it from a passage of the *Nicomachean Ethics*, in which Aristotle defines analogy as a kind of middle (*analogon meson*) between ontological extremes. This *meson* is dynamic in the sense that it describes a state of ordered becoming, splitting the difference between the absolute stasis of Parmenides and the absolute restlessness of Heraclitus.[14] Moreover, Przywara engages the long tradition of reflection on analogy that came after Aristotle, so it is unsurprising that he develops Aristotle's middle by utilizing the Thomistic distinction between essence and existence.[15] Being is analogical, then, insofar as it always describes a rest-in-motion: a complex relation *between* a thing's essence and existence, and never simply one or the other.

Once more, as in the case of Desmond, Przywara argues that such an understanding of being renders all absolute methodologies and comprehensive forms of knowledge impossible. Because our being is *in fieri*, a nonidentity between two fundamental principles, we can never attain a God's-eye view of the ontological scene. All attempts to assert one perspective (consciousness *or* its object, the ideative *or* the real, truth *or* history, etc.) as sufficient to account for the nature of being and knowing inevitably give rise to tensions that prove irresolvable within the given perspective.[16] These tensions, for Przywara, are symptoms of the more fundamental tension in our being between essence and existence—that basic distinction which, according to St. Thomas, defines us as creatures. Hence, to faithfully inquire into the "ground and end and definition" of being, metaphysics must renounce such exclusive methodologies and take its place in the "suspended middle" (*schwebende Mitte*), attending to the suspended tension (*Spannungs-Schwebe*) between various absolutes.[17] Our thinking too must be analogical: an ordered (*ana*) reasoning (*logos*) "in between" (*meson*).[18]

Second, Desmond echoes Przywara in the process of reasoning that leads him to characterize being as a between. Relevant here is what Desmond terms the "fourfold sense" of being: his insight that the space of the between is composed of an interplay between four metaphysical dimensions or senses. These are the univocal sense, which corresponds to identity and determination; the equivocal sense, which corresponds to difference and indetermination; the dialectical sense, which corresponds to identities that overcome difference and indetermination; and last, Desmond's own addition, the metaxological sense, which corresponds to irreducible difference and overdetermination.[19] In a procedure that recalls and modifies Hegel's *Aufhebung*, Desmond examines each sense of being, testing its range and explanatory power. His claim is that each of the senses proves unable to *fully* explain the happening of the between, leading the mind to relativize its insights while progressing to more inclusive perspectives.

In this way the univocal and equivocal senses relate to the dialectical and metaxological senses as points and lines relate to squares and cubes: the limited truth of each sense is exceeded by, yet integrated into, the sense that follows. Were univocity to be the only sense—unity devoid of any difference—it would be fundamentally incompatible with the dynamic nature of the between, unable to explain the many differences, changes, and ambiguities we experience.[20] Were equivocity to reign as the sole meaning of being—difference without any sense of unity—it would likewise reveal its unfaithfulness to the between, as it would deny all relation and render all things unintelligible.[21] In the end both senses betray their dependence upon one another, for they only remain consistent in light of some *interplay* between identity and difference.

Dialectic then emerges as a contender for how to understand this interplay of identity and difference. As it functions for Hegel, dialectic proposes a more extensive unity achieved in and through difference, a mediation of all that is other to the self. However, Desmond worries that a pure dialectic risks an oppressive kind of mediation, one that reduces plurality to subordinate moments of a self-mediating whole. Nonetheless, this self-enclosed system, he believes, is called into question by the experience of our own thinking, as something that is first given to us: "For thinking does not first *grant itself*; it is *granted to itself*. . . . [T]hinking is only self-determining because *it is given to itself* to be self-determining; it is granted to itself to *be* think-ing."[22] The fact that thinking is given to be at all, Desmond argues, points us toward something more original than pure dialectic.

The metaxological then arises to account for this dimension of givenness in a way that dialectic cannot. It recognizes self-mediation (thought thinking itself) as a partial truth, but it goes further by attend-ing to "intermediation" (thought thinking its other).[23] It acknowl-edges "a plurality of centers of active being" irreducible to the self, all of which are capable of entering into various kinds of relations.[24] The metaxological thereby encompasses the whole field of the between, precisely by granting a place to what remains overdetermined even as it is thought or mediated by the self.

This way of navigating the layers of being is, however, hardly original to Desmond. Przywara employs the same kind of method to arrive at his version of the *analogia entis*: one that passes through the limitations while acknowledging the partial truths of more restricted senses of being. Corresponding to Desmond's "fourfold sense" is Przy-wara's analysis of the *logoi*, or ways of ordering thought and speech about being, in section 5 of his *Analogia Entis*.[25] For Przywara, "pure" logic (*logizesthai*) is a way of ordering being that presumes its mean-ing to be singular and "immediately" given, like univocity (A = A).[26] It is, Przywara says, more suited to a divine knowledge, an attempt to comprehend the fullness of reality modeled on the idea of the One. Yet such an approach is, for us creatures, "impossible from the out-set," as it only locates meaning in one pole of any given binary we encounter (prioritizing, say, objects at the expense of concepts, appre-hension at the expense of comprehension, etc.).[27]

Przywara then proposes two senses of dialectic (*dialogizesthai*), one in which the prefix *dia-* has the connotation of keeping two terms "apart" and one in which it has the connotation of moving "through" various contradictions.[28] The former is equivocal, in that it acknowl-edges the antitheses generated by pure logic and affirms their insolu-bility. It points to the indeterminate, the incompatibility between different possibilities, and were this sense of dialectic the exclusive vantage point of metaphysics, it would amount to an admission of pure contradiction. This is why Przywara describes it as an unstable order between two poles: a frantic "back and forth" or either/or but never a harmonizing of those terms.[29] Dialectic in the second sense, which corresponds to its Hegelian usage, seeks to address this imbalance by interpreting antitheses as stepping-stones to a more encompassing kind of identity. Here the differences between the terms "spring back together all the more passionately" in the end, in a more unconditional unity, exacerbating the one-sidedness of pure logic, but now understood as the result of a process rather than something immediate.[30] In none of these perspectives, however, is anything like a lasting balance achieved.

So it is that for Przywara the imbalances of pure logic, the antithetical dialectic and the Hegelian dialectic, point beyond themselves to something more original: a *logos* of being expansive enough to do justice to both terms of a metaphysical tension without having to negate one or the other. Analogy, then, plays the same role for Przywara that metaxology does for Desmond. This point becomes clear when Przywara interprets the various "orderings" as configurations of act (*energeia*) and potency (*dynamis*).[31] As Aristotle argued, pure actuality and pure potentiality can never of themselves account for the fullness of being as we experience it. Nor can a metaphysics that merely vacillates restlessly between one extreme and the other. Only an intrinsic composition (an analogy) between actuality and potentiality, without reducing either, can account for the complexity of being. Pure logic and Hegelian dialectic are exposed as a delusional incursion into the region of the divine (*energeia*), while the antithetical dialectic represents the opposite imbalance, an excessive glorification of finite difference (*dynamis*).[32] Analogy alone represents the balance or equilibrium between them.[33]

Desmond's metaxological sense and Przywara's *analogia entis* thus serve the same function and exhibit the same structure. The metaxological relativizes the truths of the other senses as each contributes something true to the metaphysical equation. However, it alone makes room for what it is about being that remains irreducibly other, that which is too much at the beginning and remains too much at the end. Likewise, Przywara's analogy sees in the other *logoi* so many limited truths but none of which can do justice to the whole. Analogy alone articulates a balance between what is always "above" and "beyond," yet enters into relation with what is "within" and below.[34]

As metaxology gives metaphysics a structure that is simultaneously "in the midst" and always "on the way" to what is beyond it, so too does Przywara's *analogia entis* shape metaphysics as both "in" and moving "beyond": an essence that enters into composition with our existence but is always more, distinct and capable of further realization ("essence in-and-beyond existence").[35] As for Desmond, for Przywara this structure alone provides the condition for coherent thinking in the between, an approach that does not ultimately generate irresolvable contradictions. It is in this sense, as Przywara explains, that metaphysics becomes "creaturely metaphysics," a vision of being conformed to our position as finite minds (between Being and nothing, gods and beasts, etc.).[36] And to the extent that it too is both in-and-beyond, the metaxological qualifies as a "creaturely metaphysics."

There is, in sum, a profound convergence—even perhaps a formal identity—between what Przywara means by analogy or "creaturely metaphysics" and what Desmond means by metaxology. Both thinkers agree in their basic characterization of metaphysics as a "middle" or "between," spanning ontological extremes. They likewise make use of the same process of reasoning to arrive at this characterization, moving progressively from the paradoxes generated by partial truths to more comprehensive understandings of being. Finally, analogy and metaxology serve the same function and exhibit the same basic structure, preserving what about being is irreducibly "beyond" us even as we think and enter into relation with it. These parallels suggest that Przywara's *analogia entis* can be considered a kind of proto-metaxology. Moreover, they give us good reason to think that the way in which Przywara relates analogy to God can guide how theologians assess and appropriate Desmond's thinking on God.

Theological Metaphysics

Unlike many of his contemporaries, Desmond insists that reason only dispenses with the question of God at its own peril. Indeed, in his view, perhaps the most common sins of the modern ethos are its veneration of immanence and its corresponding contempt for transcendence.[37] When the philosophy of a given age sees only through the lens of the univocal, equivocal, or dialectical, and loses sight of what is overdetermined, it soon loses sight of the divine, the overdetermined par excellence. It follows that opening up a mindfulness sensitive to the givenness of being necessarily means opening a renewed approach to God within philosophy. Metaxological metaphysics is, in this sense, hyperbolic: it is the realization that the between itself constitutes a kind of sacrament of what lies beyond it. Thinking metaxologically involves, in other words, attention to the forces in the between that are not of the between.[38]

This is to say that for Desmond the metaxological applies not only to the relations between finite beings in the between but also to the relationship between creatures and God. The *metaxu* of or among beings opens out onto the *metaxu* between the community of being and its origin. The gifted character of being entails an origin that exceeds our own self-determinations, our mediations of being from the side of the self. We thus encounter a number of hyperboles, finite happenings that point us beyond themselves: "There is a thinking about the beyond in the between itself. What gives the between surpasses the between, though we face towards it, in and through the between."[39] Yet this beyond toward which we turn is unique in that it conditions even the possibility of everything other than itself. It is, as Desmond calls it, an "agapeic origin," a "possibilizing" source that gives the between its existence as a whole, in and for itself, while nonetheless existing in relation to it.[40] Thinking God metaxologically then means an understanding of the transcendent that explains the givenness of being, the givenness of the self, the relating of mind to being and being to mind, and so forth, all while upholding the distinction between God and the between, as irreducible "centers" of being in relation.

Likewise, for Przywara, the "intra-creaturely" analogy of the middle entails a more foundational version of analogy: that between God and creatures.[41] This can be inferred from how he defines the *analogia entis* in the first place, and the metaphysics corresponding to it, as "creaturely." To say that being is conditioned by a dynamic tension or real distinction between the essence and existence of all things is, in the same breath, to admit that all such things are derivative, bearing within them an ontological dependence. The analogy governing the relation between these metaphysical principles, which can be considered horizontal, opens up to a vertical analogy, that is, a relation to a "being" whose essence and existence are identical.[42] Przywara offers, in short, a vision of the middle as itself testifying to what is beyond it. It points to a God considered analogically insofar as we bear a likeness to him (a relation of essence and existence), yet remain irreducibly other to him (as the nature of those relations is infinitely different). Creaturely metaphysics, in other words, leads seamlessly into what Przywara terms "theological metaphysics" or "theo-metaphysics": the phase within metaphysics that articulates the analogy between creatures and God.[43]

Moreover, Desmond's understanding of the God-creature relation constitutes a "between" insofar as it strikes a balance between two extreme and ultimately inadequate interpretations of that relation. As was the case with his characterization of being in general, here Desmond arrives at his metaxological point of view by first identifying the problems that arise when thinking God and creation in the more limited ontological senses. These problems then lead him to find resolution in a more comprehensive view. To think God's rapport with creation on the model of a pure univocity, for instance, is, for Desmond, to think of God as perfectly and eternally determinate. Yet when God is so determinately God and thus determinately *not* the world, he is, like the Parmenidean One, rendered incapable of relating to the world.[44]

As before, pure univocity gives way to an equivocal dualism. Creation, on this view, can only be thought of in its strict identity as not-God, leaving us with the denial of any relation or mediation between God and creatures.[45] This conspiring of the univocal and equivocal senses yields a condition that Desmond associates with Gnosticism. The very being of the world as distinct from God is devalued and degraded, "for if there is a dualistic opposition between God and world," and being is thought exclusively in the purity of its origin, then "God cannot be the ground of goodness or value in the world—there can be no relation between the two."[46] Such a view, in other words, radically distorts God's transcendence.

To conceive of God and creation on the model of pure dialectic is, alternatively, to distort God's immanence. Desmond refers to the resulting God as the "erotic origin," a self-determining deity whose transcendence over creatures is seen as an obstacle to overcome on the way to a more comprehensive unity with itself.[47] This ensures, however, that there is ultimately nothing left to uphold God's distinction from the being of the world. Unsurprisingly, Desmond associates this view with pantheism, and targets Hegel as the modern champion of the pantheistic error.[48] Hegel's "counterfeit double" of God has, he writes, "its own equivocal sting to its tail."[49] By ultimately absolving God of his otherness from creation (his *Jenseits*) and including him in a self-determined whole with the world, Hegel is unable to prevent the reversal of his theology into atheism: "It is not now that we do not know God, but there is no transcendent God to know. Absolute knowing generates its humanistic double of God and inverts into atheistic critique in search of pure immanence without God. . . . The speculative access to God leads to the atheistic overcoming of God, and thus to no God."[50]

On these points as well Przywara has beaten Desmond to the punch. His understanding of the God-creature relation likewise constitutes a "middle" between similarly inadequate interpretations, and he too arrives at his analogical understanding of God by considering the deficiencies of more limited metaphysical perspectives. To envision God in the terms of pure logic, for instance, is for Przywara to occupy a purely a priori perspective, giving us a " 'God of the ideas' within the absoluteness of eidetic vision and mathematical deduction."[51] It is a view "from above to below" wholly lacking in finesse, construing God's identity so determinately that the otherness of creation in its own right is undermined. "God," then, "becomes the all," a position Przywara terms "theopanism."[52] Theopanism, which Przywara associates with the gnostics, devalues the being of creation as it can only interpret the space occupied by finite beings as not-God, and hence no-thing. Like Desmond's univocal God, this approach undermines any relation between divine and creature from the start, and thus concludes with the pure contradiction one finds in Przywara's account of dialectic (*dia-* as irreconcilable difference).[53]

To think God exclusively in terms of dialectic in Przywara's second sense (*dia-* as moving "through" difference) leaves us with the opposite extreme. Here the vantage point is strictly a posteriori, "from below to above." It begins by locating reality exclusively on the side of the world, and is thus forced to envision God as a deficient projection of the world (as in the case of secular materialism). Alternatively, in its effort to overcome the difference between infinite and finite, it ends by resolving the transcendence of God into an immanent whole with the world (as in the case of German idealism and messianism). Like Desmond, Przywara sees in this approach the signs of pantheism: if the previous error fails to uphold the otherness of creation from God, pantheism fails to uphold God's otherness from the dynamic becoming of the world. Here, inverting the logic of theopanism, "the all becomes God."[54] In both cases, however, the result is that either God or the world is lost, and thus no relation between God and the creature is actually given.

Przywara's aim in discussing these errors is to shed light on the *analogia entis* as the only relation that does justice to the ontological integrity of both God and creatures. Analogy, once more, represents an equilibrium, upholding God's transcendence ("beyond") while simultaneously affirming God's immanence to creatures ("in") who exist in their own right.[55] Unlike theopanism and pantheism, the theological version of analogy exhibits a structure of both-and rather than either/or. Just as the creaturely analogy was shown to bear the shape of "essence in-and-beyond existence," the theological analogy can now be seen in the formula "God beyond-and-in the creature."[56] And here we can see once more how Przywara claims merely to put a modern spin on a traditional Catholic principle. In this case, he refers to the teaching of the Fourth Lateran Council: "One cannot note any similarity between creator and creature, however great, without being compelled to observe an ever greater dissimilarity between them."[57] Theological metaphysics, then, is charged with describing the legitimate similarity or relation of the world to God while always renewing the irreducible mystery of God's otherness: his nature, as Przywara is fond of saying, as "always greater" (*semper maior*).[58]

As for Przywara, so for Desmond. For the latter, the metaxological proves to be the only sense capable of giving a sufficient account of the God-creature relation, resolving the anomalies that arise from attempts to pin God to the univocal, equivocal, or dialectical. Desmond likewise renounces disjunction in favor of conjunction, endorsing a structure nearly identical to Przywara's: the metaxological marks "where the energy of transcending passes from the divine to the creature, and the creature to the divine, in a porous between, itself originally given to be by the divine, the divine as *both always more* than this between *yet most deeply intimate to* it, as its mysterious endowing source and conserver."[59] Only metaxology, in other words, is able to articulate an understanding of God as "beyond," yet nonetheless "moving in, and through, and between the middle." It accomplishes this balance by describing divine otherness in terms of plenitude rather than antithesis, such that God cannot be thought to compete with creatures over the same metaphysical space.[60] Paradoxically, the freedom from this competition is what enables God's otherness to form a *community* with what he creates. The between truly resembles what is beyond it, yet such similarities always redound upon God's hyperbolic difference, "the sense of astonishing mystery" which is "always already more, always is and will be more, eternally more."[61]

It would seem, then, that Desmond's proximity to Przywara on the question of God further supports the suggestion that his metaxology amounts to a version of the *analogia entis*. In fact, this is something Desmond himself suggests when he addresses Aquinas's concept of analogy directly.[62] He refers to his own approach as "a metaxological rendition of analogy" and a "(metaxological) reconsideration of analogy" when he, like Przywara, looks back to Aquinas as a model for rethinking God in the shadow of Hegel and his progeny: "Analogy says something important not only about a middle way between univocity and equivocity, but about this very between. Analogy is itself a between, and communicates a between—and to cite the most important case, in the *likeness/unlikeness between* the creation and

God."[63] Here Desmond echoes not only Przywara but also the formula of Lateran IV: analogy, understood as a *metaxu* between God and creation, balances any similarity of terms with "an ever greater dissimilarity."[64] The likeness of creatures to God (*sunousia*, "being with") is meaningless apart from God's unlikeness (*hyperousia*, "being beyond").[65]

Desmond's claim that metaxology is "a kind of dynamized analogy" is nowhere clearer than in his understanding of the act of creation. Once more, like Przywara, Desmond sees a particular advantage to revisiting Aquinas's notion of God as analogical agent (*agens analogicum*).[66] According to Desmond, what distinguishes analogical agency is creation of the other for the other. It is not, as might be the case with a dialectical cause, creation merely as God's self-othering. Rather, "through unlikeness, it gives the release of the created other into its own being for itself." At the same time, through likeness, it upholds the creature in a network of relativities, including its relativity to "the ultimate source of all between-relations, namely, God."[67] Desmond is here, in short, identifying an analogical concept of creation with his own notion of the "agapeic origin."[68]

Desmond himself, then, supports the claim that metaxology and analogy are virtually synonymous when applied to the relation between God and creatures. As I have attempted to make clear, Desmond and Przywara converge in their basic characterization of this relation as an ontological "between" or "middle." They likewise arrive at this characterization by way of the same process of reasoning, paving a middle way between extremes that they define in nearly identical terms. Finally, their respective accounts yield the same structure, of a God both "beyond" and "in" the sphere of creaturely being. When Desmond thinks God metaxologically, therefore, his thinking corresponds to what Przywara defines as theological metaphysics: the phase of metaphysics sensitive to the rhythm of God-in-and-beyond the creature.

In other words, from Przywara's perspective, Desmond's thought not only makes sense of the complexities of being but also amounts to a kind of *theologia naturalis*—the basic insights of which align with those of Aquinas and the philosophical theology affirmed in magisterial teaching.[69] For Przywara, however, the analogy of being does not restrict itself to the philosophical domain. Rather, it continues to bear fruit within the discourses of religion and theology proper. It is just as essential, he argues, to think analogically when one deals directly with the structure of God's self-revelation in history, because analogy also names the inner rhythm of that self-revelation. If the convergence of analogy and metaxology is valid, then analogy's place in theology can function as a blueprint for bringing Desmond into even closer contact with the Christian mysteries.

CATHOLIC METAPHYSICS

According to Przywara, analogy not only describes the structure of creaturely being ("essence-in-and-beyond existence") and the God-creature relation ("God-beyond-and-in the creature"). It also names the proper relationship between philosophy and revealed theology.[70] Three points of his reasoning warrant consideration. In the first place, while these two disciplines remain distinct as to their acts and objects, Przywara maintains that "each reaches out toward the root of the other."[71] As with the previous instances of analogy, he presents this relation in terms of a traditional Thomistic principle: "faith does not destroy but presupposes and perfects reason" (*fides non destruit, sed supponit et perficit rationem*).[72] The fact that philosophy leads to certain truths about God means that in a certain sense theology is always already "in" or presupposes the philosophical. However, God is only indirectly an object for philosophy, whereas theology deals with God's own self-revelation as well as with creatures in their "objective finality" (i.e., as they are elevated by grace).[73] In this sense theology remains "beyond" philosophy, perfecting it by offering a more ultimate perspective on the realities about which it speaks. Unsurprisingly, then, their relation takes the familiar form, "theology-in-and-beyond philosophy."[74]

Second, Przywara's theological metaphysics, the part of metaphysics that deals with God and creatures, is thus revealed to involve more than merely philosophical reflection. Rather it occupies the space *between* philosophy and revealed theology. With regard to its method and the tools of its trade, he notes, it remains on the side of philosophy (it is, after all, part "of the one metaphysics").[75] But because it can arrive at the knowledge of God as "always greater," metaphysics leaves the door open for a more ultimate perspective on God and creatures, at least as an objective possibility. Revealed theology, in this sense, serves as the inner telos of metaphysics, the beyond that draws it to its "definitive actualization."[76] Theological metaphysics is then directed to revelation as the source of its principles, even as its procedures remain on the side of natural reason.[77] It is, in a certain sense, what metaphysics looks like *in the light of* revelation, when the claims of Christ and his church are taken into account. What Hans Urs von Balthasar writes of Henri de Lubac applies fittingly to Przywara as well: he occupies "a suspended middle," never considering philosophy "without its transcendence into theology," or "theology without its essential substructure of philosophy."[78]

And third, Przywara argues that the particular kind of theology toward which theological metaphysics is ordered is Catholic theology. As a matter of history, he notes, certain theologies exhibit an inner disposition toward certain kinds of metaphysics, and vice versa. For instance, theologies for which the God-creature relation is theopanistic (as in certain strands of Protestantism) rely on purely a priori philosophies. Theologies that construe the God-creature relation pantheistically (as in certain strands of Jewish messianism) naturally prefer philosophies that are purely a posteriori. Przywara's judgment is that the analogies established in creaturely and theological metaphysics only find their match in Catholicism: "For Catholic theology (alone) carries within itself, as its formal ground, the formula 'God beyond-and-in the creature,' which alone overcomes the relation between theopanism and pantheism."[79] The Catholic perspective is, in other words, the only one in which the beyond/in structure of analogy is found to be confirmed and elevated rather than implicitly rejected.[80] This is what leads Przywara to characterize analogy as a "fundamental Catholic form" (*katholischer Grundform*), a principle that implicitly structures and is ordered to the theological claims of Catholics.[81]

Przywara's central point, then, is that a metaphysics of analogy is the only one intrinsically suited to the task of relating philosophy and revelation. And on this view, with philosophy always reaching beyond itself toward revealed truths, to do metaphysics in the space between them means considering the "groundwork for the 'foundations'" of theology.[82] Theological metaphysics then does not merely represent a natural theology, a knowledge of God comfortably isolated from revelation. It constitutes a kind of *formal* or fundamental theology as well. Here analogy supplies the formal basis (*Unterhalb*) for all religions and revelations.[83] Yet because Przywara argues that analogy is internally disposed toward Catholicism in particular, "what is at issue are the *fidei fundamenta*" of the Catholic Church.[84] In this sense it is possible to consider theological metaphysics a "Catholic metaphysics":[85] a metaphysics the truths of which constitute the *Grundform* of Catholic doctrine.

In sum, thinking analogically makes possible a discourse that somehow bridges the chasm between reason and faith. In fact Przywara's descriptions of this discourse come very near to some of the ways fundamental theology was understood in the Catholic manual tradition. It is a "boundary discipline" aimed at clarifying the conditions or formal structures of what the faith reveals.[86] These foundations do not merely fall among the preambles of the faith (*preambula fidei*), the purview of philosophy. Rather fundamental theology appeals to principles of both faith and reason, often defending the possibility and credibility of the former with the methods of the latter. It concerns itself with establishing and defending the meanings and forms of "those essential truths which stand in a closer connection with the Catholic faith."[87]

By naming analogy a "fundamental Catholic form," Przywara is therefore claiming it as one of the most foundational principles upon which the meaning of revelation depends. It ensures, in other words, that God and creatures can truly be in relation without collapsing the being of one into the other. Because analogy secures similarity, it enables doctrines to communicate real knowledge about who or what God is (*quid est Deus*). But because it also judges that knowledge in light of God's infinite dissimilarity, it ensures that even the most exalted revelation is qualified by the "ever greater" depths of the unknown God.[88] This both-and, Przywara believes, even captures the inner rhythm of all such revelations: Christ as both Son of God and Son of Man, God as both three and one, creatures as both natural and graced, and so forth.

What then of Desmond? For him too the relationship between philosophy and theology ought to be understood analogically or metaxologically.[89] Just as with the previous applications, the *metaxu* between these kinds of mindfulness involves bringing them into relation without reducing one to the other. Nor, however, can philosophy and theology remain estranged relatives, as this would simply amount to another version of equivocity (the denial that Athens has anything to do with Jerusalem). Indeed, like Przywara, Desmond acknowledges that certain theologies (those with gnostic or pantheistic leanings) select for certain imbalanced renditions of metaphysics (either the univocal, or equivocal, or dialectical). In contrast the metaxological maintains a porous boundary between the disciplines, allowing them to interpenetrate without confusion and mutually benefit from an endless and open conversation. Desmond even goes so far as to suggest that part of the "moving beyond" in metaphysics includes finding its fulfillment in being drawn beyond itself to a higher discourse: "It is not faith seeking understanding; it is faith after the effort to understand that does not now dispel the mystery, but finds itself more wrapped in it than ever, more deeply struck into perplexity and praise and love at the being greater than the greatest of our thoughts."[90]

Yet if Desmond's metaxology really does coincide with Przywara's analogy and Przywara's reasoning is sound, then Desmond's metaphysics is intrinsically suited to serve not only as a (purely philosophical) natural theology but also as a fundamental theology: as a Catholic metaphysics. Desmond, of course, stops short of taking up the mantel of Catholic theology, and we need not force him to abandon this sense of methodological integrity. Nor need we deny that his philosophical insights are valid for, and capable of being appropriated by, a number of theological traditions.[91] What Przywara does help us to see, however, is that the metaxological (as a kind of "rendition" of analogy) is at least particularly reflected in the both-and, the beyond-and-in of Catholic thought. From the theologian's perspective, a metaphysics of the between appears to "contain" the formal principles governing Catholic theology, that is, those which its doctrines presuppose. Similarly, Przywara's arguments suggest that these doctrines in particular amount to a religious discourse "beyond" philosophy that, far from betraying Desmond's principles, confirm and elevate them.

In this way Przywara's example offers us a rationale for why it is that Desmond's philosophy is such a fitting "handmaiden" for Catholic theology (*ancilla theologiae*), a way of bringing him more nearly into the fold of confessional theology without denying him his disciplinary boundaries. From Przywara's perspective, metaxology is as much between philosophy and theology as it is comfortably restricted to the former. In a sense it precontains a discourse about the *katholischer Grundform*: it always already implicitly enacts a certain theology of the conditions or foundations of the faith. And if Przywara is correct, those seeking to further "theologize" Desmond need only expose the many ways in which the foundational concepts of revelation reflect the metaxological rhythm. What would it look like, for instance, to compose a treatise on the church, on sacred tradition, on historical revelation, the act of faith and the credibility of the Incarnation—all from the perspective of the metaxological mind? What would it be to offer a metaphysical defense of transubstantiation, of the persons and nature of the Trinity, of the dynamic of sin and redemption, employing the categories forged in Desmond's between? Such endeavors, it seems to me, are precisely those suited to a metaphysics between philosophy and theology.

Of course, answers to these questions exceed the scope of my contribution, the only aim of which has been to *justify* such endeavors from the perspective of both faith and reason. Expressed simply, the fruit of these comparisons is the realization that metaxology is the *analogia entis* and the *analogia entis* is metaxology. Relying on Przywara as a model helps to demonstrate that this is true with regard to the structure of being in general (the between as creaturely metaphysics) as well as with regard to natural theology (the between as theological metaphysics). These convergences support the further claim that the metaxological coincides with Przywara's *analogia entis* in a sense that more nearly addresses confessional theology, the between as Catholic metaphysics. This is to say that from the perspective of a kindred mind, the between that Desmond occupies can be viewed in the light of the *fidei fundamenta*, a metaphysics drafted into the service of the Christian mysteries. One need only plumb these depths more thoroughly and unfold the many more ways in which Desmond's thought unites the wisdom of men and the "wisdom of the cross":

> Reason cannot eliminate the mystery of love which the cross represents, while the cross can give to reason the ultimate answer which it seeks.... The preaching of Christ crucified and risen is the reef upon which the link between faith and philosophy can break up, but it is also the reef beyond which the two can set forth upon the boundless ocean of truth. Here we see not only the border between reason and faith, but also the space where the two may meet.[92]

Indeed, on Desmond's own terms, philosophy as well as Catholic doctrine are perfected in a meeting of just this sort.

NOTES

I would like to express my heartfelt gratitude to Brendan Sammon, who first introduced me to Desmond's philosophy; and to John Betz, who first introduced me to Przywara's theology.

1. See *GB*, 1–7, 18–30.

2. Both John Betz and Cyril O'Regan have gestured toward a comparison of these thinkers. See John R. Betz, "The Beauty of the Metaphysical Imagination," in *Belief and Metaphysics*, ed. Connor Cunningham and Peter M. Candler (London: SCM, 2007), 55; Cyril O'Regan, "What Theology Can Learn from a Philosophy Daring to Speak the Unspeakable," *Irish Theological Quarterly* 73 (2008): 256.

3. Christopher Ben Simpson, *Religion, Metaphysics, and the Postmodern: William Desmond and John D. Caputo* (Bloomington: Indiana University Press, 2009), 94. For other notable discussions of Desmond's theological influences and potential for theology, see Christopher Ben Simpson, "Theology, Philosophy, God and the Between," *Louvain Studies* 36 (2012): 226–38; Cyril O'Regan, "Naming God in *God and the Between*," *Louvain Studies* 36 (2012): 282–301; Renée Köhler-Ryan, "Gifted Beggars in the *Metaxu*: A

Study of the Platonic and Augustinian Resonances of *Porosity* in *God and the Between*," *Louvain Studies* 36 (2012): 256–81; John Milbank, "The Double Glory, or Paradox versus Dialectics: On Not Quite Agreeing with Slavoj Žižek," in Slavoj Žižek and John Milbank, *The Monstrosity of Christ: Paradox or Dialectic?*, ed. Creston Davis (Cambridge, MA: MIT Press, 2009), 131. Milbank in particular notes the value of interpreting Desmond in terms of the analogy of being. John Caputo also raises the question of Desmond's relation to analogy in his foreword to *The William Desmond Reader*, ed. Christopher Ben Simpson (Albany: SUNY Press, 2012), xii–xiii.

4. The German terms are taken from Erich Przywara, "Die Reichweite der Analogie als katholischer Grundform," in *Schriften*, vol. 3: *Analogia Entis, Metaphysik; Ur-Struktur und All-Rythmus* (Einsiedeln: Johannes Verlag, 1962), 247–301. Hereafter I refer to the English translation: Erich Przywara, "The Scope of Analogy as a Fundamental Catholic Form," in *Analogia Entis. Metaphysics: Original Structure and Universal Rhythm*, trans. John R. Betz and David Bentley Hart (Grand Rapids, MI: Eerdmans, 2014), 348–99. However, unless otherwise noted, citations including the title of this volume refer to Przywara's original 1932 text, *Analogia Entis*, which comprises the first part of this translation.

5. Gregory Grimes notes Desmond's "obvious relevance to fundamental theology": see Gregory Grimes, "Introduction: Theological Reflections on William Desmond's *God and the Between*," *Louvain Studies* 36 (2012): 220.

6. *BB*, xii–xiii.

7. *BB*, 50–54, 117. See also *ISB*, 236.

8. *BB*, 44–45.

9. *BB*, 44, xi.

10. *BB*, xii, 417–61.

11. *BB*, xii. Pascal's *esprit de finesse* is Desmond's preferred model for this notion. Cf. *BB*, 51.

12. *DDO*, 7; cf. *BB*, xii.

13. Przywara, *Analogia Entis*, §6, 209.

14. Ibid., 206.

15. Przywara's historical thesis is meant to trace the development of the *analogia entis* from its roots in Plato and Aristotle through its Christianized form in St. Augustine and St. Thomas. See Przywara, *Analogia Entis*, §7, 238–306.

16. Przywara traces the emergence of these tensions throughout the early sections of his *Analogia Entis*, "Metaphysics as Such." See *Analogia Entis*, §§1–3, 119–54.

17. Przywara, *Analogia Entis*, §1, 119–24; §4, 159–63; §6, 203–9.

18. Cf. Przywara, *Analogia Entis*, §5, 196; §6, 203 ff.

19. *BB*, xii–xiii; cf. *ISB*, 235.

20. *BB*, 47: "There is no such thing as absolutely pure univocity, for this would be a unity totally devoid of mediation and exclusive of differentiation. Without the latter there would be no happening of the between, no determination of diversity among beings, no speaking about being, and no articulated knowing of anything."

21. *BB*, 87: "But just as pure univocity is a limit, so it is difficult to find absolutely pure instances of equivocity, which would imply a difference without even the hint of a possible mediation. Absolutely unmediated difference seems to be absolutely unintelligible; for even to state the putative absolute difference is in some way already to transcend it."

22. *BB*, 174; original emphasis. All emphases in quoted passages are original unless otherwise indicated.

23. *BB*, 162.

24. *BB*, 178.

25. Przywara, *Analogia Entis*, §5, 192–97. In this section, Przywara begins by addressing the sense of "ordering order" that logic (*logizesthai*), dialectic (*dialogizesthai*), and analogy (*analogizesthai*) have in common. In short, he attempts to show this insofar as each Greek verb shares some form of the word *logos*, which is further specified either by the absence of a prefix (in the case of *logizesthai*) or by the addition of a prefix (*dia-* or *ana-*). His first task then is to analyze the meanings of *logos* (5.1) before describing how the "ordering" is differentiated in the specific modes of thought under consideration: pure logic (5.2), dialectic (5.3), and finally analogy (5.4).

26. Cf. John R. Betz, translator's introduction, in Przywara, *Analogia Entis. Metaphysics: Original Structure and Universal Rhythm*, 70.

27. Przywara, *Analogia Entis*, §5, 194.

28. Ibid. Desmond makes the same distinction between senses of dialectic in *ISB*, 236.

29. Przywara sees this antithetical or aporetic version of dialectic rooted in the Platonic use of the term, and he identifies its modern heirs as Kierkegaard and Heidegger. See Przywara, *Analogia Entis*, §5, 194–95.

30. Przywara sees this unitive dialectic rooted in the Aristotelian use of the term, and he identifies its modern heir as Hegel. See Przywara, *Analogia Entis*, §5, 195.

31. Przywara, *Analogia Entis*, §6, 207–9.

32. Ibid., §5, 196.

33. In section 6 Przywara spills a great deal of ink in support of the claim that analogy does not (like Hegelian dialectic) merely reassert the principle of identity in a more complex form. Rather, the mark of analogy is what he calls a "negative reductive formality," akin to how the principle of noncontradiction provides the foundation for coherent thought without itself being subject to direct proof. In this sense, analogy can constitute an equilibrium because it is the ontological equivalent of the principle of non-contradiction. See *Analogia Entis*, §6, 198–208; cf. Betz, translator's introduction, 70–71.

34. Przywara, *Analogia Entis*, §5, 196–97.

35. Ibid., §1, 124.

36. *BB*, xi.

37. *ISB*, 231.

38. *ISB*, 249.

39. *BB*, 44.

40. *BB*, 231. Cf. *GB*, 254–55; *DDO*, 183–86.

41. Przywara, *Analogia Entis*, §6, 216.

42. Ibid., §4, 155–60.

43. Ibid., §4, 170 ff.

44. *GB*, 53–55.

45. *PU*, 217.

46. Simpson, *Religion, Metaphysics, and the Postmodern*, 103. Cf. *EB*, 24; *GB*, 222–23.

47. *BB*, 242–50.

48. *GB*, 226: "As the equivocal way infiltrates the Gnostic God, so the dialectical way does the pan(en)theistic. . . . While if Hegel is the high-point of modern pan(en)theism, such premodern transcendence is reconfigured in terms of a different sense of the immanent whole, and there is no more mystery." Both Desmond and Przywara suggest that Hegel could also be seen as exemplifying the gnostic/theopanistic error. See *GB*, 217–18; cf. Przywara, *Analogia Entis*, §6, 202–3.

49. *ISB*, 241; cf. *HG*.

50. *ISB*, 241.

51. Przywara, *Analogia Entis*, §4, 164.

52. Ibid., 165. When he writes of theopanism, Przywara primarily has in mind the "dialectical" theology of the Reformation, especially in the writings of Karl Barth. However, he believes the error can be traced farther back to certain strands of Greek theology and Gnosticism. See Przywara, "The Scope of Analogy," 357–60, 388–89.

53. In *Analogia Entis*, Przywara first treats of theopanism and pantheism in section 4, before he explains the distinction between the different senses or orderings of being in sections 5 and 6. Hence he does not explicitly describe these problematics as rooted in pure logic and dialectic. He speaks rather in terms of the problematic between a priori and a posteriori metaphysics (§3, 135–54): extreme versions of the intracreaturely relation in which he sees these errors of the God-creature relation rooted. However, it is clear from the figures he describes as embodying each of these problems in section 4 (Heidegger Kierkegaard, Hegel, etc.) that these problems are interrelated. There are also other clues (ex. §6, 203) that connect the various iterations of the principle of identity (pure logic, the senses of dialectic) with theopanism and pantheism. Cf. Przywara, *Analogia Entis*, §4, 165.

54. Przywara, *Analogia Entis*, §4, 165–66. With pantheism, Przywara primarily has in mind thinkers who promote a kind of mysticism of the cosmos, including Baruch Spinoza, Hermann Cohen, Franz Rosenzweig, and Martin Buber. Hegel certainly stands as the exemplar of a unitive dialectic for Przywara; however, because he describes the patterns of a priori and a posteriori in terms of vertical direction, he more often associates Hegel with theopanism, believing that his thought begins theologically and terminates in a philosophy ("from above to below"). Nonetheless, in "The Scope of Analogy," he argues that the gnostic or theopanistic theologies generate "a pantheistic, personalistic spiritualism" in the German idealism of Baader, Schelling, and Hegel. See Przywara, "The Scope of Analogy," 359.

55. Przywara, *Analogia Entis*, §6, 219–37.

56. Ibid., §4, 160.

57. Heinrich Denzinger, *Enchiridion Symbolorum*, 43rd ed., ed. Peter Hünermann (San Francisco: Ignatius Press, 2012), 269. Cf. Betz, translator's introduction, 72–73.

58. Przywara, *Analogia Entis*, §6, 234. Read in terms of the traditional terminology, Przywara argues that the *analogia entis* is really a combination of analogies: we can affirm an analogy of attribution with God (*analogia attributionis*), insofar as creatures point beyond themselves to a divine source of their limited perfections; yet we must also acknowledge this degree of similarity as qualified by an analogy of proportionality (*analogia proportionalitatis*), which defines the infinite disproportion between how creatures and God possess the same perfections. See §6, 231–37.

59. *ISB*, 237; emphasis mine.

60. *PU*, 209.

61. *ISB*, 243, 254.

62. Desmond does discuss analogy more broadly in other words, usually in relation to metaphor, symbol, and hyperbole. See, e.g., *BB*, 211–16; *GB*, 123–25.

63. *ISB*, 232, 235.

64. *ISB*, 236. Desmond even employs Przywara's favored maxim, "Deus semper maior," in *ISB*, 242.

65. *ISB*, 255.

66. Cf. Przywara, *Analogia Entis*, §6, 219–31.

67. *ISB*, 256.

68. *ISB*, 257.

69. Przywara, *Analogia Entis*, §4, 160. Cf. §4, 186–91, wherein Przywara aligns his insights with the teaching of Vatican I.

70. Throughout the terms *revealed theology, ecclesial theology, confessional theology*, and *theology proper* are used interchangeably. They all signify theology in its straightforward, Christian sense, as ordered reasoning about God presupposing special revelation, doctrine, and identification with a particular church. These are to be distinguished from the term *theological* used to qualify *metaphysics* in Przywara's schema.

71. Przywara, *Analogia Entis*, §4, 187.

72. Ibid., 178. Przywara describes this version of the formula as the "meta-noetic," or epistemological version. He also includes the alternative version, "*gratia non destruit, sed supponit et perficit naturam*," describing it as the "meta-ontic" (ontological) version.

73. Przywara, *Analogia Entis*, §4, 170.

74. Ibid., 190.

75. Ibid., 173.

76. Ibid., 174.

77. Ibid., 172.

78. Hans Urs von Balthasar, *The Theology of Henri de Lubac: An Overview* (San Francisco: Ignatius Press, 1991), 15. Cf. John Milbank, *The Suspended Middle: Henri de Lubac and the Debate Concerning the Supernatural* (Grand Rapids, MI: Eerdmans, 2005), 5, 11.

79. Przywara, *Analogia Entis*, §4, 166.

80. This point holds true with regard to both the "creaturely analogy" and the "theological analogy." For Przywara, the latter is the "formal ground" of the former, in that it is the account of God/creation that makes possible a view of finite being as a dynamic tension or middle (essence-in-beyond-existence). Without God-beyond-in, there could be no essence-in-beyond in

the first place (as the condition for the possibility of creaturely being would not exist). See Przywara, *Analogia Entis*, §4, 160.

81. Przywara, "The Scope of Analogy," 348.

82. Przywara, *Analogia Entis*, §4, 187.

83. Przywara, "Between Metaphysics and Christianity," 530.

84. Przywara, *Analogia Entis*, §4, 188.

85. Erich Przywara, "Katholische Metaphysik," *Stimmen der Zeit* 125 (1933): 227–34.

86. René Latourelle, "A New Image of Fundamental Theology," in *Problems and Perspectives of Fundamental Theology*, ed. René Latourelle and Gerald O'Collins, trans. Matthew J. O'Connell (New York: Paulist Press, 1982), 37.

87. See John Brunsmann, *A Handbook of Fundamental Theology*, vol. 1, ed. Arthur Preuss (St. Louis: Herder, 1928), 3. Brunsmann describes fundamental theology as methodologically historical and philosophical but eventually transitioning into theology (hence, between).

88. Przywara, "Between Metaphysics and Christianity," 530–31.

89. William Desmond, "Responses," *Louvain Studies* 36 (2012): 302–15.

90. *HG*, 97–98. Cf. Simpson, *Religion, Metaphysics, and the Postmodern*, 94. Simpson rightly notes that here Desmond only speaks in general of a discourse of the religious, not necessarily of confessional theology.

91. One can agree, in other words, with Przywara's assessment of analogy and metaxology as especially fitted to the structure of Catholicism without necessarily agreeing with his *negative* empirical judgments about the other religious traditions.

92. John Paul II, *Fides et ratio* (Boston: Pauline Books and Media, 1998), §23, 36.

CHAPTER 7

Thinking Transcendence, Transgressing the Mask

Desmond Pondering Augustine and Thomas Aquinas

Renée Köhler-Ryan

Augustine and Aquinas have been Desmond's companions for some time now. Frequent quotations from Augustine, together with adoption of that saint's movement from the exterior to the interior and the inferior to the superior make that friendship quite evident.[1] Aquinas is less frequently referred to, but in *The Intimate Strangeness of Being*, Desmond describes the more systematic writer as "one of those thinkers for me whom I would call *companioning*. Such a thinker one does not necessarily make into an object of scholarly research, but yet he forms a presence as a companion."[2] This exploration does not assume that it is only because Augustine and Aquinas are both theologians as well as philosophers that they can help us know how Desmond offers something to theology. Instead, it focuses on one of their shared insights concerning transcendence to demonstrate how Desmond, in agreeing with them, vivifies an ancient intuition: through adopting

191

a mask, the human person can mediate and be mediated by the created world. This is only possible when one acknowledges that one is "nothing" in face of the "more" of God.

I endeavor to explore these points in the following way. First, I speak of masking and doubling in Desmond's philosophy. Then, I consider Augustine and Thomas in turn, in the ways that they use masks. Finally, I discuss how analogy is an appropriate way of speaking of God for all three speakers, before considering how Augustine, Aquinas, and Desmond are all thinkers of ontological peace. My exploration of Thomas is more extended than that of Augustine, mainly because I have written more extensively about Augustine elsewhere.

THE MEANING OF THE MASK:
PERSONAL ENACTMENT OF DOUBLING

Desmond's idea of the mask relies on his notion of doubling, and forms a way for him to counteract the "counterfeit double" of Hegel's God.[3] Essentially, for Desmond, Augustine and Thomas succeed in adopting masks for themselves while recognizing and expressing God's masks, because they know that a mask at its best exceeds determinate rational speculation and offers a way to know what is "more." Neither thinker explores and articulates a "counterfeit double" of God but appreciates instead that God is always beyond what can be thought and stated. For Desmond, Aquinas's understanding of plurivocity, inspired by Aristotle's *Metaphysics* as well as by Augustine's appreciation of the way that God speaks through his creation, has "metaphysical dimensions"; namely, "the plurivocity is of being itself, and not simply our ways of talking about it. Our ways of speaking it are to be true to being's way(s) of bespeaking itself—plurivocally."[4] Thinking about the mask enables one to know how a person can enter into the mystery of such plurivocity, because a mask enables the philosopher to speak about transcendence without thereby opting only for the univocal, equivocal, or dialectical. Thomas's analogical predication is blood brother to Desmond's metaxological voicing.

Such speech depends upon the personal nature of philosophical inquiry, which in turn relies upon the capacity to work with masks that both represent and point beyond what can be said. In *God and the Between*, Desmond makes this link by explaining the mask in direct relationship to the "plurivocal manifestation" of being. The mask, says Desmond, has its origins in late Roman times, as "persona" or "prosopon." Desmond will find "persona" more compelling as a way to think of the mask than "prosopon," because the latter refers more to optics, whereas "persona" connotes sound and thus the way that divine speech can sound through us, if we are porous to that possibility.[5] In any case, donning the persona, the actor became a nexus of doubleness, enabling the double mediation that Desmond speaks of elsewhere as both "self-mediation (thought thinking itself in thinking its other) and intermediation (thought thinking its other)."[6] In other words, doubleness emphasizes that self-reflection is only possible through the other and at the same time that otherness is not reducible to that mode of self-reflection. Self and other remain in fertile tension, and can mediate each other either detrimentally or effectively.

When dialectical, this mediation can become self-focused and self-enclosed, because the other is used only as a means for the self, rather than left to be in its otherness, while at the same time it is a resource for the self. Masking as metaxological mediation works in the following ways. When someone dons a mask, particularly onstage, she represents something—or someone—else while remaining herself, thus allowing something to be seen because of her disguise. Furthermore, the mask acts as a medium through which otherwise unrealizable possibilities of the human person can unfold. The mask enables intermediation, between self, world, and others, such that "there is a passage between character and enactment, between the reserve of the role and its dramatic incarnation."[7] The person, known as mask, is "at once both revealing and reserving, manifesting and intimating,"[8] so that the self is fully there but represented as holding back something of itself. What is reserved is in this case openly represented in the context of performance: the masked self undergoes a particular enactment that is of the self and yet other to the self; the self represents something that it is and yet is not.

This understanding of personhood, known *through* the mask, relies on the notion of porosity, which Desmond finds key in approaching God in any way adequately.[9] Only by allowing oneself to become as nothing can God in his otherness announce and be heard. Thereby, one becomes a passage through which transcendence speaks—a *personans* rather than a *pros-opon*, which is to say a person understood as "an acoustic passage," "a porosity of transition, in which an energy of being more original than itself passes in communication, and it is spoken or sung into being."[10] Thus can thought truly sing its other.[11]

Personal porosity, thought through the doubleness of the mask, has extraordinary implications when coupled with the notions of "more" and "nothing" that Desmond uncovers in the thought of both Augustine and Thomas Aquinas. For let us consider another way in which Desmond thinks the implications of the mask, as a device that allows discovery of what is in the self precisely through offering the pretense that one is otherwise than the self. Desmond thinks here of Prince Hamlet's taking on of mania, which almost turns upon him to take him over entirely. The mask can be deceptive, negatively pointing toward the fact that the inner person can never be completely revealed.[12] The mask makes evident an otherness to the self that is at the same time of the self. Even when one takes on a mask, one is never in complete control but instead at risk of revealing through adopting that particular mask some aspect of the very thing that one wants to hide. Kierkegaard is a case in point. Each pseudonym allows another posture of thought, so that his fervor constantly emerges, and with it a wail against systematization of the divine. Just as Pascal cannot forgive Descartes, Desmond notes that Kierkegaard cannot absolve Hegel, for reducing God to a dialectician's mask: a facade with nothing beyond or behind.[13]

Tellingly, when crossing swords with Hegel, Desmond does not call upon Kierkegaard as his boon companion so much as he does Augustine and Aquinas. The mask he adopts, like a shield, to address Hegel's "counterfeit double" takes elements of the more porous masks of Augustine, particularly in his *Confessions*, as well as the measured works of Aquinas, who patiently and contemplatively speaks but, more important, remains silent when he experiences the "something more" that he had constantly tried to approach through his philosophical work: the transcendent and personal God beyond any mode of plurivocity. Kierkegaard's "fideistic shrillness"[14] is not so helpful here, perhaps because he is "also . . . secretly infected with the godlessness he excoriates around him in modernity."[15] Unlike Kierkegaard, Thomas provides philosophical resources to counteract Hegelian occlusion by offering a way across an otherwise clogged boundary between immanence and transcendence, which is to say that together Augustine and Thomas enable us to think of the porosity between religion and philosophy, which animates philosophy and at the same time opens her to the presuppositions of the theologian. The way across is that of the "superior," the "more" to which both Augustine and Thomas constantly refer. As I argue below, each thinker achieves this by working with masks. Before doing so, though, it is important to draw attention to and links between the way that both Augustine and Thomas think of divine transcendence as both "more" and "nothing." Such a both-and way of thought would perhaps be inimical to Kierkegaard, the philosopher of the either/or; but for each thinker it is important that the "more" and the "nothing" remain in tension, such that both can be spoken as readily of us as they can of God.

The "More" and the "Nothing" in Augustine and Thomas: How to Unmask a Dialectician

Two quotations, one from Augustine and one from Thomas, allow Desmond to think of them as philosophers of the "more" and so as companions on his own philosophical journey, constantly porous as it is to divine transcendence. Augustine's *nihilne plus* and Thomas's *videtur mihi ut palea* each speak to Desmond of the nothingness which is the "return to zero"[16] without which knowledge of God and of self, as sources of transcendence in intimate relationship to each other, are impossible. In his chapter "Speculation and Representation" in *Beyond Hegel and Dialectic*, Desmond effectively brings

Augustine and Thomas together, with these two quotations, so as to challenge Hegel. These particular "mores" and "nothings" are developed elsewhere too, particularly to highlight porosity, which is essential to philosophy and theology, as they engage together and with the world. I will speak now of Augustine and Thomas Aquinas in turn, as Desmond draws from them in that particular discussion, aware that many other connections can be made throughout Desmond's work. Considering these companioning passages together provides a starting point to find Augustine, Thomas, and Desmond in the middle space between the nothing and the more.

Desmond compares Augustine to Descartes, who "on the surface . . . seems to acquiesce in Augustine's passion of knowing: *Deum et animam scire cupio. Nihilne plus? Nihil omnino* (God and the soul I wish to know. Nothing more? Nothing at all)," saying that the difference lies in this: "Augustine will say 'nothing more,' not because he has clear and distinct transparency with respect to God, but because God is the 'more' that ever resists encapsulation in clear and distinct ideas. Yet this 'more' always calls for further unremitting thought, mindfulness before the mystery of the ultimate other."[17] Descartes's mask betrays him; seeming to be like Augustine, by asking the same questions, he is instead other, closed to aspects of answers that will not directly serve his purpose. In other words, for Augustine, the "more" is a mysterious openness of otherness, into which thought can proceed and from which it need not depart—so deep are its resources for the self in search for meaning. Descartes, in contrast, takes the self and God as a starting point, from which to proceed further toward "the new science of mathematized nature."[18] Knowledge of God and the soul, he thinks, are easy by comparison. Descartes's God, then, is not Augustine's: it is no longer mysterious, and its ultimacy functions as a determinate boundary within a system—a limit rather than an overdetermined porous threshold.

Augustine's "nothing more" sets out a philosophical project intersecting with what we normally discern to be the domain of theology. He sounds out revelation to enlighten his innermost thought and being. This intimate interior self in relation to transcendence underlies all of his writings; there Augustine experiences ultimacy as the answer to his perplexity.[19] Such perplexity striving toward ultimacy is no less vivid in Thomas's thought, precisely because he acknowledges a "more" and also a "nothing more" at the heart of an experience of God's intimate otherness. For Desmond, Thomas's statement, *videtur mihi ut palea* (it seems to me as so much straw),[20] and all that implies, becomes a reflection on the speculative thought with which he has been most involved. Desmond writes:

> Aquinas tried to reconcile Athens and Jerusalem, Aristotle and Augustine, philosophy and revealed religion. Moreover, Aquinas stood in the same tradition of speculative metaphysics as Hegel. Nor should his God-service, both philosophical and religious, be in doubt, even to a professing Christian. But what happened to Aquinas at the end of speculative philosophy? What happened was a certain enigmatic silence. There came a day when Aquinas told his secretary he could not go on; indeed his sister and relatives wondered if he was perhaps mad. . . . Aquinas saw "something more" and said about all his previous thought: It seems to me as so much straw. . . . Having seen "something more," he would write "nothing more."[21]

Unlike Hegel, Thomas's questioning and his great project of synthesis was always open to the something more. Contrary to Kierkegaard, Aquinas knows that there is value in stopping thought when it really can no longer speak. That is, Aquinas draws a limit that points toward something more rather than constantly speaking of the "more" with words that might tend to lose their communicative power. Kierkegaard's great example of the silent man of faith is Abraham. If the mask of Johannes de Silentio reveals anything of the Danish philosopher, he feels defeated simply by looking at and trying to imagine the interior journey of Abraham, the father of faith, as he proceeds up the mountain to kill Isaac.[22] Kierkegaard wants to dismiss thought as insufficient before the forever unmediated and transcendent object of faith. Thomas, on the other hand, refuses to banish thought but instead sees thought for what it is, such that "compared to the excess of its transcendence, my saying of it is as nothing."[23] Before infinity, finite thought falls silent. But there is something deeply affirmative in that silence, a "so be it" of thought.[24] The "so be it" for Desmond is the human ability to make oneself as nothing toward the "more." Desmond refers elsewhere to Mary's fiat in this regard.[25]

St. Thomas looked like a madman to those around him, but he displayed idiot wisdom, in Desmond's sense of the term. His attitude and disposition represent a radical form of prayer, an opening of himself toward ultimacy.[26] Augustine and Aquinas bring together the "nothing" with the "more." Thereby they avoid fideism, and also the Hegelian both-and that Kierkegaard finds so objectionable in the Hegelian counterfeit double of God. They can make this synthesis because each has the personal experience that the "more" can be known only through personal assumption of the "nothing." That is to say, one's own nothingness is a necessary starting point. The "nothing" is also a necessary assumption in this way: the "more" is so great that there is a point at which human thought is no longer sufficient; so that "nothing" describes what can be said at the point of transcendence. Religion is never overcome by thought; instead, what it knows, in its own way, is that which thought will never fully achieve.

And so there is no simple contradiction embedded in the phrase "nothing more," which Desmond adopts with Augustine and Aquinas. Augustine wants "nothing more" than to know God and the soul, in the sense of thinking that there is nothing besides the "more" that is to be known. If I can but know the "more," he thinks, everything else will stand as it should be, as mere nothingness in contrast. Likewise, Thomas's "it is as nothing"[27] leads to the statement of his intent to write "nothing more." In place of writing, Thomas will be silent, but this silence becomes a mask, hiding and at the same time revealing what he has experienced and cannot speak—the "more" that gives thought its meaning and at the same time annihilates it. This annihilation is, however, not akin to nihilism; it is rather embedded in an appreciation that creation comes out of nothing: it is only something at all because of the "more." In this way, the "nothing more" is a response to the "nothing" in relation to the "more"—an awestruck prayer of gratitude before that which makes the "nothing" more than it could ever alone have been. Let us see how both Augustine and

Aquinas speak of the "nothing" and the "more" through masks, so as to think through the implications of masking for philosophy as well as theology.

AUGUSTINE'S MASKS: CLAMOROUS THOUGHT
AND SILENT LOVE

Augustine's "nothing more" strikes us immediately as a deeply personal philosophical project, working behind but also through the persona he offers the reader. As he masks and unmasks, Augustine's audacity makes him quite vulnerable. His quest, in its intimate dimensions, is unmasked when he gives us the *Confessions*, in which his prowess as a rhetorician (the practice of mastering masks) is evident. The *Confessions* works in several ways through masking: it provides a *persona* (the autobiographical character of Augustine himself), and it demonstrates how God presents himself to Augustine and us via masks, including that of creation itself. Thus doubling is constantly at work. We, Augustine's readers, become aware of ourselves through Augustine and his masked representation of God; and this knowledge mirrors and replicates Augustine's communication of self through the quest for knowledge of God.

While the *Confessions* as a text is punctuated with moments of self-reflection, and with questions about how and why Augustine is able to write his autobiography at all, one passage in particular is striking in this regard. It comes at the beginning of book 10, that great treatise on memory, and it captures Augustine's readiness to become as nothing before the agapeic otherness that gives himself to himself. At this point, Augustine has told the story of his conversion, and recalled the pain but also the peace of his mother's death. Having retold some of the most tumultuous moments of his life—brought them out in the open, through speech—he pauses and reflects on the act of confession. That activity takes place in Augustine's heart, because he is in the Lord's presence, but also "with [his] pen before many witnesses." Augustine may be able to fool his merely human readers—or at least try to do so—but such is not possible before God. Not to be truthful about himself, says Augustine, would be "hiding" from himself but not "myself from you [God]." Completely exposed before the Lord, Augustine acknowledges that it is for his own benefit that true confession must take place, and the mode of proper confession is especially telling: "My confession to you," he says,

> is made not with words of tongue and voice, but with the words of my soul and the clamor of my thought, to which your ear is attuned; for when I am bad, confession to you is simply disgust with myself, but when I am good, confession to you consists in not attributing my goodness to myself, because though you, Lord, bless the person who is just, it is only because you have first made him just when he was sinful. This is why, O my God, my confession in your presence is silent, yet not altogether silent: there is no noise to it, but it shouts by love.[28]

Whether being bad or good, Augustine acknowledges he is nothing. When he turns away from God, he is focused only on himself, with disgust; the joy of goodness is delight in having received all that he is from God. In either case, Augustine is "nothing." But what of the more? The more is spoken in silence, but a silence that resounds through Augustine as per-sonans rather than as prosopon. Through him God's love moves, and such love brings with it peace that is captured more in silence than in clamorous thought. In the soul's most intimate moments with God, Augustine's prayers are silent shouts: love enables the more to mask itself but not to *be* nothing.

Well might we ask then, why does Augustine bother to write at all, since silence seems so much more profound? At least one response is that in doing so he is praying, and one form of praying is to use words. With words, Augustine also thinks, making sense of himself, of how his life is situated within all of creation and the narrative of redemption. His life is also offered up to God, in ways that he hopes are completely truthful; for if they are not, then his words are meaningless. Finally, though, he writes for us, his audience, down through the ages. For us does he take up his pen, and with it he fashions a mask. That is to say, Augustine when he writes of himself presents what he can of himself, in order to form an adequate picture for his own philosophical project. He wants to know the soul and God: nothing more; and in aid of this he describes his soul in relationship with God. This seems to be, after all, the power of the mask when employed by a philosopher who knows his limits. The mask stands for the person, who finds himself situated at the very limit of thought and experience because in an intense and intimate relationship with what transcends. When Augustine's words have stopped, there is silence. But behind the words themselves, there is a still more ontological silence: the silence of love, which can never exhaust itself—even in the words of prayer.

In one way, the intimacy of Augustine's life in and with God is unmasked in the *Confessions*. In another, his words remain an essential mask, as a mediating point through which we can understand anything whatsoever about God, and about the possibilities for any relationship with God from within the middle. So, in terms of Desmond's idea of doubleness, with reference to the mask, one could suggest this: the *Confessions* as mask allows Augustine to present himself to himself, as other; that is, he forms a picture of himself for himself, and that mask becomes another through which he becomes more porous to self-knowledge.[29] That porosity, though, is only in operation inasmuch as his words carry real meaning, by remaining true to his actual relationship with God. Augustine, after all, is trained in rhetoric, which can be a powerful deceiving mask, of which the saint is well aware. To allow the mask to be true to its task, that of enabling him to open himself to the "more" by offering a representation that is both of him and yet more than he is, Augustine hopes to check himself. One of the ways that he does this is to constantly allow passages from scripture to speak for him, through him. In this way, I would suggest, he practices the art of being porous—thereby remaining alert to aesthetic happening. Likewise, he offers a point of consideration for theology—indicating that there really are moments when human speech should not be autonomously spoken, in the mode of *conatus essendi*, but received, through the powers of *passio essendi*, as the gifted words of revelation.[30]

Augustine is constantly alert to what Desmond calls the "aesthetics of happening," whereby "givenness shines forth with its own intimate radiance, coming to manifest its own marvellous intricacy of order."[31] That is, Augustine thinks of creation precisely as a mask that both conceals and reveals God. It does so by pointing to God in the fact of its givenness, or createdness. This, in any case, is one way to read another passage in St. Augustine, where he questions the whole created order, at first mistaking creatures for the Creator.[32] Listening attentively to the mask that is creation, Augustine finds that in being made by God the world presents itself as a something that reveals its own nothingness and at the same time its relationship to the "more." To Augustine's point that he wishes to know nothing more than soul and world, one might add this caveat: such knowledge is possible only because desire to know is set alight by the world in which Augustine finds himself; and without that world, neither the erotic nor the aga-peic potencies of happening would touch him. Another point from Desmond for theology, then, is one with which Augustine will agree: the concrete particularity of creation, in its elemental fullness, is a first and inexhaustible point for contemplating God.

THOMAS AQUINAS'S MASKS: SYSTEM AND THE SAP OF MYSTERY

Like Augustine, Thomas uses masks, but his at first seem less recognizable—less able to show the contours *through* the mask of what is hidden. Where Augustine speaks of his experience of God, Thomas remains for the most part silent about the particulars of his own life. In the end, though, each does fall into silence before death. Thomas refuses to write anything more, while Augustine wants only to be alone in prayer, contemplating David's psalms. Both pens take rest but finally Thomas's more dramatically than Augustine's. Des-mond has several suggestions about the masks that Thomas uses— for instance, the systematic way in which he presents the *Summa*, as well as his presentation of the five ways of knowing that God exists. One can also think of Thomas's insistence that our names for God are never entirely adequate; and one can consider Thomas's silence. Desmond sees the philosopher-saint's proclamation that "all is straw," and he can write "nothing more" as a mask that presents the "more" that he has seen. In each instance of mask, Thomas cannot help but announce something more, because his thought is always open to the transcendent Other, so intimately the center and focus of his work.

Desmond speaks of Thomas's system, particularly evident in the *Summa Theologiae*, as a mask in at least two places. The first has already been mentioned, in *Beyond Hegel and Dialectic*.[33] In *The Intimate Strangeness of Being*, Desmond speaks again of the *Summa* as system but now as a work misunderstood as solely system. "The *Summa*," he reflects, "is architectonic and systematic but differently so than the idealistic version of system." He goes on to explain that, unlike the systematizations of God by Hegel, Spinoza, and even Kant, in Thomas's *Summa*

> there is a finesse for divine mystery percolating through[,] . . . rising up from a religious ethos where, at best, the practices of prayer keep unclogged the soul's porosity to the divine. The sap of the mystery of God flows in the body of the work, though this is not always immediately evident on the surface, where some-times a kind of forensic univocity marks Aquinas's way of pro-ceeding. More rationalistic philosophers tend not to be attuned to that sap and turn Aquinas's thought into a Scholasticism closer to the prototype of modern rationalism.[34]

The surface then, with what appears like univocity, acts as a mask for what is there, running throughout the whole work. And what is there is a "porosity of religion and philosophy" mirroring the porosity of the person('s soul) to what is divine. In other words, the work as mask acts as an analogue to the person, especially Thomas Aquinas but perhaps also the *Summa*'s "witnesses," inasmuch as it allows reli-gion and philosophy to mingle. Indeed, the work for which Aqui-nas remains most famous seems paradigmatic masked porosity. The human becomes a mask that breathes and speaks—allowing to pass through as its bearer speaks systematically of rationally held beliefs, thus using the tools of philosophy, while at the same time thinking philosophically always in light of what he knows most fundamentally to be true—at a very personal and intimate level. Thomas the believer is Thomas the rigorous thinker, and the clamor of thought never blocks the flow of God's life through and in his thought.

On Aquinas's work *as* mask, Denys Turner has observed that Thomas as a person tends to slip away from us in his works. We know something of his character anecdotally, but only on "perhaps two occasions" did Thomas the man, "even in his writings[,] . . . break . . . through the impassive objectivity of his prose in an outburst of indignant rage. . . . Only very rarely would Thomas the teacher come out into the open personally, and then when the defense of his students, or the integrity of the teaching role itself, demanded it. On such occasions he was fully prepared to come out fighting, gloves off."[35] Rare may be the breakthroughs, but Turner, like Desmond, detects something of Thomas's characteristic holding back in his text. Turner suggests that Thomas's transparency necessitates that he step back, so that his students are focused not on him but on what he has to say.[36] In Augustine, personality is on show, and that personality operates as a mask allowing him to speak. For Thomas, the text, wherein we see the structure and lucidity of his thought, becomes the shining mask through which we occasionally see him but more the source of both his speech and his silences.

Such silences are essential—and here Desmond, Turner, and also Josef Pieper agree. For Pieper, Thomas's silence refers not only to what he could not say when he did not finish the *Summa*. It also pertains to Thomas's "unspoken assumptions," the most primary of which, according to Pieper, is Thomas's "idea of creation, or more precisely, the notion that nothing exists which is not *creatura*, except the Creator himself; and in addition, that this createdness determines entirely and all-pervasively the inner structure of the creature."[37] Again, an inner world is opened up with reference to silence, so that silence becomes an indicator of both a "nothing" and a "more." The silence is no mere happenstance, nor does it result from descent into madness; it is instead a mystic glimpse into the "more." That "more," according to his philosophy, is not even what one would see in the Beatific Vision but instead the perspective of what humans would have seen had they never suffered the fall into original sin.[38] Seeing more is therefore seeing as a human was always supposed to see. Thomas's lucid text can be thought in another way: as a mask that aims to show the limitations of thought in coming to know what has been lost to us, through our first parents transgressing a primal boundary whose full significance they could not realize. What the first parents saw, one might say, was their creatureliness. They were exposed, and loved in that exposure: knowing "more" through the "nothing" because the "more" loved them in that nothingness. Masks in the garden must have been other to our present imaginings. When Thomas knew this, through experience transcending fallen sensory data, it seems that he found even his own magnificent mask, as text, insufficient. How excessive must this "more" be to strike dumb one such as Thomas, even after that same dumb ox had so prolifically found his voice.

Desmond thinks of Thomas in relation to masks: through the reasoning involved in two of the five ways. Namely, in the third way (argument from possibility and necessity) and the fifth way (argument from design), Thomas proves to be a thinker of finesse rather than geometry.[39] There is, in other words, a subtlety to his thinking through these arguments that defies the limitations of mere speculation. Again, using the idea of mask helps us see this point.

In *God and the Between*, Desmond speaks about the third way as coming out of a primary affirmation of being, which relates to the "primordial affirmation of the simple elemental 'it is good to be.'"[40] The third way, says Thomas in the third article of the first part of the *Summa*, "is taken from possibility and necessity"; and he reasons that while things in nature can either be or not be, "it is impossible for these always to exist, for that which is possible not to be at some time is not."[41] For anything to be at all, then, "we cannot but postulate the existence of some being having of itself its own necessity, and not receiving it from another, but rather causing in others their necessity. This all men speak of as God."[42] Desmond finds that, contrasted with Kant's "thin" appreciation of causality, whereby an effect is completely determined by its cause, Aquinas demonstrates that "if all being is possible being, ultimately all possible being is impossible."[43] From this Desmond derives that the other about which Thomas thinks in its necessity is hyperbolic—and so, one might say, not the Cartesian

God who merely flips a switch but instead the God who "could never be a determination or determinate being."[44] For Desmond, Thomas's third way "has to do with being struck ... by the incontrovertibility of being. There is a bite of otherness in thus being struck. There is no way to sidestep being, and the inescapability of its givenness, even if there is something overdeterminate about being as thus given."[45] Thomas, says Desmond, is presenting us with what is perhaps "a thought experiment that tries to stun us into astonishment about the 'that it is,' despite the nothing."[46] Here the nothing and the more are in interplay. Behind the mask of a few lines in an article toward the beginning of the *Summa*, the reader of Thomas passes beyond, if she has the finesse to be nourished like Thomas with the same sap of a personal relationship with being, and through that with the hyperbolic. Such passing, that is to say, happens through the nothing with which we identify. Thereby one can progress to the more, which is overdetermined and thus beyond systematization.

In *The Intimate Strangeness of Being*, Desmond thinks of the fifth way as working through the mediation of a figure, which seems to be very similar in his understanding to that of the mask.[47] A figure is a representation of what one is trying to see, or "figure out," which does not pretend to give the full-blooded richness of what is the matter for thought in a particular instance. "Our need of figures in dealing with God," Desmond observes, "often reflects our figuration and reconfiguration of the ethos of being. The premodern configuring of that ethos was more porous to communications between faith and reason, theology and philosophy."[48] Thus Plato can give us the myth of the *Timaeus* as a "likely story," which is far richer than either the "Hegelian sublation of figures into concepts"[49] or Kant's "as if" whereby God serves as a regulative Idea of Reason. Both of these offer only determined human thought, unable to reach toward the overdetermined, hyperbolic terms that relate to what it is (thought here against a plurivocal index) metaphysically.[50] Aquinas can offer the argument from design, whereby we look at the world and come to know something of its cause, because thought can provide a porous way through which the "more" that is the principle and cause of the "nothing" can announce itself.

Thomas argues in the fifth way:

> We see that things which lack intelligence, such as natural bodies, act for an end . . . so as to obtain the best result. Hence it is plain that not fortuitously, but designedly, do they achieve their end. Now whatever lacks intelligence cannot move towards an end, unless it be directed by some being endowed with knowledge and intelligence. . . . Therefore some intelligent being exists by whom all natural things are directed to their end; and this being we call God.[51]

All depends, here, on how we allow ourselves to experience the world. Thomas obviously observes that things work toward their good and proper ends only seemingly of their own accord. He does and does not say what he at the same time apprehends, that God is at work behind that constant operation. Unlike Paley, the world does not seem to him mechanistic, and so God is not presumed a mechanic. And God is not simply *in* the world, contained in such manifestations, but is instead beyond it, so that Thomas through his very way of seeing and knowing the mask of creation excludes pantheism.[52]

Thomas in all of his five ways is masked and unmasked as a human being immersed in the *metaxu*. In Desmond's words, his knowledge that there is something more, and of a certain ilk, reveals him to himself as a person who is "an analogical sign whose freedom and striving to be good" are "hyperbolic signs" that, taken with the potencies of self-transcending, indicate "ultimate transcendence."[53] The person for Thomas and for Desmond, thought thus, is a figure, as a way to figure out divine transcendence; at the same time the person is more than that. For if the person in her freedom exists at all, inasmuch as hyperbole is involved in the way she is given to be, then by analogy one can find out something of the source of such self-transcending. At the very least, that origin of transcendence must have an intimate relationship to transcendence as such. The figure here, I would suggest, can be understood also as mask. The argument from design, according to Desmond's discussion, only works when the self is able, through the world, to come to know oneself as self-transcending.

Let us for a moment place this person within Desmond's metaxo-logical framework, and ask him to read Aquinas's ways from the *Summa*, penned for the author, before God, as well as for others including the reader. The potencies of masking thereby take on new meaning. For, adopting a persona and donning the mask by taking up the text and the argument, the reader can inhabit the world dif-ferently, with perspectives opened anew. Such invigorated experience, provided through the person in the experience of agapeic astonish-ment, is something that I will return to in a moment, because in order to appreciate it more fully one would need to regard what it is to see as Thomas does—discovering through creation links to God, through analogy. Crucially, Thomas's *Summa* provides a way for the witness to his task to find, through the mask of text, possibilities for seeing that might otherwise only remain hidden. Thomas's "proofs," as well as his method for saying something about God—through likeness and unlikeness to creation—facilitate such vision, through a mask that mediates self to self through the world porously known.

ANALOGY AND EXPERIENCING GOD

Such seeing leads to a different kind of mask, this time as expression of what is known and intimated. Desmond finds Thomas especially helpful, in that analogy mediates by doubling. Desmond's thoughts on analogy allow us to think Augustine and Thomas together. Meth-odologically in the *Confessions* it is true that Augustine does seem to be quite different from Thomas. He speaks first of himself and the world and usually uses the words of prayer and scripture to do so. Thomas, on the other hand, develops philosophical argument and language. Even with the seeming systematic sophistication of analogi-cal predication, however, Thomas fundamentally agrees with Augus-tine's intuition that we are always between both the "nothing" and the "more." This, I would finally like to suggest, is the main way in which Desmond brings both thinkers together. To make this point, I will briefly describe some of the main aspects of analogy, as Desmond picks them up in particular in *The Intimate Strangeness of Being*.

As just briefly explored, Desmond finds in Thomas elemental awareness that is "severely masked" by Thomas's form of "rhetorical expression." However, excess again seeps through his thinking, rooted as the latter is in prayer. Desmond's chapter on analogy enables one to see how such thought, in the mode of analogy, is a porous mode of being in the middle. Analogy enables plurivocal speaking and allows Thomas to be true to the presence of God in the world. God is not entirely of the world, but inasmuch as he is the world's cause something of him can be found in what we see and know. This is how analogy aids Thomas, Desmond, and us. For, being neither strictly univocal nor solely equivocal, analogy has the advantage of allowing one to speak of what is as what it is "like" and also what it is "unlike." Analogy, Desmond explains, "is itself a between, and communicates a between—and to cite the most important case, in the *likeness/unlikeness between* the creation and God."[54] For Desmond and Thomas alike, such speech is possible because of a fundamental relationship within being itself. We can only speak of God at all because he can be known by what he has made. When contemplating what it means to name God, Thomas describes one of the fundamental implications of analogy: "Whatever is said of God and creatures, is said according to the relation of a creature to God as its principle and cause, wherein all perfections of things pre-exist excellently. Now this mode of community of idea is a mean [*medius*] between [*inter*] pure equivocation and simple univocation."[55] I have inserted the Latin in two places here to make a point. Analogy for Thomas is a way of intermediation, between beings but also between thought and being, because of a primary ontological relationship between creature and God. We are, with Thomas, squarely in the metaxological, in the intermediating space where a certain attitude toward the world is preeminently needed. Desmond, Augustine, and Thomas again agree, for, in the same article, Thomas quotes one of Augustine's favorite passages from Paul: "the invisible things of God are clearly seen, being understood by the things that are made."[56] This quotation is obviously as much a point of reflection for Thomas as it is for Augustine, appearing again and earlier in the *Summa* when he argues that we can in fact demonstrate that God exists.[57] We can know and speak of God, the point seems clear, by looking at the world, by accepting what is given as coming from a cause that we can know and speak of—analogically. As discussed, though, it is not enough simply to see; the way in which one sees is fundamental. That is, only by being "porous" can one find God through the world, and make and speak through the appropriate mask.

ON TAKING A SABBATICAL: BEING AS NOTHING TO THE MORE

Desmond's appreciation of doubleness and masking enables one to discover the main ways he finds both Augustine and Thomas companions in thought. Each emphasizes that only in first adopting an attitude of nothingness toward transcendence can any form of self-transcendence be accomplished. Such achievement is something received, facilitated but never entirely given by striving human thought taken alone. Augustine and Thomas both demonstrate what Desmond calls a "celebrating seeing," captured but never exhausted by their adoption of masks. This seeing echoes—and so proves to be more than sight alone—the "it is good" of the Creator gazing upon the mask of his own making.[58] And that moment of utterance of the "it is good" becomes the space that Augustine, Thomas, and Desmond all share when they adopt the silence that deeply characterizes a "Sabbath for thought."

In his "Exceeding Virtue: Aquinas and the Beatitudes," Desmond emphasizes the beatitudes as "hyperbolic," "addressed to human beings in their elemental humanity," and requiring of us a "mindful porosity" in order to understand what they demand.[59] Moreover, the beatitudes exceed the philosopher's well-articulated claims that virtue is important. In particular, the first beatitude reminds us of our nothingness. "Blessed are the poor in spirit" refers to poverty not only as "a matter of removing impediments," but—and here Desmond's words about Thomas are very much in keeping with the earlier quotation from Augustine's *Confessions*—as "something more intimate to the naked soul in its exposure to God."[60] Thomas can write because he is alert to the need for such exposure, as a lived willingness to embrace the world as a means toward its maker.

This exposure opens up a manner of "celebrating seeing," which is in stark contrast to the "instrumental hypothesis that has to be mediated by evidences or sense data."[61] What will finally be seen, experienced through far more than the evidence of sensory information, is the peace of the seventh beatitude, whereby the peacemakers will be called the children of God. To know, deep down, that one is a child of God can only be mediated through the world when an attitude to that world, as also made, has already been adopted. The peace that follows from that realization is that of the Sabbath that Desmond speaks about in *Is There a Sabbath for Thought?*, where peace is the rest that comes after working. It is a stepping back from the clamors of thought of which Augustine speaks. Thomas's peace, alluded to in the beatitudes, is, according to Desmond, a vision that "makes sense of war, be it social or political or economic."[62] The revelation is, for Thomas,

> not finally other than that of Augustine's vision of peace in the *City of God*. This is a multi-layered account, as deeply ontological as it is metaphysical and theological. Ontological: it is a vision of all things being what they are by virtue of an ultimate ontological peace; to be at all is to be in the gifted peace of creation as good. No finite being could continue to be at all, without some minimal peace of that being with itself and other beings. Metaphysical and theological: in that the ultimate ground of this ontological peace of finite being lies in God, the giver of all conditions of the possibility of being at all, and the giver of finite being in its integrity.[63]

Such peace serves here not only as a point on which Augustine and Thomas and Desmond just happen to agree. It is instead the foundation for being able to know and think and speak about God at all. An acceptance that peace is more fundamental than war, that goodness rather than its absence is our ontological foundation, provides an underlying principle for Thomas's *Summa*, including its five ways, as much as it does Augustine's move from the exterior to the interior and the inferior to the superior. According to this Augustinian trajectory, the person is always the mediating point, dwelling in the center of a world and open to the ontological peace, by being porous to what is other. The person's capacity to be double, by taking into oneself what would remain otherwise only exterior, is likewise essential to Thomas's rigorous thought.

Thomas finds in Augustine a constant companion in thought,[64] and Desmond finds similar nourishment from them both; and so it is unsurprising that such strong affiliations can be drawn between their ideas. For all the ways in which their masks are different, they rest upon the same foundation, which allows them to think as well as to speak as they do. All three know that it is only when one acknowledges oneself as "nothing" that one is equal to the task of finding what is "more." Thinking transcendence at its limits means transgressing the boundaries of one's own mask, at which point the silence of prayer remains. Desmond constantly draws from the springs of these saints because they are already thinkers of the middle, porous to God's transcendent ways of speaking. Their elemental awareness is present because of that porosity, which is philosophy's true gift to theology. "The poverty of philosophy," says Desmond, "is openness to, porosity to the promise of an agapeic peace."[65] Beyond the agonistic striving of thought, there is peace; but only when the thinker, in the between of the elemental world, is porous to the agapeic promise of God's silent and masked love.

Notes

I would like to thank William Desmond for pointing to the main texts for this chapter. Thank you also to Christopher Ben Simpson for the invitation to write this chapter. It is always a gift to have the opportunity to work with such friends.

1. See, for instance, the epigraph to *GB* taken from Augustine's *Confessions*: *Sacrificem tibi famulatum cogitationis et linguae meae, et da quod offeram tibi* (St. Augustine, *Confessions*, XI, 2). For discussions of how Desmond uses Augustine's thought, see Renée Ryan, "An Archaeological Ethics: Augustine, Desmond and Digging Back to the Agapeic Origin," in *Between System and Poetics: William Desmond and Philosophy after Dialectic*, ed.

Thomas A. F. Kelly (Aldershot: Ashgate, 2007), 125–38; Renée Köhler-Ryan, "Gifted Beggars in the *Metaxu*: A Study of the Platonic and Augustinian Resonances of *Porosity* in *God and the Between*," *Louvain Studies* 36 (2012): 256–81; Renée Köhler-Ryan, " 'No Block Creation': Good and Evil in William Desmond's Augustinian Philosophy of Elemental Order," in *To Discern Creation in a Scattering World*, ed. Frederiek Depoortere and Jacques Haers (Leuven: Peeters, 2013), 207–20.

    2. *IST*, 232. Chapter 9 of this work, "Analogy, Dialectic, and Divine Transcendence: Between St. Thomas and Hegel" (231–59), is the third in what Desmond calls a "triad" of essays about Thomas. The other two in the triad are "Is there a Sabbath for Thought: Reflections of Philosophy and Peace," ch. 10 in *IST*, 312–56; and "Exceeding Virtue: Aquinas and the Beatitudes," in *Thomas Aquinas: Teacher and Scholar*, ed. James McEvoy, Michael W. Dunne, and Julia Hynes (Dublin: Four Courts Press, 2011), 28–49.

    3. On this point, it is helpful to consider some of Desmond's remarks on the need for images for thought, and when these can turn counterfeit: "Suppose we need, cannot but need, images to speak of God as original. . . . The problem of the counterfeit double is that the image will mimic as well as show the original, and mimic by presenting itself as the original. Sometimes it may seem so like the original, we have difficulty telling it is an image. If such an image, so to say, usurps the original, how can we tell this, since it looks the same as the original?" *HG*, 8–9. For the connection between person and double, see also *EB*, 190–91.

    4. *ISB*, 234.

    5. *GB*, 192. Chapter 9 in this work contains references to the "more" and the "nothing" discussed in the present chapter.

    6. See Christopher Ben Simpson, *Religion, Metaphysics, and the Postmodern: William Desmond and John D. Caputo* (Bloomington: Indiana University Press, 2009), 32.

    7. *GB*, 192.

    8. *GB*, 192.

    9. See, e.g., *GB*, 284, where *porosity* is important for us to become a "kind of nothing" capable of prayer. See also *IST*, 21–25.

    10. *GB*, 197.

    11. See, in particular, William Desmond, "Being Mindful: Thought Singing Its Other," in *PO*, 259–311.

    12. *PO*, 78.

    13. *BHD*, 156–60.

    14. *BHD*, 159.

15. *BHD*, 160.

16. *GB*, 28–29.

17. *BHD*, 156.

18. *BHD*, 156.

19. See *PU*, 11: "The middle as a dynamic field and the desiring energizing of our being there point beyond themselves. Here I would exploit Augustine's description of the double nature of his own quest for ultimacy: *ab exterioribus ad interiora, ab inferioribus ad superiora*; from the exterior to the interior, from the inferior to the superior. I interpret this to mean the following. In the middle of things—the exteriors—we come to know the dunamis of our own being as an interior middle, a mediating self-transcending power of openness. This is the first movement. The second movement is: in the interior middle, within the self-transcending urgency of desire, there is an opening to an other, more ultimate than ourselves. We are the interior urgency of ultimacy, this other is ultimacy as the superior. This superior ultimate is not identical with our own erotic self-mediation; it is irreducible to us and mediates with us—the inferior—through the agapeic excess of its unequalizable plenitude. So, in fact, this second movement also allows the possibility of a double mediation: our own erotic quest of the ultimate; the ingression of the ultimate as a superior other that interplays with the middle out of its own excessive transcendence."

20. Desmond's translation, *BHD*, 159.

21. *BHD*, 159.

22. See, in particular, Søren Kierkegaard, "Speech in Praise of Abraham," in *Fear and Trembling*, trans. Alistair Hannay (London: Penguin, 1995), 49–56.

23. *BHD*, 160.

24. *BHD*, 160.

25. *ISB*, 243 n. 9.

26. *GB*, 133. Also: Thomas's mindfulness in this regard, as prayer, is captured not only in his philosophy but also in the prayer that he wrote, *Adoro te devote*, which in part reflects upon the way that the Godhead is veiled in the mystery of the Blessed Sacrament. A veil is a kind of mask, and so perhaps here, in this prayer thought as expressive mask, the theologian could also find a porous space for thought between self and ultimate other.

27. The radical nature of such prayer is in keeping with the nature of forgiveness, as each is enabled by the agapeic. See for this Desmond's essay "'It Is Nothing'—Wording the Release of Forgiveness," *Proceedings of the ACPA* 82 (2008): 1–23. The essay draws particularly on Augustine's understanding of "nothing" as proceeding from agapeic richness.

28. Saint Augustine, *The Confessions*, trans. Maria Boulding, O.S.B., vol. I/1 of *The Works of Saint Augustine: A Translation for the 21st Century* (New York: New City Press, 1997), bk. 10, 2, 181.

29. One can think here too of the moment before Augustine's conversion, when he sees himself as though a mask has been removed: "Lord, even while [Ponticianus] spoke you were wrenching me back toward myself, and pulling me round from that standpoint behind my back which I had taken to avoid looking at myself. You set me down before my face, forcing me to mark how despicable I was, how misshapen and begrimed, filthy and festering. I saw and shuddered." Augustine, *Confessions*, bk. 8, 7, 16; 148.

30. See, in particular, *GB*, 33–36.

31. *GB*, 134.

32. *Confessions*, bk. 10, 9. Augustine questions various beautiful aspects of creation, which reply that they are God but instead are, like Augustine, made by God. Their reply, he says, is "their beauty." Thus, a statement of the aesthetic.

33. *BHD*, ch. 3.

34. *ISB*, 243.

35. Denys Turner, *Thomas Aquinas: A Portrait* (New Haven, CT: Yale University Press, 2013), 35–36.

36. Ibid., 36.

37. Josef Pieper, *The Silence of Saint Thomas*, trans. John Murray, S.J., and Daniel O'Connor (Chicago: Henry Regnery, 1957), 47.

38. Thomas Aquinas, *De Veritate*, q. 1, a. 18, in *The Disputed Questions on Truth*, trans. Robert W. Mullitan, 3 vols. (Chicago: Henry Regnery, 1952), 344.

39. For an explanation of these terms, which are frequent in Desmond's writings, see *IST*, 191–93.

40. *GB*, 131.

41. Thomas Aquinas, *Summa Theologiae*, I, q. 2, a. 3; trans. Fathers of the English Dominican Province, 5 vols. (New York: Cosimo Classics, 2007), vol. 1, 13.

42. Aquinas, *Summa Theologiae*, I, q. 2, a. 3.

43. *GB*, 132.

44. *GB*, 133.

45. *GB*, 133.

46. *GB*, 133.

47. Desmond speaks of this way of "figuring" in "Analogy and the Fate of Reason," in *The Oxford Handbook of Catholic Theology*, ed. Lewis Ayres

and Medi-Ann Volpe, Oxford Handbooks Online, 2016, DOI:10.1093/oxfordhb/9780199566273.013.4.

48. *ISB*, 244.

49. *ISB*, 245.

50. *ISB*, 247.

51. *Summa Theologiae*, I, q. 2, a. 3 (p. 14).

52. *ISB*, 249.

53. *ISB*, 249.

54. *ISB*, 235; original emphasis.

55. *Summa Theologiae*, I, q. 13, a. 6 (p. 64).

56. Rom. 1:20; *Summa Theologiae*, I, q. 13, a. 6 (p. 64).

57. *Summa Theologiae*, I, q. 2, a. 2 (p. 12).

58. See *EB*, ch. 5, "Ethos and Metaxological Ethics," 163–220.

59. See Desmond, "Exceeding Virtue," 29.

60. Desmond, "Exceeding Virtue," 34.

61. Ibid., 39.

62. Ibid., 47.

63. Ibid.

64. See Introduction to *Aquinas the Augustinian*, ed. Michael Dauphinais, Barry David, and Matthew Levering (Washington, DC: Catholic University of America Press, 2007), xxiv: "We might say . . . that Aquinas is an 'Augustinian' in the sense that, like all of Augustine's greatest interpreters, he engages with and elaborates upon Augustine's insights in a manner that challenges us to think afresh about the realities known and loved by Augustine."

65. *IST*, 349.

CHAPTER 8

Rolling with Release into the Future

William Desmond's Donation to a Natural Theology of the Arts

CHRISTOPHER R. BREWER

In this essay I consider the donation of William Desmond to natural theology along two lines, the first beginning with his call "for more adequate metaphysical reflection on the ontological character of the ethos."[1] I argue, with reference to his 1999 essay, "God, Ethos, Ways," that Desmond offers an alternative perspective on natural theology from continental philosophy. Second, and more specifically, I consider Desmond's donation to a natural theology of the arts in relation to the work of Howard E. Root (1926–2007). In his 1962 essay, "Beginning All Over Again," Root argued that natural theology had become malnourished, and this as a result of theology's isolation from the arts.[2] I argue that Root's project might benefit from Desmond's discussion of Hegel's double evaluation of art, as well as Desmond's further consideration of the power and limits of art in relation to the question of history. Consideration of Desmond leads not only to the possibility of a renewed natural theology but also to a reformulated version of Root's natural theology of the arts. Desmond has suggested, "Sometimes we need to rock backwards to get out of a rut and budge the jam and then roll with release into the future. Philosophy in the *metaxu* has to move with something of this rocking motion—and with it releasing promise. Rocking back allows forward release."[3] With that in mind, I turn to consider Desmond's call for more adequate metaphysical reflection as an alternative perspective on natural theology from continental philosophy.

"GOD, ETHOS, WAYS"

In his essay "A Perspective on Natural Theology from Continental Philosophy," Russell Re Manning argues that, despite "something of a block to any interest in natural theology," continental philosophy "is vitally marked by an engagement with issues that are essential to natural theology."[4] Acknowledging that "the central features of natural theology, as normally conceived, seem to be strikingly absent from the writings of continental philosophers,"[5] Re Manning suggests that "all is not as it seems on the surface."[6] While helpful in drawing our attention to a perspective on natural theology from continental philosophy, Re Manning fails to engage with or acknowledge Desmond.

Desmond argues that "the ways" (a.k.a. "the arguments for God's existence," "the proofs") cannot be abstracted from "the ethos" (a.k.a. "the ontological ethos," "the between"). More fully, he argues that "we do an injustice to the 'proofs' if we abstract them from the ontological context in which they are formulated; we have to acknowledge a complex interplay of ways and ethos. The result is not only a task for rethinking the ways, it is also a task for more adequate metaphysical reflection on the ontological character of the ethos."[7] We might here observe the importance of the ethos in Desmond's consideration. All too often natural theology is thought to be synonymous with ways or proofs, but Desmond calls for a deeper mindfulness, that is, a mindfulness of the ethos. Put simply: the ethos matters, and it has, in Desmond's estimation, received far too little attention.

But what is the ethos? Desmond explains: "Ethos is more primordial; a way formulates a more definite passage of thinking out of the overdetermination of ethos; a way also makes determinate what otherwise is indefinite in the ethos."[8] Put differently, the ethos is, as Christopher Ben Simpson explains, "the matrix or milieu of all our subsequent (if always already present) constructions."[9] In other words, we find ourselves in the middle (a.k.a. "the ethos," "the milieu of being"), and this is where metaphysical thinking takes shape.[10] In addition to this primal ethos, Desmond names a second ethos, "the reconfigured ethos," which, as Simpson explains, "is made up of the more determinate judgments and valuations that we come up with to get a handle on the fullness of the between."[11] One might thus speak of the ancient ethos, the modern ethos, and so forth. In any case, it is this second ethos that the ways all too often reflect. More fully, Desmond explains:

> There is first an ontological ethos of what I call the between; we are in this between and our participation shapes its form. Our participation contributes to this *second* ethos which is the *reconfigured* ethos, in light of our fundamental perception and presuppositions, and basic sense of good and evil, and so on. Then there are ways, arguments, proofs; most of these reflect the second ethos; not many put their roots into the primal ethos; and if they do not, they will tend to reflect, shall we say, the preoccupations of the *Zeitgeist*, perhaps the idolatries and bewitchments.[12]

The problem, it seems, is that natural theologians have failed to mind the first ethos. Desmond is thus concerned to recover a deeper mindfulness: a mindfulness of the first ethos.

Considered from this perspective, Desmond's donation to natural theology is nothing less than the whole of his metaxological musings, concerned as they are with the primal ethos. Now this may leave one wondering where to begin for there is, it might be said, a "too muchness" to the musings.[13] If one wanted a systematic account, I would say begin with the first thing Desmond wrote and read straight through. Less daunting, perhaps, and more helpful to my mind, is a selective approach, one beginning as I have here with "God, Ethos, Ways."

Besides providing an alternative perspective on natural theology from continental philosophy, and by "alternative" I mean an alternative (or supplement) to "the theology of the faithless" Re Manning describes, Desmond's essay provides a key to, and overview of, his donation to natural theology.[14] Returning to the beginning of that essay, we read:

> A common view of the arguments for God's existence sees them as neutral uses of reason that are purportedly convincing, or not, on the basis purely of a reason separate from any religious claims of revelation or faith. Their neutrality guarantees their appeal to reason, considered as a power common to all human beings, transcending the differences of Greek, Jew, Christian, Moslem, infidel and so on. These differences are not relevant, it is claimed. I suppose that this view of the proofs is now widely criticized, not only by those not religious but also by believers.[15]

Desmond then rehearses the criticisms of these two views. Those not religious attack the proofs on "evidentiary or rational grounds."[16] This is the "enlightenment critique."[17] Believers, on the other hand, "embrace a not dissimilar view to press the necessity of a commitment of faith."[18] This Desmond calls "fideistic self-legitimation."[19] While these two views may at first glance appear dissimilar, Desmond argues that they share a common problem. Each "operates in terms of ontological presuppositions inadequately thematized."[20] He then argues against the aforementioned neutralized view, contending that "the ethos" (i.e., the ontological context of the ways) is itself not neutral.[21] This deeper mindfulness of "the ethos," I argue, constitutes the first portion of Desmond's donation to natural theology, and the second, which I will now discuss, is a metaxological reformulation of the ways in that context.

Desmond begins with Kant's critique of the ontological way and, drawing upon the preceding discussion, argues that it is based upon an understanding of the ways that reflects the second ethos, more specifically, the modern ethos characterized by Cartesian dualism. But what is this understanding of the ways? It is, according to

Desmond, a univocal understanding, and Kant's critique, a reminder of equivocity. Desmond affirms Kant's reminder but argues that "the presuppositions of univocity themselves remain inadequately criticized."[22] He pursues this critique elsewhere. More relevant here is his suggestion that Kant's turn to transcendental inwardness failed "to explore more deeply the so-called concept of God that we might find in immanence."[23] This leads Desmond to consider Anselm's version of the ontological proof, a version whose milieu was "one of prayer and meditation."[24]

While more could be said with regard to Desmond's metaxological reformulation, I here wish to pursue a third aspect of Desmond's donation, related to but distinct from the second: the previously mentioned interplay of ethos and way. Desmond explains:

> The point of the interplay and ethos is that there is no such univocal way; for such a way is itself a derivative from the interplay of ethos and way; and the deeper truth of the search for God has to be approached in terms of that interplay and not just in terms of the produced configurations of the interplay, be these very powerful and suggestive as 'proofs' that *probe*. The ontological way ought to be understood in light of this, I suggest: what is deep about it is that the probe of the concept of God in inwardness itself can have the effect of loosening the bewitching effect of a finite configuration of the ethos, and open us, through the passageway of inwardness, into the excess of overdetermination where the signs communicating God are all the more powerful, more powerful even in their essential ambiguity.[25]

In addition to a deeper mindfulness of the ethos, and the resulting reconfiguration of the ways, Desmond here wants to draw our attention to the *interplay* of ethos and way. But what does this mean? Desmond answers: "The interplay means that ways must be returned to the ethos and understood in their relativity to that context."[26] The first sentence in the above quoted paragraph calls for this return. The second then explains what this looks like with reference to the ontological way. I will return to discuss Desmond's description of proofs as " 'proofs' that *probe*" in a moment but first need to say something about Desmond's call for the ways to be returned to the ethos so that they might be understood in that context. One might think this nothing more than a recognition of cultural embeddedness, but, as Desmond explains, "to reroot them is not just to tell a historical, hermeneutical tale relative to the suppositions of a particular era that we have now outgrown (it is not a question of historical relativism merely: this may have some application to the human reconfiguration of the ethos but not to the primal ethos). Rather it is also a question of a systematic exploration of the fundamental ontological presupposition at stake in the primal ethos, refracted through the reconfigured."[27] More than a call for recognition of cultural embeddedness, which has to do with the second ethos, Desmond's call is a call for a deeper mindfulness, that is, a mindfulness of the first ethos. Aware of the first ethos, one then becomes mindful of the interplay between ethos and way, and this leads to metaxological reformulation.

Returning to Desmond's description of proofs as " 'proofs' that *probe*," I wish to make two observations, the first in relation to what Re Manning has referred to as "a widely accepted and deeply ingrained standard narrative of the rise and fall of natural theology"[28] and the second in relation to prayer. Like Re Manning, Desmond rejects this standard narrative, the so-called demise of natural theology.[29] Desmond argues that "there can be no end to philosophical reflection on ways to God: not only on the ways already formulated but on the keeping open of those ways and the probe for new ways that reflect current configurations of the ethos."[30] Proofs probe, and the natural theologian is, like the philosopher, "a perpetual beginner."[31] Second, Desmond describes this probing, with reference to Anselm, as a kind of prayer. "Prayer and thought pass into one another," he says, but then, in the endnote, he asks, "*Fides quaerens intellectum*: prayer seeking thought? And thinking comes to a limit where it becomes a praying . . . ?"[32] The first movement here is more or less familiar, but the second less so. What does he mean by this? What is this thinking that becomes a praying, and how is it related to prayer seeking thought? Desmond unpacks this elsewhere, noting:

The standard form of "being between" religion and philosophy is the one inherited from a long tradition and expressed in this quest: *fides quaerens intellectum.* While not denying this, I would ask about the less evident quest of *intellectus quaerens fides.* I do not just mean the converse of the first. There is a more radical "between," as it were, "beyond" the satisfactions of determinate cognition concerning finite things and processes, and the excellences of self-determining knowing at home with itself. Something more than the warrants of science and the self-determinations of moral autonomy is solicited from us.[33]

But what is this something more solicited? The short answer: Faith beyond the loss of faith.[34] And what does this mean? Briefly: metaphysical thinking, according to Desmond, begins with astonishment. Astonishment, however, leads to perplexity, and perplexity to curiosity. And what does he mean by curiosity? Simpson explains: "Curiosity is driven toward definiteness, determination, and univocity."[35] It is "the principal understanding of mindfulness as such in the modern ethos."[36] Returning to Desmond's "less evident quest of *intellectus quaerens fides,*"[37] we might begin to put this together. This thinking that becomes a praying (i.e., faith beyond the loss of faith) is "beyond" astonishment, perplexity, and curiosity. Curiosity, after all, breaks down. But there is, for Desmond, a breakthrough beyond this breakdown. Perplexity returns, and this "second perplexity" leads to "second astonishment." It is not my concern here to unpack this movement. Rather, I simply wish to observe, in relation to Desmond's " 'proofs' that *probe*," that this probing "beyond" curiosity is, according to Desmond, like prayer.[38] More could be said along these lines, particularly in relation to the hyperbolic, but that would take us too far from Desmond's essay.[39]

I have, in this first section, argued that Desmond offers an alternative perspective on natural theology from continental philosophy. In what sense alternative? First, Desmond is interested in those things which Re Manning suggests the continental philosophers are not (e.g., "the canonical arguments for the existence of God").[40] Second, Desmond's prayer seeking thought is, it seems to me, distinct from "the theology of the faithless" Re Manning describes.[41] For Desmond, proofs probe like prayer, and the natural theologian is, like the philosopher, "a perpetual beginner."[42] It seems fitting, then, that we turn now to consider Desmond's donation to a natural theology of the arts in relation to Root, and more specifically, his essay "Beginning All Over Again."

"BEGINNING ALL OVER AGAIN"

Root was dean of Emmanuel College, Cambridge, when he suggested to his senior colleague Alec Vidler, then dean of King's College, Cambridge, that they might convene a small group "with a view to discussing their dissatisfaction with the state of English, or at least of Anglican, theological thought and to consider what might be done about it."[43] And what was the nature of their dissatisfaction? They were, according to Vidler, dissatisfied with neo-orthodoxy's jargon and the neglect of natural theology.[44] Their discussion, and the later conference at Launde Abbey in Leicestershire, resulted in the publication of *Soundings: Essays Concerning Christian Understanding*. Probably the most influential volume of essays in postwar British Christianity, *Soundings* preceded, in more than one sense, John Robinson's well-known and much-discussed *Honest to God*.[45]

In his *Soundings* essay, "Beginning All Over Again," Root argued that the problem of natural theology could be attributed to a single sentence from Descartes and "that a restoration of natural theology will finally depend upon the abandonment of our present understanding of what it is."[46] I will begin with Root's 1962 call for, and contribution to, a natural theology of the arts and then proceed to discuss Eric Mascall's 1963 critique of Root. Mascall thought, wrongly in my opinion, that Root meant to neglect tradition. Contra Mascall, I argue that Root was calling for the *ressourcement* of tradition via the arts, and this based upon my recent discovery of Root's unpublished 1972 Bampton Lectures in an uncataloged box in the Lambeth Palace Library archives.[47] These lectures provide additional insight into Root's 1962 call for a natural theology of the arts. His discussion of the arts, however, requires a deeper mindfulness. In an effort to resource Root's *ressourcement*, I will draw primarily from Desmond's *Art and the Absolute*, as well as his more recent *Art, Origins, and Otherness*.[48]

In his 1962 essay, Root observed, "Most people who think about these things at all agree that natural theology is in a poor state. Ninian Smart has aptly called it 'the sick man of Europe'. Everyone has his own ideas about the reason for this *malaise*. Not everyone agrees that it is unfortunate. There are theologians who would be glad to let the sick man die."[49] For Root, however, "to accept this situation would . . . be the acceptance of a betrayal and the beginning of the end of faith."[50] The problem, according to Root, was that natural theology had been "weakened by malnutrition."[51] He explained: "For decades, if not generations, Christian faith has lived in a state of imaginative impoverishment. How should it not? The Church has lived in almost total isolation from the arts. Academic theology has lived on its own fat. The supply of fat is running out."[52] From Root's perspective, theology had become irrelevant and uninteresting, having failed to engage individuals "at the deepest levels of thought and imagination."[53] This led him to conclude, "The starting-point for natural theology is not argument but sharpened awareness. For the moment it is better for us that the arguments have fallen to pieces."[54]

This conclusion caused quite a stir, such a stir, in fact, that Eric Mascall (1905–93), coming from the perspective of historical theology, wrote a book-length response.[55] In his polemical "Introduction," Mascall critiqued "Dr. Vidler's Leadsmen (for that would seem to be the right term by which to describe them)"[56] and argued that "the book suffers . . . from three serious deficiencies. First, it fails to ask the really fundamental questions. Secondly, it looks to the wrong quarters for its answers. Thirdly, it fails to look to the quarters in which the answers might be, and to a large extent are already being, found."[57] Five chapters follow Mascall's introduction, and the first is chiefly concerned with Root's essay "Beginning All Over Again." Mascall's critique might be summed up in the following four points: Root (1) neglects tradition, (2) conflates natural theology and apologetics, (3) repudiates logic in favor of art, and (4) gives insufficient criteria. He suggested, "Many of the Leadsmen . . . seem to have lost all confidence in the tradition that they have received and to envisage their task simply as, in Mr. Root's phrase, 'beginning all over again,' as if we had nothing to learn from nineteen centuries of Christian experience."[58] This, I argue, was a gross misreading of Root.

Root, far from neglecting tradition, was arguing for its *ressourcement*. The problem, to his mind, was that natural theology had become synonymous with "the philosophical practice of the last two or three hundred years."[59] He explained:

At the beginning of the *Meditations*, Descartes wrote: 'I have always been of the opinion that the two questions respecting God and the soul were the chief of those that ought to be determined by help of philosophy rather than theology, for although to us, the faithful, it is sufficient to hold as matters of faith, that the human soul does not perish with the body, and that God exists, it yet assuredly seems impossible ever to persuade infidels of the reality of any religion, or almost even any moral virtue, unless, first of all, those two things be proved to them by natural reason.' The whole problem of natural theology might be written as a gloss on that revealing sentence.[60]

For Root, Descartes represented "the conventional understanding of natural theology,"[61] one in which "there are two ways to knowledge (or kinds of knowledge) of God's existence. For the believer it was given. . . . For the unbeliever, it could be gained by rational argument."[62] The problem, of course, was that "rational argument could take the unbeliever only as far as the bare belief that God exists. To learn more he would have to humble himself before revelation."[63] Root continued: "We are so used to this model that we usually fail to notice its oddity. . . . Reason is thereby likened to a railway line which takes one to a frontier station. There the line ends. We all have to get off the train."[64] And what did he mean by this? He explained: "What the railway-line analogy brings out is that one conventional model will not do at all. If this is in fact what natural theology does it should come as no surprise that both theologians and philosophers would well like to be rid of it. It simply does not work."[65] Why? Root answered: "Our thinking is still confined to the familiar grooves: natural and revealed; reason and faith. It may seem paradoxical, but there would be point in saying that a restoration of natural theology will finally depend upon the abandonment of our present understanding of what it is."[66] And here his *ressourcement* becomes clear.

Root's discussion of "get[ting] ourselves out of the familiar grooves"[67] is consistent with the *ressourcement* emphasis "to reconnect nature and the supernatural."[68] As Hans Boersma has argued, "the group of theologians that became known as *nouvelle théologie* or the movement of *ressourcement*" was concerned with the "rupture between theology and life,"[69] and sought "to enter into dialogue with contemporary philosophical developments."[70] Root shared these concerns, and his essay should be read as just this sort of attempt. Far from neglecting tradition, Root was arguing for its *ressourcement*, advocating what he would in his 1972 Bampton Lectures call a "backward-looking" radicalism.[71] Along these lines, Desmond has suggested, "The philosopher may indeed be a perpetual beginner, but there is, so to say, an age in that perpetual beginning."[72]

Rocking back (i.e., a backward look, or perpetual beginning with age) allows forward release, what Root referred to as the re-creation of tradition. More fully, he explained: "Each theological attitude or position (I prefer these words to the word system) is, if you like, a constellation; itself and not some other thing, yet in relationship with other constellations of theological thought because of a shared totality of tradition. No two will make use of precisely the same elements in that tradition, or arrange and highlight the elements in quite the same way. Each, to that extent, will be re-creating tradition and, in turn, its re-creation will become part of the on-going tradition."[73] The resources for this re-creation "may not always be found in the most obvious places. . . . The most important imagery from the past lies not in the most obvious but, often, in the nearly concealed."[74] And what did he mean by that? He explained: "There is . . . a vast supply of Christian imagery associated with what we call religious experience. . . . Anything from pop art to the most impenetrable avant garde may touch off the spark and thereby start the process of image-making, or imagery-inspired invention."[75] Adding to the list of resources, he mentioned novels, poetry, television, pop songs, and modern art before concluding, "The problem about resources is not that they are not there but that, as theologians, we have not had time to seek them out where they are."[76]

All this being said, what is Desmond's donation to a natural theology of the arts in relation to Root? Desmond comes alongside Root, resourcing his *ressourcement* with a deeper mindfulness. Desmond's donation is, here again, nothing short of the whole of his metaxological metaphysics. That said, I mention two points in relation to Root. First, Desmond, like Hegel, both defends and criticizes art. "This important relation," he says, "is a delicate balance of subordination and openness: a certain subordination of art to philosophy, a clear openness of philosophy to art."[77] Desmond continues, "The view defended here is that we must take fully into account the *twofold* character of Hegel's response to art: that he *both* defends it and criticizes it. I will suggest that the ambiguity of this response is not the result of a simple confusion of thought but that it points to the possibility of a positive relation between art and philosophy."[78] And what, more specifically, is this relation? "According to Desmond's reading, "art and philosophy work as complementary modes of articulation, one oriented to imaginative concreteness, the other to conceptual concreteness."[79] More fully, he explains that "philosophy cannot consist in just *reducing* art to concepts, or of merely using it for the illustration of some more generalized abstractions. Their relation works in two directions. Philosophy explicates and brings to self-consciousness the richness made present in art. But also, the concreteness of art continues as a basic challenge to philosophy, challenge for it to overcome its own tendency to reduce experience to generalized abstractions."[80] This double reading—power and limits—seems consistent with Root's *ressourcement* but offers a deeper mindfulness by locating the problem of resources within a larger conversation, that is, "philosophy's relation to its others."[81]

In *Philosophy and Its Others*, Desmond argues that "philosophy cannot just hold a conceptual monologue with itself in which it rests satisfied to merely reformulate the voices of its others in its own terms. It must listen to the voices of the others. Whenever appropriate it must let its own voice be reformulated under the impact of their otherness. When it does reflectively try to voice these others, it must genuinely try to respect what these other voices *on their own terms* bring to the metaxological between."[82] Along these same lines but with reference to theology rather than philosophy, David Brown has noted:

> A constant temptation among Christians when looking at art or music is to view their role, when legitimate, as at most illustrative, confirming or deepening faith but never challenging or subverting it. It is therefore hardly surprising that there is so much bad Christian art and music around, if even the more informed among us want to keep their influence in a safe pair of Christian hands, such as Rembrandt or Rouault in art, Bach or Bruckner in music. The more liberal minded, in spreading the net more widely, may believe themselves immune from such criticism, but often the same fault is still there: art seen as merely illustrative of what is already believed on other grounds.[83]

In light of the above, Root might be metaxologically reformulated, his discussion of "constellations" relocated in "the between," and the related discussion of resources understood along the lines of "a delicate balance of subordination and openness."[84]

From this perspective, art has something distinctive to contribute. Thus Root's closing admonition: "Let the voices speak."[85] At the same time, Root would, I think, have acknowledged, as Desmond does, that "art cannot be the *sanctus* [sic] *sanctorum* in which the burden carried by religion, science and metaphysics can be sustained, and renewed."[86] Yes, powers, but also limits. Without limits, we end up with something like Jeffrey L. Kosky's suggestion "that one need not look only to traditional religion or religious traditions for refuge from the vicissitudes of human being in the world set up by modern disenchantment."[87] He argues that we might dwell "in this in-between, never fully enchanted, never fully disenchanted, never fully secular, never fully religious."[88] But Kosky's "in-between" is equivocal, and thus, as Desmond puts it, "distorted, because truncated."[89] More faithful to Root and compatible with Desmond, I think, is Brown's balance of powers and limits, a contemporary answer to Root's call.[90] In any case, Desmond resources the *ressourcement*, and this with Hegel's double evaluation of art.

Second, Desmond, attempting "a more 'open' reading of Hegel,"[91] argues for the open wholeness of the artwork, and this, I argue, has implications for Root's "constellations" and the *ressourcement* of tradition in relation to a natural theology of the arts. Desmond argues:

> The sense of an end that art may offer us, then, need not force us into any spurious "closure" of history. Hegel has frequently been attacked as offering such a closure. The wholeness of the art work, in its gathering of past greatness, in its rich presentness, in its openness to futurity, undermines any such closure. The "open" wholeness of the art work need not be identical with "totalitarian closure." The story is not finished in this closed sense. But this need not entail the denial of any possibility of the sense of an end: the end "opens" out precisely because what its wholeness makes manifest is the sense of the presence of infinite inexhaustibility.[92]

According to Desmond, the artwork gathers past greatness in rich presentness while remaining open to the future. Is this not in some sense similar to Root's backward-looking radicalism that re-creates tradition and, in so doing, becomes part of an ongoing tradition? Are these "constellations" not open wholes, perfect and complete yet open-ended?

Along these lines, Desmond discusses art in relation to the question of history.

> The attractiveness of this suggestion in relation to history resides, I think, in the character of this perfection. For this perfection we find in art displays, even in its completeness, an open-ended side. So, for instance, perfection in art is not something achieved just once, where prior to perfection there was only a long ascent, mere stepping stones to this point, and where subsequent to the point of perfection all that awaits us is a long decline or decadence. Perfection, once achieved, is something to be achieved again and again. Its realization is open to a plurality of possible actualizations.

The perfection of this art work, or even of that artistic movement, does not preempt the possibility of other future instances
of perfection.[93]

Desmond here offers a metaxological reformulation of Hegel's perfection as open to "future instances of perfection."[94] He notes several
pages later, "The art work exhibits a certain wholeness, but if we attend
to this we find there is a kind of compacted fullness which seems to be
inexhaustible in terms of finite analysis. For this compacted fullness
of the art work is not just a recollective gathering up of the past. It is
also a kind of implicit spanning of the future. The art work is always a
promise of repeated reinterpretations, repeated resurrections."[95]

Talk of open wholes in relation to tradition calls to mind Lieven
Boeve's "Christian Open Narrative."[96] According to Boeve, "every
shift in context constitutes a challenge to the Christian tradition to
reformulate itself in dialogue with the relevant context."[97] Boeve,
however, emphasizes discontinuity (i.e., "rupture").[98] Closer to what
Root had in mind, I would argue, is Brown's notion of an open tradition.[99] Brown has argued that modernism's "principal fault" was "its
contempt for tradition."[100] Against this, Brown argues that traditions
should be "allowed to function as open, both towards their past and
to the wider context in which they are set."[101] Here, then, we have a
backward-looking radicalism, one that understands both powers and
limits, and the notion of an open tradition. Considered from this perspective, Brown's work might be seen as having answered Root's call.
In any case, Desmond's donation to Root is twofold: (1) Hegel's double
evaluation of art resources Root's *ressourcement*; and (2) Desmond's
more open reading of Hegel, resulting in the metaxological reformulation of Root's "constellations," now open wholes.

CONCLUSION

I began by arguing that Desmond offers an alternative perspective
on natural theology from continental philosophy. Unlike "the theology of the faithless" that Re Manning describes, Desmond's natural

theology is a faith beyond the end of faith. I then argued, in relation to a natural theology of the arts, that Desmond resources Root's *ressourcement* with a deeper mindfulness. More specifically, he draws attention to art's power and limits, as well as a more open reading of Hegel where the artwork and history are understood in terms of the open whole. Taken together, these might serve as a second, more sufficient response to Mascall. Desmond's donation to natural theology, as well as a natural theology of the arts, is significant, and though my consideration here has been selective rather than systematic, it nevertheless contributes to the possibility of natural theology's forward release.

Notes

I am grateful to David Brown, Michael Burdett, and Andrew T. J. Kaethler for their helpful comments on an earlier version of this essay.

1. William Desmond, "God, Ethos, Ways," *International Journal for Philosophy of Religion* 45 (1999): 14.

2. Howard E. Root, "Beginning All Over Again," in *Soundings: Essays Concerning Christian Understanding*, ed. A. R. Vidler (Cambridge: Cambridge University Press, 1962), 1–19.

3. *DDO*, xxvii.

4. Russell Re Manning, "A Perspective on Natural Theology from Continental Philosophy," in *The Oxford Handbook of Natural Theology*, ed. Russell Re Manning (Oxford: Oxford University Press, 2013), 263. See also Christopher R. Brewer, review of *The Oxford Handbook of Natural Theology*, ed. Russell Re Manning, *Journal of the Evangelical Theological Society* 56, no. 2 (June 2013): 448–52.

5. Re Manning, "A Perspective on Natural Theology from Continental Philosophy," 263.

6. Ibid., 264.

7. Desmond, "God, Ethos, Ways," 14.

8. Ibid., 23.

9. Christopher Ben Simpson, *Religion, Metaphysics, and the Postmodern: William Desmond and John D. Caputo* (Bloomington: Indiana University Press, 2009), 26.

10. *BB*, 44.

11. *BB*, 44.

12. Desmond, "God, Ethos, Ways," 23; original emphasis. All emphases in quoted passages are original unless indicated otherwise.

13. Desmond speaks of the " 'too muchness,' the overdeterminacy of being in which we participate." William Desmond, "Wording the Between: Being Philosophical: On Metaphysics as Metaxological," in *The William Desmond Reader*, ed. Christopher Ben Simpson (Albany: SUNY Press, 2012), 226.

14. Re Manning, "A Perspective on Natural Theology from Continental Philosophy," 267.

15. Desmond, "God, Ethos, Ways," 13.

16. Ibid.

17. Ibid., 14.

18. Ibid., 13.

19. Ibid., 14.

20. Ibid.

21. As Simpson explains, "Our dwelling in this most basic given ontological ethos is not neutral; the ethos manifests the worth of being, the value inherent in the given, its hospitality to the good (*EB* 23, 177; *AOO* 292). The ethos is charged with value." Simpson, *Religion, Metaphysics, and the Postmodern*, 26.

22. Desmond, "God, Ethos, Ways," 17.

23. Ibid., 18.

24. Ibid., 21.

25. Ibid., 24; cf. *GB*, 131–32; William Desmond, "On God and the Between," in *Between Philosophy and Theology: Contemporary Interpretations of Christianity*, ed. Lieven Boeve and Christophe Brabant (Farnham: Ashgate, 2010), 124–25.

26. Desmond, "God, Ethos, Ways," 25.

27. Ibid., 28.

28. Russell Re Manning, Introduction to Re Manning, ed., *The Oxford Handbook of Natural Theology*, 2. It should be noted that Re Manning is there arguing against this standard narrative.

29. See Christina M. Gschwandtner, *Postmodern Apologetics? Arguments for God in Contemporary Philosophy* (New York: Fordham University Press, 2013), 1.

30. Desmond, "God, Ethos, Ways," 25.

31. *IST*, 107.

32. Desmond, "God, Ethos, Ways," 9, 9 n. 8; cf. Re Manning, "A Perspective on Natural Theology from Continental Philosophy," 266–68.

33. *IST*, 19.

34. For the long answer, see Simpson, *Religion, Metaphysics, and the Postmodern*, 34–45.

35. Simpson, *Religion, Metaphysics, and the Postmodern*, 38.

36. Ibid., 39.

37. *IST*, 19.

38. Desmond defines prayer as follows: "Prayer is waking up to the already effective communication of the divine in passage: not just our communication with the divine, but our being already in that divine communication, within which we participate, now in sleep, now more mindfully awake. Prayer is awakening to the passing communication of the divine in the finite *metaxu*. We do not produce it; it is not the result of our determination or self-determination; we are 'determined,' or better, released into the middle where we can sink deeper into ontological sleep, or begin to awake more fully to what communicates us to be at all" (*IST*, 130).

39. For Desmond's discussion of the hyperbolic, see *GB*, 116–58, esp. 134–41.

40. Re Manning, "A Perspective on Natural Theology from Continental Philosophy," 263.

41. Ibid., 267.

42. *IST*, 107.

43. Alec R. Vidler, *Scenes from a Clerical Life: An Autobiography* (London: Collins, 1977), 176; cf. John S. Peart-Binns, *Bishop Hugh Montefiore* (London: Anthony Blond, 1990), 109–15.

44. Vidler, *Scenes from a Clerical Life*, 177–78.

45. John Robinson, *Honest to God* (London: SCM, 1963). For additional context, see Sam Brewitt-Taylor, "'Christian Radicalism' in the Church of England, 1957–70" (DPhil thesis, Mansfield College, University of Oxford, 2012).

46. Howard E. Root, "Beginning All Over Again," in Vidler, *Soundings*, 10.

47. Howard E. Root, "Papers of Howard Root," Lambeth Palace Library, Acc 2010-17, 5 boxes, Uncataloged accession, 1960s–2000s. Rediscovered April 2014 with the help of Laura Elliot, library assistant at the Lambeth Palace Library. I am grateful to the Trustees of Lambeth Palace Library for access to this material. These papers have now been cataloged and are available for research: Howard E. Root, "Sermons, Essays and Lectures by Howard Root: The Bampton Lectures—Oxford," Root/1/2, Archives and Manuscripts, Lambeth Palace Library, London. For a critical edition of the

text, see Howard E. Root, *Theological Radicalism and Tradition: "The Limits of Radicalism" with Appendices*, ed. Christopher R. Brewer (London: Routledge, forthcoming).

48. More could be said, if space allowed, in relation to *GB*, 116–58 in particular. These two works, however, contain the bulk of Desmond's reflections on art, and so here seem particularly relevant.

49. Root, "Beginning All Over Again," 3. See also Ninian Smart, "Revelation, Reason and Religions," in *Prospect for Metaphysics: Essays of Metaphysical Exploration* (London: George Allen and Unwin, 1961), 80–92; Ninian Smart, "Soft Natural Theology," in *Prospects for Natural Theology*, Studies in Philosophy and the History of Philosophy, vol. 25, ed. Jude P. Dougherty (Washington, DC: Catholic University of America Press, 1992), 198–206.

50. Root, "Beginning All Over Again," 6.

51. Ibid., 19.

52. Ibid.

53. Ibid., 17.

54. Ibid., 19.

55. Eric Mascall, *Up and Down in Adria: Some Considerations of "Soundings"* (London: Faith Press, 1963).

56. Ibid., 10.

57. Ibid., 14. In reading this I couldn't help but think that if John Updike's *Picked-Up Pieces* (New York: Random House, 1966) had been published several years earlier Mascall might have avoided this adventure in missing the point. Updike there advised, "Try to understand what the author wished to do, and do not blame him for not achieving what he did not attempt" (xvi). Root never claimed to ask, or attempted to answer, "the really fundamental questions" (Mascall, *Up and Down in Adria*, 14). In fact Root noted, "The one thing we can be sure of is that answers to the fundamental questions, even presuming we know which questions should be asked, will not come easily or quickly" (Root, "Beginning All Over Again," 12–13).

58. Mascall, *Up and Down in Adria*, 11.

59. Root, "Beginning All Over Again," 7.

60. Ibid.; Desmond, "God, Ethos, Ways," 23.

61 Root, "Beginning All Over Again," 8.

62. Ibid., 9.

63. Ibid.

64. Ibid.; cf. *GB*, 78 n. 4.

65. Root, "Beginning All Over Again," 9–10.

66. Ibid., 10.

67. Ibid., 11.

68. Hans Boersma, *"Nouvelle Théologie" and Sacramental Ontology: A Return to Mystery* (Oxford: Oxford University Press, 2009), 5. See also David Brown, "Sacramentality," in *The Oxford Handbook of Theology and Modern European Thought*, ed. Nicholas Adams, George Pattison, and Graham Ward (Oxford: Oxford University Press, 2013), 615–31.

69. Jean Daniélou, "Les orientations présentes de la pensée religieuse," *Études* 249 (1946): 7; quoted in Boersma, *"Nouvelle Théologie" and Sacramental Ontology*, 2.

70. Daniélou, "Les orientations présentes de la pensée religieuse," 3.

71. Root, "The Limits of Radicalism," "Papers of Howard Root," 3:2.

72. *IST*, 107.

73. Root, "The Limits of Radicalism," 4:6.

74. Ibid., 5:9–10.

75. Ibid., 5:10.

76. Ibid.

77. *AA*, 2.

78. *AA*, 2.

79. *AA*, 30.

80. *AA*, 31.

81. *PO*, 1.

82. *PO*, 5.

83. David Brown, "The Glory of God Revealed in Art and Music: Learning from Pagans," in *Celebrating Creation: Affirming Catholicism and the Revelation of God's Glory*, ed. Mark Chapman (London: Darton, Longman, and Todd, 2004), 44–45; republished as "Learning from Pagans," in David Brown, *Divine Generosity and Human Creativity: Theology through Symbol, Painting and Architecture*, ed. Christopher R. Brewer and Robert MacSwain (London: Routledge, 2017), 38.

84. *AA*, 2.

85. Root, "The Limits of Radicalism," 8:12.

86. *AOO*, 289–90.

87. Jeffrey L. Kosky, *Arts of Wonder: Enchanting Secularity—Walter DeMaria, Diller + Scofidio, James Turrell, Andy Goldsworthy* (Chicago: University of Chicago Press, 2013), xiii.

88. Ibid., 177.

89. *BB*, xii.

90. In addition to Brown's Oxford University Press volumes (1999–2008), see Robert MacSwain and Taylor Worley, eds., *Theology, Aesthetics,*

and Culture: Responses to the Work of David Brown (Oxford: Oxford University Press, 2012).

91. *AA*, xix.

92. *AA*, 75.

93. *AA*, 68.

94. *AA*, 68.

95. *AA*, 70–71.

96. Lieven Boeve, *Interrupting Tradition: An Essay on Christian Faith in a Postmodern Context*, Louvain Theological and Pastoral Monographs 30 (Louvain: Peeters, 2003), 101.

97. Ibid., 22.

98. Ibid., 34–35.

99. David Brown, *Tradition and Imagination: Revelation and Change* (Oxford: Oxford University Press, 1999), 5–8.

100. Ibid., 11.

101. Ibid.

CHAPTER 9

The Impatience of Gnosis

Cyril O'Regan

There is still much to be done in terms of translating the philosophical work of William Desmond, which seems to flow more or less unceasingly. I myself have contributed a number of essays and reviews over the years,[1] am currently finishing up a monograph on his work, and expect to continue to write about him more or less indefinitely. The reasons for my interest are not hard to state. First, while the recovery of metaphysics in analytic philosophy has long been on its way, such is not the case in the continental philosophy tradition which Desmond and I share. Kant, Husserl, Heidegger, and later various stripes of postmodern thought have united to make metaphysics more or less verboten. Desmond is perhaps the thinker who has most relentlessly and successfully challenged this orthodoxy from within continental philosophy, and thereby joined ranks with the Platonic, Aristotelian, and Thomistic resisters. Second, and relatedly, it is not the case that Desmond has issued manifestos complaining that rumors of the demise of metaphysics have been greatly exaggerated, or that he has

produced pamphlets of scholarly invective against the regnant orthodoxy or set forth a program of rehabilitation for what might after all
be a non–terminally ill discourse. Desmond is distinguished in that
he has fully rendered a metaphysics which he judges to be the need
of the current age, which does not seem to be able to release itself
from the grip of the either/or of clear and comprehensive explanation of the density, ambiguity, multiplicity, and plural relationality of
reality or no explanation at all. The three-volume construction of the
metaphysics of the between, or a metaxological metaphysics, reveals
the need for it by the very performance of it.[2] This performance is
as copious and versatile as could be imagined, and can be complexly
identified as phenomenological in intent, Aristotelian in its commitment to the particular—what Desmond calls the "idiotic," and the
definition of philosophy as constituted by wonder—and Platonic in
its range and its insistence on the horizon of transcendence. But it
is ultimately constructive and systematic and admittedly perspectival
rather than a view from nowhere, even if the perspective is complex
and enfolds a multiple.

Third, although the articulation of his metaphysics is not strictly
speaking hermeneutic, throughout Desmond's work as a whole and
even the trilogy, the range of conversation with the philosophical
tradition is enormous. In addition to classic figures such as Aristotle
and Plato and the continental philosophers mentioned above, one
would certainly have to mention Hegel and Nietzsche. At the same
time the range of conversation with art and religion has been equally
enormous,[3] and reveals the nature of philosophy to be more nearly
a wisdom discourse than an enterprise of problem solving with its
stipulation as to what is or is not a proper question and its advisories
about proper technical competence. Fourth, and relatedly, Desmond's
thinking has demonstrated a marvelous hospitality to Christianity in
general. His work has also evinced an interest in dialogue with theology in particular, both of the past and of the contemporary scene.
This is so despite the fact that Desmond is prepared to agree with
some of theology's critics that historically it has been guilty of an
inclination to rationalism and too anxious to operate in the mode of
proof. Exploration of the fourth contribution is a particular avocation

of this commentator, and provides the proximate site of my essay. Now, though there is much to add to what I have already in print on the porousness of philosophy and theology, I would like to write on something at once more specific and more in keeping with the generativity of Desmond's thought, which lies as much in suggestion and intimation as in an explicit thematics. My specific topic is how gnosis is both explicitly and implicitly treated in Desmond's work. Needless to say, such an exploration runs the risk of reducing Desmond to the same, by capturing his remarks within an ongoing project of my own.[4] Nonetheless, I want to shed light on the light Desmond's reflections on Gnosticism shed on ongoing attempts to think both the nature of Gnosticism and, especially, the complex nature of the relations between myth, Christianity, and philosophy that it conjugates and how in turn this illuminates various forms of modern philosophical, theological, and literary discourse.

In carrying out this task I focus on the two main textual sites in Desmond's oeuvre where Gnosticism is especially prominent. The first site is to be found in *God and the Between* (chapter 10).[5] Here Desmond provides a scintillating account of ancient Gnosticism in which, notwithstanding its event character, the content of knowing itself has the epistemic-ontological form of doubling, which results in the generation of the material, historical, and social world that serves as a block on knowledge and that, from an axiological point of view, represents not only an absence of value but also an absolute disvalue. The second site is Desmond's reading of Hegel's speculative thought in *Hegel's God: A Counterfeit Double?*[6] Here my interest is not to judge the adequacy of Desmond's reading—I am entirely sympathetic to it[7]—but rather to consider that if Desmond is right in his exposé of Hegel's God in its complex relation to world and humanity as a counterfeit of the standard Christian view, whether this amounts to making the claim that Hegel's speculative thought is in effect a modern Gnostic confabulation. The condition of this question is the identification of Gnosticism with a transgressive hermeneutic that repeats and distorts a prior form of religious thought which has symbolic, narrative, and conceptual potency and a community referent. As a useful shorthand we can speak of this form of doubling as "hermeneutic doubling."

Crucially, I ask the question whether and how epistemic-ontological and hermeneutic doubling contributes to illuminating the nature of Gnosticism and shedding light on its capacity to appear in the modern world in which Christianity is on trial if not evacuated. I argue that Desmond's insights are such that his more or less unsystematic reflections help correct misinterpretations and assist significantly in constructing a much more sophisticated account of the nature of Gnosticism as well as help us discern recurrences in modern discourse. In line with my view of the importance of "epistemic-ontological doubling" and "hermeneutic doubling," the first two sections examine these contributions in turn. In the third section I join these contributions to discussion of a number of more episodic features of Desmond's reflections on Gnosticism which usefully complicate the picture of Gnosticism and thus which we might keep in mind should we be interested in tracking the actuality and possibility of the return of Gnosticism in the modern period.

GNOSIS AND EPISTEMIC-ONTOLOGICAL DOUBLING

Desmond's most focused discussion of Gnosticism is chapter 10 of *God and the Between* and is one of the number of important chapters on God(s) in part 3, which also includes chapters on pantheism, mysticism, theism, and the divine names. To say that the level of reflection is on a par with the other chapters is to pay Desmond a significant compliment, since these chapters are not only among the best in the book, but, arguably, among the best chapters to be found in any part of the trilogy. What stands out as usual is the quality of the thinking and the finesse of Desmond's judgments. Nonetheless, one should not undersell the scholarship. Desmond has paid a steep price for admission. He shows familiarity with the texts of Nag Hammadi (206 n. 2), which are the main independent source of our knowledge of myth-laced narratives that seem parasitic to the main religious and philosophical traditions of the ancient world. The various narratives, which stage an event of epistemic transformation, are wildly experimental at best, bizarrely phantasmagoric at worst, and obsessed with the tragedy of perfection lost and regained. Even if Desmond does not offer detailed exegeses of these narratives, he demonstrates that he has read widely. Among a variety of texts he cites are *The Apocryphon of John*, *The Origin of the World*, *Hypostasis of the Archons*, and *The Tripartite Tractate*.[8] Desmond also shows that he is familiar with the heresiological material and evinces a high regard for Irenaeus (212).[9] By the same token he is aware of the way in which Gnosticism is also a trial for ancient Neoplatonism, as evinced in the denunciations of it in the *Enneads* (212–13). And he demonstrates a good measure of awareness of the commentary tradition broadly consisting of historical studies in which the emphasis falls heavily on philological considerations, and also of the broad-based "philosophical" studies which have not given up on definition and which are eager to explore whether ancient Gnosticism manifests itself in modern forms of discourse.[10] Despite the affinity between philosophy and theology espoused throughout the text, and fully endorsed elsewhere in his oeuvre, Desmond is anxious to avoid playing the role of heresiologist. Accordingly, he insists he is not going to judge Gnosticism by the level of deviance from the canonic narrative or narratives (205).

The sum of Desmond's reading does not rise to expert knowledge. Nor does Desmond claim it does. In order of importance Desmond makes two main contributions to understanding Gnosticism. The first and most basic contribution is his diagnosis of epistemic-ontological doubling as a unique feature of Gnostic texts despite their manifest variety and heterogeneity. The second, and related, claim is that it makes sense to speak of modern as well as ancient forms of Gnosticism, albeit acknowledging that modern forms may be much more affirming of the world and history than the ancient varieties. Around these two interconnected contributions is a constellation of suggestions whose pertinence becomes clear in the modern reception and repetition of ancient Gnosticism: these include the willful and self-conscious construction of metanarratives that produce the event of knowing and intercalate a special community. Relatedly, although the overcoming of alienation and the trajectory to the "beyond" is usually cast as the move from evil to the good, since the good as such does not seem to have ontological anchor in Gnosticism, exhibition of transcendence can be exhibited in practices and forms of life which are daimonic or demonic. In addition, while Gnostic texts explicitly denounce sexuality, as a group, arguably, they constitute the most sexualized of all the ancient texts in their obsession with couplings and birthings and their reveries on androgyny and the calamity of sexual difference.

From the start Desmond makes a telling intervention. Agreeing for argument's sake that while the common identification of Gnosticism as being dualistic is not incorrect, he announces that he prefers to speak of doubles and doubling as a discrimen. He proceeds: "The notion of doubles and doubling qualifies dualism by the equivocal sense of being, and thereby offers more supple means of dealing with dualism but with the subversion of dualities and the surpassing of opposition. It also allows us to underline the crucial significance of the counterfeit double" (206). Sticking to the negative for the moment, it is obvious that the most prominent feature of the relativization of "dualism" as the fundamental explanatory category in the study of Gnosticism is that this ignores the point of emphasizing rupture and alienation, which is precisely to overcome it and recuperate the aboriginal perfection. Thus, in a sense it would not be wrong to subjoin "recuperative" to the complex category of epistemic-ontological coupling. Desmond reinforces this point throughout the chapter. His reading slightly later in the chapter on the Sethian Gnostic text *The Origin of the World* provides just one example (213).[11] He further weakens the claims of dualism to be an explanatory category by suggesting that perhaps Gnostic texts are not always exclusively dualistic in orientation and that they might best be arranged along a monist-dualist spectrum (211). Here Desmond is being intuitive rather than hermeneutic, since he does not adduce texts from Nag Hammadi which admit of a monistic reading. As a matter of fact, however, Desmond's intuition finds support in modern scholarship on Gnosticism which underscores the monistic tendencies in *The Gospel of Truth*,[12] arguably, the jewel of the Nag Hammadi Library and possibly the Valentinian text of the same name mentioned by Irenaeus in *Adversus Hairesis*.[13]

The negative is in the service of the positive proposal that Gnosticism be seen as characterized by the dynamic of doubling or splitting at the most fundamental level of a reality which characteristically is described in epistemic terms, for example, Pronoia, Ennoia, Protennoia, Sophia, and so forth. The doubling proceeds from the unitive base of reality, on one axis through generations of pairs to the creation of the world through a demiurge (209), and on another through mimicry, for example, Sophia and the Demiurge trying to replicate the unique productivity of the unitive Father. The doubling, Desmond seems to suggest, is paradoxical. It is impatient insofar as its epistemic-ontological splitting is dynamically iterative, but otherwise doubling is a pathos, that is, something that happens to the divine who would not be split. Now it is at the level especially of the mimicry of the hypostasis (Sophia or otherwise) and the demiurge that one introduces the notion of the counterfeit double, that is, the reproduction of an activity and/or a reality which is the very opposite of the exemplar. One is speaking, therefore, of a subversion of the fundamentally imitative and participative nature of the image vis-à-vis the archetype that is the lingua franca of the ancient world and not merely a Platonic possession. The material temporal world in a quite literal sense is a misbegotten mess that functions as a countermimesis to the divine world. The material world is, as *The Gospel of Truth* (28.28–32.12) puts it,[14] a nightmare from which the "knower" should awake, a view which eerily anticipates a saying of James Joyce.

Given the nature of Desmond's overall project, which is a philosophical rather than philological or theological consideration of Gnosticism, the dominant register of the counterfeit double or doubles is epistemic-ontological. But in practice, and perhaps in principle, Desmond finds it difficult to avoid speaking also of both the counterfeit double and doubling more broadly in a hermeneutic register. With regard to the former Desmond cannot avoid noticing that the demiurgic figure seems to be a pastiche of the God of Hebrew scriptures (218). While avoiding the heresiological mode, nonetheless, Desmond feels he can enlist Irenaeus in making the general point about the phenomenon of the hermeneutic doubling or misrepresentation of an established form of discourse, which—although these are not his precise terms—amounts to a form of parasitism. He quotes a rather long passage from the preface (2) to *Adversus Hairesis*:

> Error, indeed, is never set forth in its naked deformity, lest, being
> thus exposed, it should at once be detected. But it is craftily decked
> out in an attractive dress, so as, by its outward form, to make
> it appear to the inexperienced (ridiculous as the expression may
> seem) more true than truth itself. One far superior to me has well
> said in reference to this point, "A clever imitation in glass casts
> contempt, as it were, on the precious jewel the emerald (which
> is most esteemed by some), unless it comes under the eye of one
> able to test and expose the counterfeit." (212)

Now it is true that in quoting this passage, which carries normative
force, Desmond himself does not entirely escape evaluative judgment.
Desmond remains on the side of the original, not the supplement,
which disarticulates it and replaces it with a rival narrative scheme that
makes a claim to truth.[15] Still it is not a little interesting that Desmond
quotes this more formal passage from the preface to *Adversus Hairesis*
rather than the more stridently evaluative passage in book 1 (1.8; also
1.11) in which Irenaeus, using the striking visual metaphor of painting,
suggests that Gnostic interpretation redraws the portrait of God as sovereign and king as a dog or a fox. If evaluation is difficult—maybe even
impossible to edit out—when one is discussing doubling, judgment
should be left as open as possible. At a minimum an order is established: evaluation presupposes the observation of the phenomenon of
the hermeneutic doubling and the generation of a textual counterfeit
double. It should be noted that Irenaeus is no crutch for Desmond. He
is aware of other heresiological accounts of Gnosticism, for example,
Epiphanius. Yet he is struck by the genius of this particular church
father in providing a general characterization of the counterfeit. In
addition, he indirectly acknowledges the power of Irenaeus's figure of
methamorttein, which can be taken to mean the refiguration of God in
and through the refiguration of the biblical narrative.[16]

As suggested already, Desmond does not place upon his short
chapter the impossible burden of providing a genetic account of the
return of Gnosticism in modernity. But he does make it clear that
the case can be made. Logically speaking, a main focus of continuity would necessarily be the phenomenon of epistemic-ontological

doubling isolated by Desmond as a defining feature of ancient Gnosticism. Perspicaciously, Desmond rules out straightforward repetition. If there is repetition, it necessarily will be nonidentical in kind. The actual, as well as expected, differences are spelled out perspicuously in the following passage which charts the many expressions of a fundamental shift in vector from "beyond" to "here," from transcendence to immanence.

> In ancient Gnosticism the absolute One is utterly beyond the counterfeit creation, for this world here and now is the domain of the mimicry of spirit, hence the need of a world-denying flight. In more modern forms, it seems all but the opposite, in that the absolute One must be redoubled in absolute immanence, which is now the pleroma to be realized through the self-becoming of the absolute One. In one, flight to the hyperbolic transcendence as world denying, in the other flight from transcendence to absolute immanence. In the latter, the inward way becomes utterly immanent: history becomes the dialectical process of realizing the divine spark initially implicit in, sleeping in the process of equivocal becoming. Ancient form: an ascetic "Platonic" response to the given world as a counterfeit double. Modern form: a non-ascetic "Hegelian" response to the counterfeit doubles of an alien transcendence. One a version of "Christian" gnosis as world-denying; the other, a version of "Christian" gnosis as world affirming. But the terms in both are more or less set by dualism and dialectic, with the equivocal double as the fall from, or immanent self-alienation of, the absolute One. (217)

A few remarks on this rich description of the contrast between ancient and modern forms of Gnosticism are in order. First—to repeat—Desmond is persuaded that modern forms of Gnosticism do exist. Second, he obviously thinks that Hegel's thought is a good candidate, but given the scare quotes Hegel is more than a proper name and the real or implied author of one of the major philosophical opuses in major philosophy. He is also a stand-in and a cover term for speculative discourses in the modern period. The pansophism of the seventeenth-century theosophic mystic Jacob Boehme, who influences Hegel, comes to mind, as does the work of Schelling, whom Boehme influences even more. Third, although the binary world denying and world affirming is standard usage in much commentary on Gnosticism, Desmond refuses to allow it to be a free radical and to determine interpretation of Gnosticism. It is connected with the iterative doubling and recuperation of such doubling, which in a real sense provides the definition of dialectic. Still one should also be reminded of the converse, that is, the irreducibility of what we might call an existential pathos, disregard of which might handicap us in fully appreciating Gnosticism and recognizing its return in modern discourses.

Desmond illuminates by remaining on the level of description and not offering an explanation for how it is historically possible to move from one type of Gnosticism to another. The closest he comes to the explanatory is when he suggests that despite the almost overwhelming emphasis on transcendence in ancient Gnostic texts, there might be latent reserves of some degree of positive evaluation of the cosmos. Desmond does not develop this line of inquiry, which would necessarily require both close reading of Gnostic texts and the elaboration of concepts that point to subtle subversions of the would-be univocal Gnostic stance that the counterfeit double of the created world is negative without remainder.[17] In any event, should one have the ambition of an actual explanatory theory of Gnostic return, much more than this would need to be done. This would include tracking the historical transmission of accounts of Gnosticism, figuring the point of entrance into modernity, determining the role the biblical text plays as subtext for hermeneutic violation, and isolating the basic convictions of modernity and its hermeneutic strategies vis-à-vis the Bible and ancient philosophy. Desmond inadvertently provides a hint with regard to the last mentioned point by underscoring that Hegel knew and appreciated ancient Gnosticism. Hegel does this in his *Lectures on the History of Philosophy*.[18] Hegel's view of ancient Gnosticism is strikingly similar to that put forward by Desmond in *God and the Between*. That is, epistemic-ontological doubling and the generation of a reality countermimetic to the aboriginal perfection are constitutive. Hegel suggests an amendment to Gnosticism as he finds it presented in the available historiographies of the eighteenth century.[19] The amendment appears to be completely friendly, and Hegel implies it is at least implicit in ancient Gnosticism, thus justifying the following emendation of Gnostic narrative: the iterative splitting to the point of antithesis is not really something that happens to the really real, which is unitary. Rather splitting is always an action, because always under way. This means that the primordial unity is merely a function of grammar; it is always already left behind in the movement toward rather than from perfection: the movement and the result, therefore, constitute epistemic and ontological perfection. Thus, relative to the impatience—or in Hegel's term, the "restlessness"—of the epistemic-ontological doubling exhibited in classical Gnosticism, it is greatly exacerbated in Hegel. It would not be incorrect to say that impatience is absolutized. As is also the teleological pattern, which means that the circular pattern of ancient Gnosticism is broken. There is a return to unity; but whereas in the case of classical Gnosticism we are talking about a *restitution in integrum*, here we are talking about a perfection that is a result rather than a given, a surplus—quite literally a surplus value—of knowledge and reality.

The primordial nature of splitting is the reserve in ancient Gnosticism, one might even say ancient Gnosticism's dirty secret. From Hegel's point of view, pulling the thread in this way shows how Gnosticism can transform itself into German Idealism. It is no accident that early in his career Hegel was extremely interested in showing the difference between German Idealism and all modern philosophy that preceded it, which belonged, in his view, to the order of reflection (*Reflexion*).[20] Reflection is characterized by a mode of thought distinct from the phenomenon under conceptualization and proceeds essentially by hypostatizing particular aspects of it which consequently cannot be integrated into a whole. In contrast, speculation is a form of thought that moves with the reality about which it would speak: thus differentiating features is a form of self-differentiation. Rodolphe Gasche is correct to draw attention to the Latin root of *speculation*, which is *speculare* (to mirror or to see) and *speculum* (mirror).[21] German Idealism in general and the thought of Hegel in particular is constituted by mirroring or doubling which finds a limit (counterfeit double) only for it impatiently and restlessly to overcome it. But speculation also suggests—and this is crucial for Desmond—that mir-roring is self-reflexive, indeed self-reflexivity, and that, therefore, we can talk about *self*-doubling and *self*-mediation. This is the realization of speculation in the full and proper sense, of which ancient discourses of Gnosticism provide at best antecedents.

GNOSIS AND HERMENEUTIC DOUBLING

Hegel's God: A Counterfeit Double? is not shy about answering its own question in the teeth of the evasion in the Hegel establishment of such normative questions and the prohibition of the kind of reply supplied by Desmond. Desmond, however, not only arraigns, but convicts. Given the relative self-sufficiency of the text whose aim is to contribute to Hegel studies, as well as the fact that Desmond does not explicitly tie the language of "counterfeit double" to Gnosticism or its return in the modern period, one has to thread carefully in establish-ing a link between this text and Desmond's discussion in *God and the Between* of Gnosticism in general and the "counterfeit double" in par-ticular. Still Desmond is such a systematic thinker that the recurrence of locution can hardly be accidental. To keep to the lexical connection, it does seem obvious that "counterfeit double" has a different inflec-tion in the Hegel book than it has in *God and the Between*. Specifi-cally, whereas in *God and the Between* the term referred in the main to the emergent material world as the counter-divine, here it concerns the misrepresentation of a prior—perhaps canonic—discourse. Mis-representation is demonstrated in and by how key Christian symbols are "misprisoned"—to use Harold Bloom's Shakespearean locution—and ultimately how Christian narrative as a whole has been rotated more or less on a 180-degree axis to issue in a developmental ontology. Now it is likely that even at this stage Desmond is aware of the Irenaeanorigins of "counterfeit double," which, of course, is nothing less than the translation of the German *Doppelgänger*. And if this is the case, it seems fair to insist that Desmond is capitalizing on the sec-ond, more hermeneutic form of doubling implied in Irenaeus's trope of *methamorttein*. At the same time, however, no more than in the case of Irenaeus does Desmond really segregate hermeneutical from epistemic-ontological doubling and vice versa. Hermeneutical doubling involves substantive epistemic-ontological doubling; conversely, epistemic-ontological doubling presupposes hermeneutic doubling.

The charge of hermeneutic doubling and its necessary link with epistemic-ontological doubling is indicated from early on in chapter 1 where Desmond speaks to "refiguration." Refiguration implies an important alteration of religious discourse which necessarily involves a refiguration of the meaning of the divine (2). In terms of entire chapters the hermeneutic sense of the "counterfeit double" is most nearly to the fore in chapter 2, which has as its actual theme speculative philosophy's redoubling of religion. As a term *religion* is at once generic and specific: generic, in that Desmond wants to underscore Hegel's claim that philosophy understands better than any religion its intentionality, the inclination of its symbols, and the level of achievement of its practices and forms of life; specific, in that the religion of interest is Christianity, which from the time of the *Phenomenology* Hegel routinely casts as the full realization and perfection of all religion. Desmond is fully aware of how Hegel has cast Christianity as a phenomenon, whose aim of achieving intimacy with the divine through symbol, practice, and form of life exceeds its grasp. Desmond thinks it fair to ask the question whether Hegel distorts the meaning of Christianity, especially if one allows the phenomenon some measure of autonomy and self-definition enabled by the sources of scripture and tradition. Desmond focuses on belief or doctrine more than he does on scripture. But anything that Hegel says with respect to the biblical text, undoubtedly, would prove grist for the mill in Desmond's exposé of the profound hubris of speculative philosophy vis-à-vis Christianity. Hegel routinely adduces his Lutheran credentials, but from the beginning of his philosophical career he has no compunction about standing outside ecclesial interpretation. Thus, his early "theological" writings (1795–99)[22] offer in quick succession Kantian ethical interpretations of the biblical text, taken initially to be the best option to disclose its meaning, truth, and meaningfulness, and a more romantic interpretation, redolent of Herder and Lessing, which views biblical symbols to be important because of their community context and reference as well as their pneumatic and eschatological valence.

Arguably, because of his view of how the Protestant principle operates Hegel feels little or no compunction about his systemically nonecclesial, perhaps even antiecclesial hermeneutic. The Protestant principle of the autonomy of the subject in interpreting scripture remains Lutheran to the extent to which the axiom of *sola scriptura* is constitutive. But Hegel seems to have controverted the Lutheran axiom when he avers in *The Lectures on the Philosophy of Religion* that the biblical text is a "wax nose" that admits of just about any interpretation.[23] And he performs the relative lack of importance of the biblical text by paying much more attention to the doctrines which have emerged over time in and through a mixture of biblical interpretation and attempts to respond to difficulties in interpreting God and the God-world and God–human being relations. As Desmond rightly underscores, Hegel is relentlessly critical of the theological tradition. For example, the Hegelian reading of the classical doctrine of creation—often expressed as *creation ex nihilo*—is thoroughly corrosive. From Hegel's point of view, the doctrine of creation—but arguably all doctrines—supposes and reinforces the divine as a totally other. Hegel's speculative dialectic is calculated to make divine transcendence redundant, thereby opening up the space in which the divine and human belong together and interdefine each other. Ever a metaphorical thinker, Desmond speaks of Hegel's "airbrushing out of the picture the transcendence of the Other" (58). Desmond is not consciously recalling Irenaeus's metaphor of the "picture" of the divine and the divine-human relation that is being distorted in and through Gnostic interpretation of canonic scripture; nonetheless, the metaphor of "airbrushing" evokes it. Indeed, the metaphor of "airbrushing" also is resonant of the passage from the preface (2) to *Adversus Hairesis*, quoted by Desmond in chapter 10 of *God and the Between*, in which Irenaeus speaks to the superior attractiveness of the simulacrum over the original.

Another more nearly hermeneutic rather than substantive feature of Hegel's doubling of Christianity drawn attention to by Desmond is the negative relation to Judaism (106–7, 122 ff.).[24] Importantly, this negative relation is constitutive rather than contingent, even if the motivation has more to do with Jewish survivals in Christianity than with Judaism itself. Desmond is fairly schematic: the crucial survival is the Jewish conviction of the absolute transcendence of God. But, of course, Desmond is fully aware that involved in the acceptance of the transcendence of God are negative postures toward the world, history, human autonomy, and the value of institutions. Relatedly, Desmond draws attention later in *Hegel's God* (153) to the famous Zusatz to *Encylopaedia* #24.[25] There, after the manner of the kind of transgressive interpretation of Genesis 1:3 routine in ancient Gnostic texts and drawn attention to by Irenaeus, the God of Hebrew scriptures is exposed as a God jealous of the innate divinity of human being and anxious to keep humanity in submission.[26] In fact, Hegel recalls the Ophitic Gnostic tradition in suggesting that the truth of the divinity of human being is spoken by the serpent who is the proper figure of gnosis. In contrast, the God of Hebrew scripture is not a truth-teller. He is either lying—in which case by implication he is Satan—or self-deluded in that he does not know that he does not know the truth.

The above is one of the very few places in *Hegel's God* where Desmond explicitly speaks to the issue of Hegel's hermeneutic of scripture rather than doctrine. In line with some other commentators and critics on Hegel, Desmond remarks on the way in which Hegel calls attention in the *Phenomenology* and the *Lectures on the Philosophy of Religion* to Jacob Boehme, and to his figuration of Lucifer as the "Son" of God and specifically his fall as the ground of the historical-material world as the antithesis of the pure divine (154).[27] The fall of Lucifer provides a *mythologem* of the world as the epistemic-ontological counterfeit double, which Desmond emphasizes much more in *God and the Between*. Boehme's theosophical reflections represent a kind of mediating layer between biblical interpretation and doctrine that shows the prospect of shifting from hermeneutic to epistemic doubling which is characteristic of classical Gnostic as well as Hegel's texts. Needless to say the connection between the two forms of doubling hardly rests on Hegel's s recall of the German theosophist, about whom Hegel gushes in *Lectures on the History of Philosophy*.[28] The connection between the two forms of doubling is evident already in

Desmond's very early discussion of refiguration in which the term is the generation of a "surrogate of the God of religious transcendence" (2). Throughout *Hegel's God, speculation* is used more as an adjective than a noun—although there is also a sense in which it functions as an adverb, that is, as connected with the operation of self-doubling.

This comes out most clearly in the connection of speculation with the movement of dialectic, which Desmond suggests is a movement of eros in the strict sense (112), that is, a movement from emptiness to fullness in and through the generation of a counter-divine which, paradoxically, is the condition of the possibility of the perfect divine not-other than world and humanity. Again, Desmond is fully aware that Hegel accepts with sangfroid that his erotic divine has been anticipated in modern thought by Jacob Boehme (154). Desmond notes the obvious dissonance of this view with that of the received Christian tradition. Specifically, the erotic view obviously does not rhyme with the Christian view of divine agape and the view of the world as gift which can only be distorted by making it an instrument of divine becoming. Notwithstanding the obvious utility of Desmond's reading of Hegel for theology and especially for theological apologetics, *Hegel's God* is intended mainly for philosophers. Thus, while it is philosophically relevant to point out how Hegel has distorted Christianity despite his intention to save it, nonetheless, logically speaking, the rehabilitated version of Christianity could be construed as superior from an alethic, semantic, and performative point of view. Even more if this hermeneutic operation is true to the nature and task of philosophy and neither effects nor symptoms a sea change, then *eo ipso* it is justified. Desmond judges, however, that such is not the case, and by doing so allies himself—at least functionally—with another critic of Hegel, who also happened to articulate the *metaxu*, that is, Eric Voegelin.[29] Knowledge of the erotic divine from the vantage point of its self-reflexive term means for Desmond nothing less than the subversion of philosophy which is grounded in wonder (*thaumazein*). In addition, the agonistic nature of eros suggests that Hegel departs from the economy of Neoplatonism which holds on to the agapeic view of the divine and the mimetic nature of the material and human world.

Desmond is cognizant in *Hegel's God* that the symbol of the Trinity is more than congruent with the erotic God of speculative Idealism. This is the subject of chapter 4. Desmond does not draw attention to the irony of the alliance between Hegel's refigured divine, which is inclusive of world and humanity, and the Christian doctrine regarded by Enlightenment and post-Enlightenment thinkers as in principle the least recuperable of all Christian doctrines.[30] For Hegel, however, the value of the Trinity lies in supplying a schematic of the erotic divine which proceeds by doubling or self-doubling until it reaches the nadir of the world of nature and finite spirit only then to double back. Given the largely hermeneutic use of "counterfeit double" in this text, Desmond does not speak of Hegel's construction of the material world as the counterfeit double. Since, of course, Hegel construes the material world as the antithesis of the theo-logical or theo-onto-logical divine world, nothing really prevents an identification actually made in *God and the Between*. Desmond realizes that Hegel's articulation of a trinitarian schematics is decidedly unorthodox. Indeed, he seems to have grasped that the erotic self-doubling of the divine is such that it deconstitutes the relation between the immanent and economic Trinity, making the former depend as much on the latter as the latter on the former. There are also lexical indicators of a profound refiguration of the Trinity and its missions. First, there is the absence of any referral to conciliar definition or to magisterial figures such as Augustine, Gregory of Nazianzen, Aquinas, or even Luther and Calvin. Second, with regard to anticipators of Hegel's trinitarian schematics, there are odd references in *Lectures on the Philosophy of Religion* to Philo and Proclus in the ancient world—neither of whom is Christian—and to the agonistic trinitarianism of Jacob Boehme at the dawn of the modern period.[31]

Stranger, however, than all of these is Hegel's reference in *Lectures on the Philosophy of Religion* to Valentinus.[32] Desmond does not expatiate on the point, but it is worth noting that the reference is not adventitious. In his *Lectures on the History of Philosophy* Hegel makes much of the philosophical value of the Valentinian school providing a template for a trinitarianly shaped divine which is radically self-doubling and recuperating. The only retardation to bringing out the full radicality of an always already dynamic and erotic divine is the postulate of unity as a backdrop to which doubling is regarded as an event of a contingent sort. Hegel espies the latency for the dropping of this assumption. When he comes to discussing philosophical thought in the modern period, he credits Boehme as a thinker who first makes this narrative—and trinitarian—move of thinking of the movement of doubling or differentiation as primordial.[33] Given the trajectory of modernity in which all its beginnings, whether Luther, Descartes, Bacon, or Boehme, point toward definite and definitive dénoument, and given Hegelian ascesis of pure thinking, which leaves the existing subject in brackets,[34] Hegel can claim without an iota of embarrassment that all these beginnings are realized in his speculative system. Sticking to Boehme and his positive relation to speculative thought found unacceptable to Christianity,[35] for Hegel it follows pretty automatically that the real intent of Gnostic insight is realized in the modern period. It is true that the line of progression from Valentinus through Boehme to Hegel is not what is most remembered when one reads Hegel's texts. What is remembered of his speculative historiography is the movement from classical thought, which is objective in orientation, through the emergence of the modern, which is subjective in disposition, to speculative Idealism, which successfully unites and balances subject and object. Still, the Gnosticism-Boehme-Hegel thread was important enough for one of Hegel's most talented students, Ferdinand Christian Baur, to write the nineteenth-century classic text on the return of Gnosticism in the modern period, that is, *Die christliche Gnosis*, which successfully meshed Hegel's story of progress in getting the status of divine self-doubling right with the very best available studies in the history of ancient Gnosticism.[36]

In Excess: The Core and the Supplement

I have identified Desmond's main contribution to the understanding of Gnosticism as consisting of his recognition of the phenomena of epistemic-ontological and hermeneutic doubling. Although I assigned the first to *God and the Between* and the latter to *Hegel's God*, I was careful to spell out the approximate nature of the contrast. Evidence of hermeneutic doubling can be found in the third volume of the trilogy, and conversely, evidence of epistemic-ontological doubling can be found in *Hegel's God*. Still at the very least the assignations have pragmatic value, perhaps a bit more, since one can speak of different dominant-recessive relations in each text, which necessarily have both since the relation between the two forms of doubling is hard to repress: on the one hand, the refiguration of the transcendent divine naturally points to a transgressive mode of interpreting the biblical text and its subsequent theologization; on the other, the refiguration of the biblical text and its subsequent theologization issues in a refiguration of the Christian God and this God's relation to the world and humanity. In the latter case, there is the dissolution of transcendence into immanence and the concomitant absolving of the asymmetrical relation between God and the world and God and human being. In addition, while Desmond does not provide a theory of Gnostic return, in the two books under discussion he is affirmative about its prospects, and suggests at least the following: (1) given its speculative nature, German Idealism is a prime suspect for Gnostic return; (2) candidates for Gnostic return will illustrate the two features of doubling that Desmond takes to define ancient Gnosticism, that is, epistemic-ontological and hermeneutic doubling; and (3) candidates for Gnostic return will exacerbate epistemic-ontological doubling, making divine eros absolutely radical, and absolutely impatient, in a way that was at best merely latent in ancient Gnosticism.

Now if the above represents the core contribution, the two texts under scrutiny offer a number of supplements which function as advisories with respect to all attempts at a theory of Gnosticism in general and a theory of Gnostic return in particular. I will speak to two closely related supplements. First, although Desmond does not foreground the existential experience of alienation in the manner of early twentieth-century scholars and aficionados, and seems to be persuaded that the experience cannot function in an explanatory fashion with respect to Gnosticism, nonetheless, he advises against too summarily dismissing the existential dimension.[37] The turn to epistemic-ontological dynamics and hermeneutic doubling, though crucial, needs to supplemented by attention to the rage against disorder felt toward a world regarded as a *Doppelgänger*. The corollary is that while historiographers of Gnosticism such as Hans Jonas and pundits of Gnostic return such as Eric Voegelin may fall short in their conceptual and taxonomic grasp, nonetheless, they are right to insist that the horror of the material temporal world is an important note of Gnosticism.

A second and closely related supplement is Desmond's sober emphasis on the relation between discourse and practice; the former is both guide and summary of the latter; the latter concretizes a stance and requires a discourse of legitimation. For Desmond, the stance of the Gnostic, modern or ancient, is unequivocally sovereign with regard to the world and expresses itself in an ethos of contempt rather than gratitude regarding the existence and form of the world. The evidence in Gnostic texts suggests, Desmond believes, that sovereignty can be illustrated in stances toward the world as different as radical ascesis and antinomianism. Desmond's basic intuition seems to be that with regard to modern forms of thought which are plausible candidates for Gnostic ascription, it is more likely the case that sovereignty will take antinomian form and display a deliberate transgressive attitude toward social norms, natural law, and would-be divine commands. Desmond's concept "erotic sovereignty" is borderline pleonastic in that acquisition and instrumentalization of world and others is built into the term *sovereign*. Almost, but not quite, since the self-aggrandizement is the means by which one enacts the claim of ontological specialness. The focus on "erotic sovereignty" is powerfully suggestive and encourages the search for diagnosis of its presence in modernity. Here Nietzsche as its central promoter and Dostoyevski and Kierkegaard as therapists might prove to be central.

More to the point here, however, is the tantalizing suggestion made by Pierre Klossowski that the discourse or discourses of sovereignty of Sade are essentially "Gnostic."[38] At one level, Klossowski manages to say no more than that the repetition of violation of others enacted by the sovereign or would-be sovereign—there are pretenders who will be found out—is a mark of their absolute alienation from material bodies, time and history, social custom and religious rule. Considered thus, one can think of Sade as the practical realization of the disembodied and disembedded *ego cogitio*. However provocative this connection is, more relevant to my theme is Klossowski's analysis wherein he links the practice or practices of the rule of sovereignty with metanarratives about the overcoming of a morally vacuous and intrinsically violent Nature.[39] The practices are entirely antinomian in nature. This means that the practices offer only an inverted expression of the Gnostic "blessed rage for order"—to borrow a famous phrase from Wallace Stevens. Phenomenally, the Gnostic is characterized by the transgression of order experienced as a counterfeit; the Gnostic is constituted by the infernal rage for disorder. All of this tracks what Sade obsessively writes about sovereignty in *Juliette*, *Justine*, and *120 Days of Sodom*, in which the masters endlessly exploit those constituted as slaves.

Sade, however, also sets in train a line of reception, which functions for Klossowski and others as an alternate "sacred" line of discourse whose central purpose is to disenlighten the Enlightenment. The nineteenth-century writer Lautréamont's *Maldoror* enjoys pride of place in this sacred line.[40] The antihero Maldoror's killings, mutilations, and rapes have as their aim outraging moral and social norms and exposing the weakness of the legislative God of Judaism and Christianity, who is a demented and aging drunk, no match for the virile and ascendant antihero. Bataille is especially interesting, for three reasons. First, without waiting for the literary critics and cultural historians, he essentially inserts himself in the Sadean line.[41] Second, he connects his own thought with that of Gnosticism, although he insists that the Gnosticism is oriented toward matter as the very site of transcendence: it is the body that expresses the outrage against the limits of the human condition which include religious and social norms. Third, throughout his oeuvre Bataille is in constant critical conversation with Hegel,[42] opposing his nonknowledge—secreted through transgression—to Hegel's absolute knowledge. Knowledge is thus event. The event, that is, the event of transgression, admits of repetition, and thus by implication it can proceed without finality. These three features suggest that if Hegel allows Gnostic attribution, he might have a Sadean double in modernity, where antinomian practices are key and are supported by the transgressive hermeneutic of the text, ideological substance, and ethos of the Christian tradition. This is a tantalizing suggestion, indeed one that seems confirmed in Derrida's divagations in *Glas* in which the bell tolls for the absolute knowledge of Hegelian speculation which bears a violent relation to all particularity, including the particularity of the Jew.[43] The chosen bell ringer is Jean Genet, whose dreamily rhapsodic iterations of violation and self-humiliation challenge Hegel's exclusion of singularity, but also his affirmation of the Trinity and his bourgeois embrace of the family in which the Father is the head of the household. Perhaps Derrida does not quite canonize Genet. But still, by pitting him with more nearly heavyweight thinkers such as Bataille and even Lacan, Derrida could be accused of dangerously elevating the Sadean tradition.

Now, *erotic* does not necessarily connote "sexual" either in the two texts under review or in Desmond's work as a whole. Still, throughout his work Desmond recognizes that the enactment of sovereignty plausibly takes place on the sexual plane, and also that ancient Gnostic texts are both heavily sexualized and riddled with a perverse politics of the demonization of the "female." Hegel's inversion of classical Gnostic hatred of the world might suggest that this will not be borne out in his oeuvre. True, there is plenty in Hegel's view of women and marriage for feminists to object to,[44] but assigning women a complementary but subsidiary role in a marriage can hardly be classed as demonization. Nor can his functionalization of the role of women in the creation of children, who reproduce the conditions of reproduction, be cast in an obvious Gnostic light. For typically in Gnostic texts reproduction is a sign of materiality that grants power to the spurious God who rules over it. Hegel's discourse on recognition in general,[45] and the mutual recognition of man and woman in particular, presents a challenge that a Gnostic return thesis will eventually have to meet. Similarly, with Hegel's relatively positive view of reproduction. Even more generally, one can say that all of Hegel's talk about ethos and his positive description of modern ethos (*Sittlichkeit*) in which we find the rule of economics, as well as law and the state, constitute a real challenge to sticking Hegel with a Gnostic label. Even if all these challenges could be met and one could bring in the verdict that Hegelian thought as a whole can rightly be called Gnostic, the conclusion would have to be drawn that performatively this is a very different form of Gnosticism than that spoken of by Irenaeus and illustrated in the texts of Nag Hammadi. Importantly, however, the antinomian attitude is repeated in modern texts with copious outlining of sexual transgression. Sexual violence can be considered under the auspices of regime, as is the case in Sade's *mathesis universalis* of sexual degradation in which bodies are reduced to orifices to be penetrated and opportunities for mutilation, with death the ultimate goal. The death of the violated sexual body is sovereignty's exclamation point, even if it also signals defeat. Or transgression can be understood to be both more episodic and more creative, thus upsetting iteration that might be conceived as the introjection of normalizing rationality. Both Bataille's reflections on pornographic imagination and his own pornographic performance[46] instantiate this second type, which wallows in and hallows the sovereignty enacted in perverse sexuality.

Concluding Remarks

William Desmond is that remarkable kind of thinker who unites the "much knowing" and "deep knowing" that Heraclitus separates. His competence extends over the entire range of philosophy, and especially philosophy in the classical and modern period. His range of reference outside philosophy, and especially with regard to religion and art, is extraordinarily impressive. Throughout his work Desmond interprets major thinkers, but he never forgets that it is the business of philosophy to think rather than render the thoughts of others. His major contribution lies in his vast refurbishing of metaphysics carried out in his great trilogy. All three of these texts are major orchestrations involving clearing away what is dead and reinvigorating and developing what shows signs of life. Discussion throughout is extraordinary in its depth, but equally so in its range and variability. The latter lends the labile quality to Desmond's work and exhibits what he—on the authority of Pascal—calls finesse. What is, perhaps, beyond extraordinary is that Desmond can touch on a topic such as Gnosticism, which is somewhat peripheral to him, and say something that is truly memorable and that makes a difference. When Desmond speaks to epistemic-ontological and hermeneutic doubling, he makes a real contribution to the understanding of Gnosticism that exceeds that of the philologists and also most modern thinkers interested in whether there are Gnostic elements in modern thought. When Desmond constructs Hegel as offering a *Doppelgänger* of Christianity and espies the links between Hegel's speculative thought and that of Gnosticism, he has opened up a major vista of exploration. When he writes about the differences between classical Gnosticism and the modern forms and suggests that one element of explanation of the movement from one to the other lies in the "reserve" of ancient Gnosticism to be both more developmental and teleological in its overall ontology, we are stunned into admiration and cannot help but say, "Thank you."

NOTES

1. For articles on William Desmond by Cyril O'Regan, see "Metaphysics and the Mextaxological Space of the Tradition," *Tijdschrift voor Filosofie* 59, no. 2 (Fall 1997): 531–49; "The Poetics of Ethos: William Desmond and the Poetic Redemption of a Platonic Archeology," *Ethical Perspectives* (Fall 2002): 272–302; "Metaxological Metaphysics and the Repetition of Vico," in *BSP*, 65–91; "What Theology Can Learn from a Philosophy Daring to Speak the Unspeakable," *Irish Theological Quarterly* 73 (2008): 243–62; "Naming God in *God and the Between*," *Louvain Studies* 36 (2012): 282–301. In addition, see the reviews by Cyril O'Regan of *BB* and *PU*, *Modern Theology* 13 (Spring 1997): 289–93; *EB*, *Modern Theology* (January 2003): 149–51; and *Hegel's God: A Counterfeit Double?*, *Clio* 33, no. 4 (Summer 2004): 251–57.

2. *BB, EB, GB*.

3. See especially *AA, AOO*; see also *PO*. While art is not the only other in this text, it is, nonetheless, a very important other. Desmond has just completed another major manuscript which features the disclosive potential of art.

4. See Cyril O'Regan, *Gnostic Return in Modernity* (Albany: SUNY Press, 2001); *Gnostic Apocalypse: Jacob Boehme's Haunted Narrative* (Albany: SUNY Press, 2002). My recent *The Anatomy of Misremembering: Von Balthasar's Response to Philosophical Modernity*, vol. 1: *Hegel* (New York: Crossroad, 2014), addresses the issue of the return of Gnosticism throughout. Articles that bear on the ongoing project of tracking the return

of Gnosticism in modernity include "Hegel and Anti-Judaism: Narrative and the Inner Circulation of the Kabbalah," *Owl of Minerva* (Spring 1997): 141–82; "The Impossibility of a Christian Reading of the *Phenomenology of Spirit:* H. S. Harris on Hegel's Liquidation of Christianity," *Owl of Minerva* (Fall–Winter 2001): 45–95; "Balthasar and Gnostic Genealogy," *Modern Theology* (Fall 2006): 609–50; "Hegel's Retrieval of Philo and the Constitution of a Christian Heretic," *Studia Philonika Annual* 20 (2008): 243–62; "Voegelin and the Troubled Greatness of Hegel," in *Eric Voegelin and the Continental Tradition: Explorations in Modern Political Thought,* ed. Lee Trepanier and Steven McGuire (Columbia: University of Missouri Press, 2010), 44–63; "Hegel, Sade, and Gnostic Infinities," *Radical Orthodoxy: Journal of Theology, Philosophy, and Politics* 1, no. 3 (September 2013): 383–425.

5. *GB*, 205–24. The full title of chapter 10 is "God(s) Gnostic: On Passing through the Counterfeit Doubles of the Divine."

6. See *HG*.

7. I make my sympathies for Desmond's reading of Hegel clear in my review in *Clio*. Although my work on Hegel has somewhat of a more theological focus, there is a major overlap between Desmond's and my own work on Hegel, the major example of which is *The Heterodox Hegel* (Albany: SUNY Press, 1994). This close relation is even indicated by the respective titles of our major writing on Hegel.

8. Other Gnostic texts referred to in the chapter include *Allogenes, Trimorphic Protennoia,* and *The Gospel of Philip.*

9. See *GB*, 213 n. 10, where Desmond refers to my analysis of Irenaeus and my "Irenaean" self-ascription in *Gnostic Return in Modernity.*

10. In addition to his knowledge of Irenaeus's *Against Heresies* (205 n. 1), the texts of Nag Hammadi, and my own work (207 n. 3, n. 4; 212 n. 9; 213 n. 13), Desmond shows knowledge of some of the classic commentary literature. These include Kurt Rudolph, *Gnosis: The Nature and History of Gnosticism,* ed. Robert McLachlan Wilson (San Francisco: Harper and Row, 1987) (205 n. 1); Hans Jonas, *The Gnostic Religion,* 2nd ed. rev. (Boston: Beacon Press, 1963) (206 n. 2). As an example of a historicist-philological treatment of Gnosticism, which proscribes definition and prohibits speaking of Gnosticism outside its original environment, he cites Michael Allan Williams, *Rethinking "Gnosticism": An Argument for Dismantling a Dubious Category* (Princeton, NJ: Princeton University Press, 1996). As is evident in Desmond's treatment of my own work, he is obviously more in favor with those scholars who are open to thinking that Gnosticism can be conceived as returning in modern discourses. Among those whom he cites

are Michael Pauen, *Dithyrambiker des Untergangs: Gnostizismus in Äesthetik und Philosophie der Moderne* (Berlin: Akadamie Verlag, 1994) (207 n. 4), and Eric Voegelin, *Science, Politics, and Gnosticism* (Chicago: Henry Regnery, 1968) (222 n. 25).

11. In his discussions of the texts from Nag Hammadi—much of it pursued in the notes—Desmond does not distinguish, as many contemporary scholars of Gnosticism do, between the Sethian brand of Gnosticism, which seems to have Hebrew scripture in its sights, and Valentinian Gnosticism, which refigures the New Testament as well as Hebrew scripture. See my discussion of this in *Gnostic Return in Modernity*, 266 n. 4, 267 n. 12.

12. William R. Schoedel is the scholar of Gnosticism who has most emphasized the monistic tendencies of the *Gospel of Truth*, thereby upsetting the received wisdom that Gnosticism is through and through dualistic. See "Gnostic Monism and the Gospel of Truth," in *The Rediscovery of Gnosticism*, vol. 1, ed. B. Layton (Leiden: Brill, 1979), 379–90; "Typological Theology and Some Monistic Tendencies in Gnosticism," in *Essays on the Nag Hammadi Texts in Honour of Alexander Böhlig*, ed. Martin Krause (Leiden: Brill, 1972), 88–108. Other well-known scholars persuaded that the *Gospel of Truth* gives the lie to anything like a dualistic consensus include Benoit Standaert and Cullen Story.

13. For critical reflections on this point, see Kendrick Grobel, *The Gospel of Truth: A Valentinian Meditation on the Gospel* (New York: Abingdon Press, 1960); also Benoit Standaert, "L'Évangile de vérité: Critique et lecture," *New Testament Studies* 22 (1975): 243–75.

14. Here I give the paragraph and line numbers of the Robinson edition of the *Nag Hammadi Library* used by Desmond (205 n. 1). For my discussion of this passage, see *Gnostic Return in Modernity*, 111.

15. The language of "counterfeit double" signifies the rejection of anything like the logic of supplementarity performed by Gnosticism in the ancient world and promoted by Derrida as a key feature of postmodern discourse.

16. See my discussion of *metharmottein* in *Gnostic Return in Modernity*, 148–59.

17. For example, in *Tripartite Tractate*, while the text supposes as with other Gnostic texts that creation represents a fall from the pleroma, it goes on to suggest that the fall might be purposeful and issue in a different and superior kind of perfection. See my discussion of *The Tripartite Tractate* in *Gnostic Return in Modernity*, 118–31.

18. *Lectures on the History of Philosophy*, vol. 2, trans. E. S. Haldane and F. H. Simson (Lincoln: University of Nebraska Press, 1995), 396–99.

19. See my somewhat detailed discussion of Hegel's sources when it comes to Gnosticism as well as Kabbalah in "Hegel's Retrieval of Philo as the Constitution of a Christian Heretic."

20. Here *Glauben und Wissen* (1802) represents a watermark in Hegel's production in its pointed opposition between speculation and reflection. For a convenient translation, see *Faith and Knowledge*, trans. W. Cerf and H. S. Harris (Albany: SUNY Press, 1977).

21. For an illuminating discussion of Hegel's rejection of reflection in favor of speculation, see Rodolphe Gasché, *The Tain of the Mirror: Derrida and the Philosophy of Reflection* (Cambridge, MA: Harvard University Press, 1986), 13–105. For a discussion of the "mirror" roots of "speculation," see 43–44; also 16.

22. I am speaking of texts such as "The Positivity of the Christian Religion" and "The Spirit of Christianity and Its Fate," which can be found in *Early Theological Writings*, trans. T. M. Knox (Philadelphia: University of Pennsylvania Press, 1971), 67–181, 182–301, respectively. This text represents a translation of *Hegels theologische Jugendschriften*, ed. Herman Nohl (Tübingen: Mohr, 1907). The ascription "theological" rather than "political" has increasingly come under pressure in recent years. For the most recent example, see Peter Wake, *Tragedy in Hegel's Early Theological Writings* (Bloomington: Indiana University Press, 2014).

23. See *Lectures on the Philosophy of Religion*, vol. 1: *Introduction and The Concept of Religion*, ed. Peter C. Hodgson, trans. R. F. Brown, Peter C. Hodgson, and J. M. Stewart with the assistance of J. P. Fitzer and H. S. Harris (Berkeley: University of California Press, 1984), 1824 Lecture, 123. As Hodgson points out in note 29, Hegel likely borrowed the term from Lessing. But the term was in circulation from the Reformation and dates back to the pre-Reformation period. The expression may very well date to the twelfth-century theologian Alain de Lille.

24. There is a good amount of literature on this topic. For a review of the literature, as well as the suggestion that Hegel adapted to Kabbalah in the service of an anti-Judaism agenda, see my article, "Hegel and Anti-Judaism."

25. The Zusatz to *Encyclopaedia* #24 is not unique in this respect. For similar discussions of the Genesis fall story with the same pro-serpent slant, see *Lectures on the Philosophy of Religion*, vol. 3: *The Consummate Religion*,

ed. Peter C. Hodgson, trans. R. F. Brown, Peter C. Hodgson, and J. M. Stewart with the assistance of H. S. Harris (Berkeley: University of California Press, 1985), 1821 MS, 104–6; 1824, 207; 1827, 302.

26. In contradistinction to classical Jewish and Christian interpretations of creation, Gnostic texts, both Sethian and Valentinian, depict the Creator as jealous of potential prerogatives of human beings. Sethian texts, which offer a pastiche of the biblical Creator God under the figure of Yaldabaoth—a mixture of Sabaoth with Hyle—are particularly virulent on this point.

27. This is a point I underscore in my treatment of Hegel's view of creation in *The Heterodox Hegel*, 151–69.

28. For Hegel on Boehme, see *Lectures on the History of Philosophy*, vol. 3, trans. E. H. Haldane and F. M. Simson (Lincoln: University of Nebraska Press, 195), 188–216.

29. Interestingly, Voegelin—with whose work Desmond is not entirely unfamiliar—is (a) aware of the Platonic origins of the *metaxu*, whose classical textual sites are the *Republic* and the *Symposium*, and (b) uses *metaxu* as a critical lever against Hegelian thought which would transcend it in the apotheosis of absolute knowledge (*absolut Wissen*). I discuss the relevant texts in my article "Voegelin and the Troubled Greatness of Hegel," 44–63. I also explicitly make the connection between Desmond and Voegelin on *metaxu* (61 n. 4).

30. This is a point very much to the fore in *The Heterodox Hegel*. For a more compact expression, see my article "The Trinity in Kant, Hegel, and Schelling," in *The Oxford Handbook on the Trinity*, ed. Gilles Emery and Matthew Levering (Oxford: Oxford University Press, 2011), 254–66. Others who have pronounced on the unusual importance of the Trinity in the light of its modern marginalization include Dale M. Schlitt and Peter C. Hodgson. For Schlitt, see *Hegel's Trinitarian Claim: A Critical Reflection* (Leiden: Brill, 1984); for Hodgson, *Hegel and Christian Theology: A Reading of the Lectures on the Philosophy of Religion* (Oxford: Oxford University Press, 2005). For a critical engagement with *Hegel's God*, see Hodgson, *Hegel and Christian Theology*, 247–58.

31. See *Lectures on the History of Philosophy*, vol. 2, 387–94, 432–50.

32. *Lectures on the Philosophy of Religion*, vol. 3, 1821 MS, 85. As Hodgson observes in fn. 84, Hegel gets most of his information from August Neander's text, *Genetische Entwicklung der vornehmsten Gnostischen Systeme* (Berlin, 1818). In the 1824 Lectures Valentinus is not mentioned by name, but the Valentinian material of the 1821 MS is repeated, though in reduced form (196–97). Similarly with the 1827 Lectures (287–88).

33. Neither is it accidental that in the *Lectures on the Philosophy of Religion* Hegel follows his avowal of the Gnostic contribution to trinitarian thought with an affirmation of the contribution of Boehme. See *Lectures on the Philosophy of Religion*, 1827, 289–93.

34. Thereby earning the undying hostility of Kierkegaard.

35. Boehme's own thought was found unacceptable to Lutheran orthodoxy in his day and throughout the seventeenth and eighteenth centuries.

36. Ferdinand Christian Baur, *Die christliche Gnosis, oder die christliche Religionsphilosophie in ihrer geschictlichen Entwicklung* (Tübingen, 1835).

37. Perhaps the major criticism that Desmond makes of *Gnostic Return in Modernity* and *Gnostic Apocalypse* is their relative neglect of the existential dimension of Gnosticism. See his review of both volumes in *Tidjschrift voor Filosofia* 64, no. 3 (2002): 607–11.

38. Pierre Klossowski, *Sade mon prochain* (Paris: Seuil, 1947).

39. See Klossowski's introductory essay, "Nature as Destructive Principle," in *120 Days of Sodom and Other Writings*, trans. Austryn Wainhouse and Richard Seaver (New York: Grove Press, 1966), 65–86. This reproduces Bataille's introduction to the Précieux edition of *Les 120 Journées de Sodom*. A longer, more developed version of the thesis is to be found in *Sade mon prochain*.

40. *Les Chants de Maldoror* is the main text produced by Comte de Lautréamont (Isidore Lucien Ducasse; 1846–70) in his very short life. The text that ties together Lautréamont and Sade is Maurice Blanchot's *Lautréamont et Sade* (Paris: Éditions de Minuit, 1963).

41. For Bataille, see his *Literature and Evil*, trans. Alistair Hamilton (New York: Marion Boyars, 1985). The chapter on Sade (103–29) is foundational for a genealogy that includes Baudelaire and Genet. For his reflection on "sovereignty," see *The Accursed Share*, trans. Robert Hurley (New York: Zone Books, 1993).

42. See Georges Bataille, *The Unfinished System of Non-Knowledge*, ed. Stuart Kendall, trans. Michelle Kendall and Stuart Kendall (Minneapolis: University of Minnesota Press, 2001).

43. For an analysis which reads Derrida's powerful text on Hegel (1976) as being careless with regard to the Sadean tradition that he deploys, see my article "Hegel, Sade, and Gnostic Infinities."

44. The literature on Hegel and feminism in the past twenty-five years is not insignificant. At root is the work of Judith Butler and her classic text, *Subjects of Desire: Hegelian Reflections in Twentieth-Century France* (New York: Columbia University Press, 1999; originally published 1987).

45. Robert R. Williams has made this topic his own. See, among other texts, *Recognition: Fichte and Hegel on the Other* (Albany: SUNY Press, 1992); *Hegel's Ethics of Recognition* (Berkeley: University of California Press, 2000).

46. Bataille wrote novellas rather than novels. Two of the many examples written before World War II are *Story of the Eye*, trans. David Bergelson (New York: City Lights, 2001); *Blue of Noon*, trans. Harry Matthews (London: Penguin, 2012).

CHAPTER 10

The Silences of the Between

Christological Equivocity and Ethical Latency in Desmond's Work

JOHN PANTELEIMON MANOUSSAKIS

What is god, or what is not god, or what is in between—
What mortal says he has found it by searching the farthest limit?
                                        —Euripides, *Helen*, 1137–39

William Desmond is arguably in our times the last metaphysician. In making this assertion I am thinking of his work as a meditation of being, especially what he calls the *conandus essendi*, or, more recently, the intimacy of being—especially since for Desmond *being* is not the Being beyond beings, a hidden, mystical and mystifying being, but rather, to use his terminology, idiotic, aesthetic, erotic, and agapeic—and all four at once. Such a complex meditation, if it is not to remain descriptive, needs to allow itself to stand in the face of the fundamental question of metaphysics, namely, why there is something rather than nothing?, and, in doing so, to posit the question of being's origin, that is, of its causes (ontological be-causes). To speak of being's be-cause is of course to think of what comes to be, of be-coming, and indeed a becoming that, *at some time*, came to be; that is, it began. Be-causes, be-comings, and beginnings: it is this conceptual trinity that inspires Desmond's work of the between,[1] a work that, following Aristotle's definition of metaphysics as the knowledge of "the first beginnings and causes" (τῶν πρώτων ἀρχῶν καὶ αἰτιῶν, A 928b9), can be properly called *metaphysical*.

Is it on account of such metaphysical orientation that a double omission is detected in Desmond's work—the lack that perhaps grounds his works by precisely being the very lack of a ground (*Abgrund*)—when one observes, or rather fails to observe, any substantial treatment, apart of a few references in passing, of sin, even when writing on ethics, and of Christ, even when writing on God?[2] I would, therefore, venture to discuss what Desmond does *not* say. I want to speak of his silences, for they speak more loudly than his words.

Desmond's God: "He who shall not be named"

In book 3 of the *Confessions* Augustine reads Cicero, and thus philosophy makes its first explicit appearance in the dramatic unfolding of history that the structure and the narrative of the *Confessions* represents. Yet, ironically, philosophy was found lacking in one particular respect: the name of Christ. His name was not spoken.

> In the customary course of study I had discovered a book by an author called Cicero, whose language is almost universally admired, though not its inner spring. This book of his is called the *Hortensius* and contains an exhortation to philosophy. The book changed my way of feeling and the character of my prayers to you, O Lord, for under its influence my petitions and desires altered.... Only one consideration checked me in my ardent enthusiasm: *that the name of Christ did not occur there*.[3]

This is ironic because philosophy since its beginning is concerned with beginnings: it is the beginning as such that interests philosophy; the beginning is interesting (and hereby a paradox lies concealed, for the interesting is already and always in-between and thus in a difference from the beginning that is not indifferent to us). Nevertheless, philosophy ever since its beginning has been interested with beginnings, and thus one would have expected, Augustine suggests, that the name of him "who is the beginning"[4] might have been spoken.

Perhaps philosophy, like the young Augustine of book 3, is blind to *that* beginning—the beginning which is "in the beginning"—for it thinks of it (and of him) as the in-between, and so exceptionally, unsurpassably, the *metaxu* par excellence, that is, as the mediator. For Christ is also inter-esting and more so as Christ—that is, as the one who came to be between beings (*inter-esse*) and in our midst (*entos humon*; Luke 17:21).

For philosophy, however, things are otherwise: while recognizing and acknowledging the fundamental difference and thus the distance between "what is god" and "what is not god"—to return to the Euripidean epigram that opens this essay—nevertheless a different answer or name is given to "what is in between" these two poles: for the Greeks, as it is perhaps expected, it was a Christ-less philosophy (thus Augustine's disappointment), but for Desmond's philosophical work it seems to be an equally disappointing mediation that takes place by means of a Christological equivocity of sorts.[5] Desmond argues that "we need a finessed, transdialectical *logos* of the *metaxu*."[6] The question is, is it not such a *logos* precisely *the* Logos? Is it not the Chalcedonian formula precisely such a "finessed, transdialectical *logos*" of the Logos as the *metaxu* par excellence?

Unless Desmond is still thinking of philosophy as the *between* the world of God (or gods) and the world of "what is not god" that transfers (hence the original meaning of *translation*) something from the one world to the other, thereby establishing a communication, if not a communion, between the two orders. This metaxological function of philosophy was thought as particularly suitable for a daemon—that is, for a being who, on account of being a demigod, partakes of both realms, the human and the divine, being strictly speaking neither. Diotima gives us a memorable account of philosophy's demonic features in Plato's *Symposium*:

They are messengers who shuttle back and forth between the two, conveying prayer and sacrifice from men to gods, while to men they bring commands from the gods and gifts in return for sacrifices. Being in the middle of the two, they round out the whole and bind fast the all to all. Through them all divination passes, through them the art of priests in sacrifice and ritual, in enchantment, prophecy, and sorcery. Gods do not mix with men; they mingle and converse with us through spirits instead, whether we are awake or asleep. (*Symposium*, 203a)[7]

Interestingly, for Plato the daemonic force best suited for this mission was Eros—an Eros who, as Plato through Diotima describes him in the lines that follow, found its closest resemblance in the person of a philosopher, and indeed the philosopher par excellence, Socrates. Let us leave aside for now this moment when philosophy, hermeneutics, and erotics converge into a single point, as it deserves its own proper treatment. Instead, we will follow Diotima's axiom cited above: "Gods do not mix with men." For the excursion to the idyllic landscapes of Greek philosophy has confirmed in the most explicit way the problematic of the absolute disparity between God and humans, and thus, by implication, it has opened for us the question of theological impossibility. For if theology is merely *our* discourse about God and nothing more, then it cannot make any pretense to know its object: such "theology" has rightly been called an anthropomorphism[8] and a conceptual (self-) idolatry.[9] If, on the other hand, theology is our discourse about God on the basis of and in response to God's always prior address to humanity, an address that was initiated by God's self-revelation and that unfolds as an invitation to a dialogical conversation, then the human *logos* about the divine Logos (theo-logy) cannot be anything else than *the logos of the Logos*: in other words, it is of paramount importance that the Fourth Gospel calls God's self-revelation "the Logos" (the Word) who was "in the beginning" and who was eternally "with God" and who "was God" (John 1:1); for only as *logos*, as word, as discourse—a discourse that proceeds from God and is God—can God's self-revelation ground theology, now properly so understood. Theology as *the logos of the Logos* points to a hermeneutic uniqueness of a truth—indeed, *the* Truth, "I am the truth" (John 14:6)—that offers itself as interpretation and, moreover, as a self-interpretation.[10] A truth that is hermeneutical through and through.

"What is god, or what is not god, or what is in between?"—that was the tragic poet's question that guides my reflections here. It is important to notice that the poet poses the question in terms of "what is god"—*die Gottefragen?*—and what is not god. The question of humanity is raised only negatively—that is, incidentally, as if "what is god" were a more readily available question; as if one knew the answer to that question better, and therefore "what is not god" needed only to be asked in light of that first question and its corresponding answer. Yet does the question "what is not god?" point immediately at man? What is that that is not god? It is not the godless for sure, nor is it the ungodly. It is not even the "mortal" which the poet mentions in the next line. For "what is not god" is the mortal only in one aspect—that is, only in respect to god's immortality. What, then, "is not god"—especially if we assume, as the chorus in *Helen* does, that one should begin with the question of god (of what god is)—that is, we should begin with the beginning and from the beginning? What is *not* god is what god is *not*: namely, this *not*. *What is not god is not.*

And yet, this *not* can be seen, and even see itself, and it can be spoken of, and even speak of and for itself, in light of what-is-god. But precisely because it can do so, it can also easily forget that seeing itself and speaking of itself is made possible only in a light and in a *logos* that does not belong to it. Therefore, this *not* can mis-take itself as that light and that *logos*; that is, it can assume that it is self-illuminated (*autophoton*) instead of the recipient of a light external and quite foreign to itself (*heterophoton*). It is in this mistaken assumption that the problematic of sin opens up.

Sin

The metaphysical beginning—that is, the preoccupation with beginnings—seems to function as a way in which one could speak of sin without lifting the veil over sin's proper face (in fact this manner of speaking is that veil itself). Here sin becomes philosophical—but isn't this philosophy's sin? Isn't this *our* sin qua philosophers, namely, that when it comes to sin all we can do is run back to the beginning and speak the language of being?

Language suggests a closer association of sin with ontology than one might assume. Perhaps in sin the connection between the ontological and the ethical remains intact. Thus, we trace the origin of the word *guilty* back to the Latin adjective *sons, sontis*—with probable derivation from the verb *esse,* "to be." If, on the other hand, we think for a moment along the path of the Greek language, then we are presented with a vocabulary familiar from Greek tragedy that includes such terms as *hubris* and *hamartia,* even though there is a term closer to our philosophical home, namely, that of *aitia*—a term whose translation into the Latin as *causa,* and thereby into "cause," Heidegger has rightly protested as misleading.[11] It would be closer to its Greek meaning if we were to think of *aitia* as, for example, in *aitiatike,* that is, the *accusative* case ("das, was ein anderes *verschuldet*"). When the philosopher speaks of causes and causality, he stands at the tribunal of reason as the accuser. To call the cause of a becoming—since only that which be-comes is in need of a "be-cause"—is to accuse, to proclaim that which comes-to-be as guilty.

Nothing is more familiar to philosophy and to philosophers than accusations. The first, and therefore the oldest, of them is the accusation of being—in the double sense: of having been, of having come-to-be (recall the μὴ φῦναι of the tragic hero),[12] and of that accusation that only being, being itself, can pronounce. Perhaps it was Anaximander who first adopted the language of crime and punishment in philosophy, as a surviving fragment of his thought (DK 1) seems to suggest. According to this fragment, Anaximander must have seen the world as an immense crime scene where the crime of being is continuously committed. "Things" are coming to being, and that means that a moment ago they were not. Being is not theirs, for it can be taken away from them, as indeed it will, "paying penance and being judged for their injustices, in accordance with the ordinance of time."[13] In a work unpublished during his lifetime, a youthful Nietzsche imagines Anaximander addressing beings thus: "Why are you here? Your guilt,

I see, causes you to tarry in your existence. With your death, you have to expiate it."[14] The first accusation, then, that philosophy investigates, is that of being itself, of a certain unlawfulness in our origin, and in front of such accusation, we stand all equally guilty—an original guilt.

So much with *aitia* then. However, one cannot think of *aitia* without conjuring up its twin concept, namely, *arche*. In Aristotle's *Metaphysics* the two terms occur almost always together; wisdom, as we have seen, is the knowledge of τῶν πρώτων ἀρχῶν καὶ αἰτιῶν (A 928b9). So once more the question of beginnings presents itself—*protai archai*—a word that thanks to its Latin translation as *principium* has come to mean not only the beginning but also the principle. What does it mean, then, to have a beginning—an *arche*—to find oneself already under the principle of the *principium*—of the beginning?

The answer now offers itself: having a beginning means above all that one is not *anarchic*, that one recognizes oneself at the very least as a derivative, secondary being—a being whose very being, precisely because it had a beginning, cannot therefore mistake itself as its own beginning, that is, as *autarchic*. It is the impossibility of such an autarchic being that becomes thematized in the book that so erroneously has been taken to be an autobiography, namely, St. Augustine's *Confessions*. That impossibility is before anything else demonstrated performatively: thus in the first book we are met with the difficulty of beginning, especially of beginning at the beginning (as an autobiography ought); since we are beings that have already begun, we find ourselves already in *media res*, *meta*-beings (*meta-onta*) in the twofold sense that the *meta* has for Desmond's work: after but also in the midst. On the other hand, an autobiography that begins is a contradiction in terms for the only being that can lay claim to autobiography in the strict sense is precisely a being without a beginning. Yet the *Confessions* begin and appropriately not *sub propria voce sui* but through the voice of another, that of the psalmist. Book 1 speaks of the origins of man, not only of *this* man who recalls his childhood in Thagaste, but of man in general, of mankind as such, and, therefore, of the origins of sin. Already in the opening lines the theme of death and sin—and of their connection, which is traced back to the primordial Garden that St. Augustine's narrative so skillfully reenacts in the

Garden of the stolen fruit—that is, the theme of death as the result of sin, is announced: "homo circumferens mortalitatem suam, circum-ferens testimonium peccati sui et testimonium, quia superbis resistis" (I, i). *Pride*, namely, the refusal to recognize one's origin, or better yet the refusal to recognize *that* one has an origin,[15] becomes the *begin-ning* of sin. So here sin begins with the denial of the beginning. Thus the Wisdom of Sirach affirms that "pride is the beginning [the *arche*] of all sin" (10:13).[16] Let it be noted that pride is, incidentally, auto-biography's motivating thrust, which, it should be now made clear, far from being synonymous with confession, is its very opposite. A confession in its threefold sense of confession of sins, profession of faith, and praise—all three, by the way, intrinsically connected as each one constitutes a logical progression in the spiritual life—is nothing but the acknowledgment that everything one has and is, *except sin*, is given from God.[17] The condition that excludes sin leads to the para-doxical conclusion that the only thing that properly belongs to me and furthermore the thing that by a sinister *principium individuatio-nis* defines me is my sin. The only thing, therefore, that one could legitimately be proud of is sin itself, but since sin is nothing more, as we have seen, than pride, the only thing that one could be proud of is one's own pride.[18] Here sin is revealed as an empty structure that seeks self-affirmation by running amok, that is, by pointing back at its emptiness.[19] It is in this sense that one can say that the origin of sin is sin, and that sin begets sin, which is to say, in agreement with the scholastic tradition, that sin does not have a proper cause, but it is only a presuppositionless negation.[20] At the same time, one becomes aware of the irony in the autobiographical effort, for the self-narrated self has nothing to say, no matter how verbose it may otherwise be.

This denial of the origin, the forgetfulness of the beginning, can be also expressed differently as the denial of mediation and interme-diation. Under this concept, sin is the desire for immediacy in two senses: (a) in time—as that which, unable to suffer the passing of time, becomes averse to time itself and to history; and (b) as that which, unable to wait for the Other, seeks to bring about what is to take place on its own and by itself, becoming averse to any form of depen-dency on the Other. Kafka must have had this in mind when he wrote,

"There are two main human sins [*Hauptsünden*] from which all the others derive: impatience and indolence. It was because of impatience that they were expelled from Paradise; it is because of indolence that they do not return. Yet perhaps there is only one major sin: impatience. Because of impatience they were expelled, because of impatience they do not return."[21]

The first man sinned insofar as he wanted to achieve *without waiting* what was promised to him anyway but in time. When the Serpent promises our ancestors that eating of the forbidden fruit will make them "like God" (Gen. 3:5), he promises them in fact what has already been planned by God as humankind's destiny: its *theosis*. The object of sin here is neither different from nor contrary to God's will; rather sin consists entirely not on what one desires but on *how* one desires, that is, on this double immediacy. What our ancestors heard in the voice of the Serpent was the seduction of the "here and now."

It is in this sense that sin can have its beginning only at the very beginning, at the very inception of time, when one cannot measure time, or by faking such timelessness. Thus, it is necessary *not* to avoid the controversial position that affirms the existence of sin already *at* the beginning of history, dispelling any notions of primordial perfection. Even though one can argue that there was no moment in history when man enjoyed a sinless state of perfection, history does not begin with sin or even less because of it, as Kierkegaard, for example, seems to think. For him, "without sin there is no sexuality, and without sexuality, no history."[22] I believe that Kierkegaard thinks of sexuality, in particular sexual difference, as the result of sin only with respect to man for whom, on account of his corporeal nature, sin could be thought of as having such an effect—otherwise, he would have to explain why sin did not result in sexual differentiation when angels sinned. Yet he is right in asserting that an angel has no history. "Even if Michael had made a record of all the errands he had been sent on and performed," he writes, "this is nevertheless not his history."[23] Still, to make history the aftermath of sin, or worse, the means of its punishment and correction, creates some inescapable perplexities.[24] Instead, history, which was never for the Creator an afterthought, *even if man had not sinned*, is God's means of a perfection yet to be achieved, the means by which such a perfection can be reached, as we expect eschatologically.

In fact, I would like to suggest, taking my prompt from St. Augustine's *Confessions*, that time as a movement toward perfection is at the same time the means of sin's undoing. For sooner or later (i.e., in time), the *posse peccare* has to crumble under the confession of the *non posse non peccare*—admit, that is, that its capability is nothing more than its incapacity to transcend itself; its freedom is only a condemnation to repeating itself. In time, that is, in that very repetition, the sinner recognizes himself as such and despairs over his sin.[25] But his desperation at this point is already the birth pangs of his salvation—for a sin recognized as sin constitutes already a moment *after* sin, that is, a sin already delivered at the hands of time, and the hands of time, following St. Irenaeus of Lyon, are nothing else than the hands of God.[26]

It is, therefore, a characteristic of sin as such to be devoid of continuity. By this I don't mean to deny the habitual nature of sin, but only to call attention to its mode of existence which is no other than that spasmodic repetition which Kierkegaard has called "the sudden."[27] Like a tic, sin repeats itself almost compulsorily—although its compulsion is but an illusion facilitated precisely by its lack of continuity and can be exposed as such through the lens of mediation. As a series of spasms do not make a gesture, let alone a movement, so the repetition of sin over a given amount of time fails to make up the content it lacks. It fails to arrive somewhere for in a strange way sin does not move, it only jumps.[28] Thus, sooner or later (i.e., in time and over time), sin, no matter how enticing its promises and phantasmagoric its fantasies, must yield to *boredom*. In boredom, however, sin has left the timelessness of the sudden and has already become subjected to the mediation of the temporal; in other words, it can now look at itself and become aware of its emptiness—that is, sin becomes perceptible as sinful.

There is, therefore, no need to emphasize at this point that boredom (as well as anxiety) is a category available to us only *after* sin; and, therefore, Origen's explanation of the creation of the world—a creation which for Origen is still understood in terms of a catastrophe, in its literal sense of a "turning downward"—by appealing to the boredom (*koros*) that the souls had experienced in their eternal preexistence suffers from the grave mistake of conceiving boredom *before* the beginning, indeed as the reason for which creation began.[29] The mistake is quite obvious: in a timeless state of existence boredom makes little or no sense.

It follows that that which makes sin perceptible as sinful, to the sinner himself above all, and thus opens the way for repentance is mediation as, first, the reflection that can be afforded only by distance in time (diachronicity), and, second, as intermediation through the relation with the Other against whom I have sinned. In fact, both of these parameters are articulated in the famous parable of the prodigal son.

> There was a man who had two sons. The younger one said to his father, "Father, give me my share of the estate [δός μοι τὸ ἐπιβάλλον μέρος τῆς οὐσίας/da mihi portionem substantiae]." So he divided his property between them [διεῖλεν αὐτοῖς τὸν βίον/divisit illis substantiam]. Not long after that, the younger son got together all he had, set off for a distant country [εἰς χώραν μακράν/in regionem longinquam] and there squandered his wealth [διεσκόρπισε τὴν οὐσίαν αὐτοῦ/dissipavit substantiam suam] in wild living. (Luke 15:11–14)[30]

"Father, give me my share of the estate." What did the prodigal son ask for? His share of the estate, says the English text, translating a Greek word with many and important meanings: give me, says the Greek text, "μέρος τῆς οὐσίας"—give me, that is, a part of *being*, give me part of your paternal *essence*. What the prodigal son asks for is, in a deeper sense, impossible. Either he asks for a share in the father's fatherhood, he asks to become his own father, to give birth to himself, or he asks that *being itself* be given to him, that his being might be given. Yet what sense does it make for one to ask to be given that which one already is? "Give me my being, father," says that being who is a being given. That life is given can mean two different things to different people: either it can mean that life as given is a gift over which one is full with gratitude, or it can mean that life is *a* given, something over which I have no choice, and therefore no freedom.

Life itself, insofar as it is given, constricts and constrains my freedom. Thus the givennness of life can give rise to two opposing experiences: on the one hand, that of gratitude and thanksgiving; on the other, that of imprisonment from which one desperately seeks to free oneself, seeking an alleged independence.

What the prodigal son really asks for in asking for his share of "the estate"—even if we were to understand "the estate" according to the language of the parable in purely pragmatic and practical terms, as referring to his property—is nothing more than his freedom. The very figure of his father is a reminder that everything he has, his life included, is not his but something for which he ought to feel indebted to someone else. And a man who feels indebted, that is, under debt, cannot presumably feel free. It is freedom that the prodigal son longs for, the kind of freedom one understands under the prized word *independence*. He simply wants to be independent. Even such independence is bought on the price of a being that is divided, of a division engrafted in the heart of being. "Διεῖλεν αὐτοῖς τὸν βίον"—the verb διαλαμβάνω means "to divide, to separate, to cut off," but also "to grasp separately."[31] The passage, then, speaks of a life seized, claimed, and, as such, separated and torn into pieces. The prodigal's life is not any more the life of his father but his own. Like Oedipus in Thebes, he replaces his father by becoming the father of himself and thus fatherless.

As soon as he has left the paternal house, he finds himself in a "distant land." But what land can be distant from the Father who holds all in his hand? Is there a place devoid of God? To look back at the series of perplexities with which Augustine chooses to open his *Confessions*: "No, my God, I would not exist, I would not be at all, were you not in me. Or should I say, rather, that I should not exist if I were not in you, from whom are all things, through whom are all things, in whom are all things?" (I.2.2 [p. 40]). "The distant land" is nothing more than *the land of distance*, a land in which everything is presented in some distance, no matter how close we come to people and to things. It is a world that is fragmented—into so many fragments as are many people and places there; fragmented into gender and race, into different languages and ethnicities, into different social classes, separated from each other and ultimately from ourselves.

In such a land, one cannot but "squander his wealth"—again, the Greek text is helpful: "καὶ ἐκεῖ διεσκόρπισεν τὴν οὐσίαν αὐτοῦ": there one *scatters* one's life and oneself; in this land, which we call our world, one cannot but be a scattered being. As scattered, we desire our lost unity, we desire to be one again, to be *whole*. First, to be one again with ourselves, for not unlike that demon who, when questioned about his name, answered "legion" (Mark 5:9), *each of us is many*. That is why the return to the Father begins with a return to oneself: "εἰς ἑαυτὸν δὲ ἐλθών/in se autem reversus" (Luke 15:17), which we translate "when he came to his senses," even though a more faithful translation would have rendered it "having returned to himself." Indeed, one can be distant, not only from others, but from oneself; and the return to the Other takes place by a turning toward oneself. For no matter how much we try, no matter how much we love each other, our efforts remain frustrated, our intimacy with one another never quite succeeds in making us one. Hence that sense of failure, of a desire unsatisfied and unsatisfiable that awaits us at the end of our efforts. The land of distance is not so much a land defined by geography but rather by a way of being, our way of life, which is to say that we do not reside in the land of distance but rather we have become *it*: each in his and her way making out of ourselves, as Augustine says, a wasteland ("et factus sum mihi region egestatis," II.10.18).

> After he had spent everything, there was a severe famine in that whole country, and he began to be in need [ὑστερεῖσθαι/egere]. So he went and hired himself out to a citizen of that country, who sent him to his fields to feed pigs. He longed to fill his stomach with the pods that the pigs were eating, but no one gave him anything. (Luke 15:14–16)

The Greek verb employed here to denote a need that is most physical, namely, hunger, means primarily "to come late," "to be too late." Ὑστερέω implies a lack or want first and foremost in terms of lateness (ὕστερος).[32] The prodigal son was, like Augustine, late ("Late have I loved you"; X.27.38). This ethical lateness is first inscribed and awakened in the body.

Sin cannot be conceived *in abstracto*, that is, outside and without the relation between the sinner and the Other to whom the sinner is accountable. That Other, on the other hand, cannot be the sinner himself, as if that to which the sinner is accountable could be his own sense of duty, "the master [who] lies in us,"[33] or his conscience. Such a misinterpretation would have returned us to the beginning of this essay and the beginning of sin indicated by such notions as autarchy and autonomy. Furthermore, there is not such thing as a consciousness, in the strictest phenomenological sense, which could stand alone without being in reference to and in relation with an Other. "The *inescapability of the other* is undeniable."[34] No, first and foremost sin presupposes the very relation it is understood to have damaged; it presupposes the dialogue that sin has interrupted. The essential background of sin, therefore, without which the concept of sin would have been canceled out, is what Paul Ricoeur has called "the fundamental situation of a man who finds himself implicated in the initiative taken by someone who, on his side, is essentially turned toward man; ... [namely] a god who is anthropotropic—before being anthropomorphic."[35] That is why, for Ricoeur, "sin is a religious dimension before being ethical; it is not the transgression of an abstract rule—of a value—but the violation of a personal bond."[36] A phenomenological description of sin, therefore, cannot but begin by focusing on the structure of being-before-God, of being-in-relation, or, to use just one word, of being a *prosopon*. I have analyzed elsewhere the phenomenology of *prosopon*,[37] and so there is no need to return to that analysis here. It would be sufficient to ask, "if sin is primarily the rupture of a relation,"[38] then how can we best envision the character of that relation?

Nietzsche, in his *Genealogy of Morals*, puts forward a creative interpretation of guilt (*Schuld*) that traces its origins back to debt (*Schuld*).[39] The most fundamental of debts is, according to him, that which is owed to one's ancestors; it is, in other words, an ancestral debt, being indebted for one's origin, an indebtedness that requires from the members of the tribe a repayment in the form of "sacrifices[,] ... feasts, music, honors; above all, obedience." Nietzsche's analysis concludes with the hypothesis that the first gods, the very concept of divinity, emerged out of such a contractual relationship with one's ancestors—invested now for the first time with divine attributes on account of one's fear for them.[40] History keeps adding to the original, ancestral debt interest to such an extent that it reaches a symbolic proportion that is beyond repayment. Eventually, only a god would be able to pay back what is owed to god, a god that would become man in order to sacrifice himself in satisfaction of humanity's debt. That's the "stroke of genius on the part of Christianity" for Nietzsche, namely, that "God himself sacrifices himself for the guilt of mankind, God himself makes payment to himself, God as the only being who can redeem man from what becomes unredeemable for man himself—the creditor sacrifices himself for his debtor, out of *love* (can one credit that?), out of love for his debtor!"[41] Taking a step that anticipates Freud, Nietzsche argues that, at some time in history, the relationship between two individuals, namely, creditor and debtor, was internalized in a single individual. Of course, as long as that contractual relationship was external and intersubjective, it did not constitute guilt *as such*. It became that when indebtedness and correspondingly the feeling of "being-indebted-to," that is, the feeling of an unsettled account, of unfinished business, is transferred within oneself, becoming thus intrasubjective.

It is precisely this line of thought that Heidegger picks up in the famous analysis of sections 57 and 58 from *Being and Time*, where the silent call that conscience itself is pronounces only one verdict and always the same: "guilty."[42]

Heidegger's idea of life as "a series of repayments on a loan that you did not agree to, with ever-increasing interest that will cost you your life," that is, life as "a mort-gage,"[43] takes us back to Anaximander's fragment. Yet in the time between Anaximander and Heidegger a decisive transformation took place to which philosophy ought to pay attention. I speak of the almost imperceptible change from the neutral "the one" (τὸ ἕν) to the masculine "the One" (ὁ εἷς), that is, of the movement from impersonal being to a *personal* God. In Greek the difference is mostly in the definitive article, and in English it is inaudible, but it is a difference big enough to make all the difference in our discussion for, being in relation with a personal God, being must also be understood as personal, and between persons the primary relation goes under the name of either *eros* or *agape*.[44] It is telling that in the prophetic utterance sin takes the form of an accusation for *adultery*.[45] In turning away from God to other self-made gods, and offering to them what one ought to offer only to God, not only are we proven unfaithful, but we have shown ourselves guilty of a certain religious promiscuity. Thus the other side of adultery is, sensibly enough, *idolatry*.[46] In the prophetic language adultery becomes the most eloquent metaphor for idolatry, yet idolatry itself can, in turn, become a metaphor for sin in general. After all, as we have seen, sin is nothing else than the positing of the self as its own self-made idol. Thus, the Great Canon, which is sung in the Orthodox Church during the last week of Lent, puts such an anguished confession in the mouth of the faithful with great clarity: αὐτείδωλον ἐγενόμην, "I have become an idol to myself" (*Great Canon*, Ode 4). Self-idolization becomes, therefore, the final accomplishment on a course that began with the denial of beginning only in order to end in the self-denial of one's end.

NOTES

The chapter epigraph is from *The Complete Greek Drama*, ed. Whitney J. Oates and Eugene O'Neill Jr., trans. E. P. Coleridge (New York: Random House, 1938),

1. Were we to assign each of these concepts to one of the three metaxological volumes, I would suggest that be-causes corresponds to *BB*, becomings to *EB*, and beginnings to *GB*.

2. "Though we do not yet speak that name." *GB*, 118.

3. Augustine, *The Confessions*, III.4.7–8, trans. Maria Boulding (New York: New City Press, 1997), 79–80. My emphasis.

4. Cf. *Confessions* ("This eternal Reason is your Word, who is the Beginning"), XI.8.10 (p. 291), alluding to John 8:25.

5. So the majority of references to Christ in *GB* are to a Christ that serves merely as an example (see esp. 187, 338, 145)—in a sense not different from the Christological exemplarism one meets in Kant's *Religion within the Boundaries of Mere Reason*. Desmond avoids assigning to Christ's role and place any uniqueness as the in-between par excellence, or if he alludes to such an exception (as on pp. 186, 194, and 196) this is done in Christianity's name while carefully avoiding any personal endorsement.

6. *GB*, 117.

7. Translation by Alexander Nehamas and Paul Woodruff, in John M. Cooper, ed., *Plato: Complete Works* (Indianapolis, IN: Hackett, 1997), 486.

8. Beginning with the Greek poet Xenophanes, this line of criticism culminates in Schleiermacher's rethinking of Christianity along the principles of Enlightenment and, further still, in Freud's construction of religion as a neurosis.

9. See the work of Jean-Luc Marion, in particular, *The Idol and Distance*, trans. Thomas A. Carlson (New York: Fordham University Press, 2001).

10. Thus Hans Urs von Balthasar writes, "Who can understand that this does not give rise to two truths, because there is only one truth that is itself interpretation?" *Theo-Logic, II: Truth of God*, trans. Adrian J. Walker (San Francisco: Ignatius Press, 2004), 15.

11. See *The Question Concerning Technology*, trans. William Lovitt (New York: Harper and Row, 1977), 7 (from where the German citation in the next sentence comes as well); and also "On the Essence and Concept of Φύσις in Aristotle's *Physics* B," in *Pathmarks*, trans. Thomas Sheehan (Cambridge: Cambridge University Press, 1998), 188.

12. Sophocles, *Oedipus at Colonus*, 1225 (the phrase is given an older provenance that leads back to Homer; see *Homeri Opera*, vol. 5, ed. T. W. Allen [Oxford], 288).

13. Anaximander's fragment DK 1, from *Die Fragmente der Vorsokratiker*, ed. Hermann Diels and Walther Kranz (Zurich: Weidmann, 1996), vol. 1, 89. My translation.

14. Friedrich Nietzsche, *Philosophy in the Tragic Age of the Greeks*, trans. Marianne Cowan (Chicago: Henry Regnery, 1962), 48. Nietzsche sees in Anaximander a predecessor of Schopenhauer (46) and doesn't hesitate to identify Anaximander's "indefinite" (*apeiron*) with Kant's *Ding an sich* (47). A quite different interpretation of the same fragment is offered by Heidegger in his 1946 essay, "Anaximander's Saying" (in *Off the Beaten Track*, trans. Julian Young and Kenneth Haynes [Cambridge: Cambridge University Press, 2002], 242–81). Heidegger's rendering of Anaximander's fragment—now beyond recognition—reads, "along the line of usage; for they let order and reck belong to one another (in the surmounting) of disorder" (280).

15. On autonomy's denial of the origin, see *EB*, pt. 1, esp. 27–38.

16. This idea becomes the subject of St. Thomas's discussion on sin, especially as sin "causing" sin, in *Summa Theologica*, II, q. 84, a. 2 (see also note 20 below).

17. Although a leitmotiv throughout the *Confessions*, this theme finds its first and more succinct articulation in the coda of book 1: listing the gifts he has received, Augustine declares them to be just that: *at ista omnia dei mei dona sunt*. This becomes, naturally, the occasion for thanksgiving: *gratias tibi de donis tuis*. More important, however, are the concluding words of this book: *quia et ut sim tu dedisti mihi*, "Being itself, my being, has been given to me."

18. *EB*, 8. "The will that wills itself is a double will," Desmond writes, "not redoubling itself in an ecstasis of self-transcending but doubling itself against itself in a self-undermining self-apotheosis, a self-hating self-love" (*EB*, 288).

19. "It is the self-consummation that consumes itself and only itself, and in its own self-consumption it finds the bitter taste of its own nothings. . . . Despair here is an empty self full of itself, circling on empty in its own lacking fullness with self" (*EB*, 289).

20. See St. Thomas Aquinas, *Summa Theologica*, II, q. 75, a. 1, where sin is defined as a negation with a deficient or an accidental efficient cause. Of sin as the "cause" of sin, see q. 84. On evil, in general, St. Thomas, following Dionysius (*de Div. nom.* IV), believes that it is, properly speaking, without a cause, or if a cause is to be assigned, then that cannot be but the good (see *Summa contra Gentiles*, 3.10). That God cannot be the cause of sin, see *Questiones Disputatae de Malo*, q. 3. a. 1–2.

21. Franz Kafka, *The Zürau Aphorisms of Franz Kafka*, trans. Michael Hofman (New York: Schocken Books, 2006), 5 (translation modified).

22. Søren Kierkegaard, *The Concept of Anxiety*, trans. Reidar Thomte and Albert B. Anderson (Princeton, NJ: Princeton University Press, 1980), 49.

23. Ibid.

24. For example, the creation of the world is not anymore the outcome of God's love and freedom, but the necessary result of man's sin. Thus, God would have been bound by necessity, for he either would have to accept the fall or take advantage of it in order to save man. In the latter case, where God leaves man to go through history, a history that is apparently defined by evil, then God seems to collaborate with evil and the question of theodicy is raised with particular acuteness. Why didn't God simply forgive man? Why does he punish man? And if the fallen condition of man is God-given, why "at the end of times" does he send his own Son to undo what he has done? Why does not God do in Paradise what he did in Gethsemane? Why had he to wait?

25. "That this desire desiring itself may end up in despair . . . is imaged in the story of Don Juan. . . . [T]he life of simulated desire of desire seeks its final 'freedom from' when it wills to be 'free from' *itself*. It cannot bear its own

emptiness; it would be free from itself in a self-negation that would negate all" (*EB*, 288; original emphasis).

26. In the twentieth chapter of the fourth book of his *Against the Heresies*, Irenaeus employs the image of the two hands of God saying, "For God did not stand in need of these [beings] . . . as if He did not possess His own hands. For with Him were always present the Word and Wisdom, the Son and the Spirit, by whom and in whom, freely and spontaneously, He made all things" (IV.20.1). However, the operation of the two hands of God is not restricted only in the creation of the world, but extends much more profoundly in the unfolding of the *economy*, that is, in the salvation of man through history; thus "the Spirit indeed working, and the Son ministering, while the Father was approving, and man's salvation being accomplished" (IV.20.6). The Word's incarnation, in particular, recapitulates times: "now this is His Word, our Lord Jesus Christ, who in the last times was made a man among men, that He might join the end to the beginning" (IV.20.4). This same idea is brought to a bold summation toward the end of the fourth book: "By this arrangement, therefore, and these harmonies, and a sequence of this nature, man, a created and organized being, is rendered after the image and likeness of the uncreated God—the Father planning everything well and giving His commands, the Son carrying these into execution and performing the work of creation, and the Spirit nourishing and increasing [what is made], but man making progress *day by day*, and ascending toward the perfect, that is, approximating to the uncreated One" (IV.38.3; my emphasis).

27. See, e.g., "*The demonic is the sudden*" (original emphasis) and "the negation of continuity is the sudden." Kierkegaard, *The Concept of Anxiety*, 129 ff.

28. See Kierkegaard's comments on Mephistopheles's jump in Bournonville's *Faust* (*The Concept of Anxiety*, 131–32).

29. "The creation of all rational creatures consisted of minds bodiless and immaterial without any number or name so that they all formed a unity by reason of the identity of their essence and power and energy and by their union with and knowledge of God the Word; but that they were seized with weariness [*koros*] of the divine love and contemplation, and changed for the worse, each in proportion to his inclination in this direction; and that they took bodies." Origen, *De Principiis*, II, viii, 3. This quotation comes from a series of anathemas directed against Origen by the Fifth Ecumenical Council (Second Council of Constantinople) in 553. In the same chapter, Origen had given his version of the etymology of the word *psyche* from the verb *psychesthai*, "to grow cold," in order to express the same idea.

30. NIV translation. Within square brackets I have given first the original Greek text and then the Vulgate's Latin translation.

31. Liddell and Scott, *A Greek-English Lexicon* (Oxford: Clarendon Press, 1996), under the entry διαλαμβάνω.

32. It is of interest to see how this term is used elsewhere in the scriptures and especially in the eschatological parables of the Gospel of St. Matthew. In the parable of the two sons, the father sends his first son to work in the vineyard, but he refuses; "but later [ὕστερον] he changed his mind and went" (21:29). Here the word *later* is used together with a verb denoting repentance, or changing one's mind (μεταμεληθείς). In the parable of the tenants that follows immediately after this one, the term is employed as an indicator of the time the father sent his own son to the vineyard (21:37)—a reference to the incarnation, and thus to the eschatological fullness of times.

33. Immanuel Kant, *Religion within the Boundaries of Mere Reason*, trans. Allen Wood and George di Giovanni (Cambridge: Cambridge University Press, 1998), 48.

34. *EB*, 31.

35. Paul Ricoeur, *The Symbolism of Evil*, trans. Emerson Buchanan (Boston: Beacon Press, 1967), 51.

36. Ibid., 52.

37. See my *God after Metaphysics* (Bloomington: Indiana University Press, 2007), esp. chs. 1 and 2.

38. Ricoeur, *The Symbolism of Evil*, 70.

39. Nietzsche, *Genealogy of Morals*, 63. That idea is facilitated, of course, by the fact that in German the two terms are identical.

40. Nietzsche, *Genealogy of Morals*, 89. The ancient practice of worshipping the ghosts of one's ancestors, especially that of the paterfamilias (see, e.g., the cult of Lares in Roman religion), seems to offer some evidence in support of Nietzsche's theory.

41. Nietzsche, *Genealogy of Morals*, 92; original emphasis.

42. "All interpretation and experience of conscience agree that the 'voice' of conscience somehow speaks of 'guilt.'" Martin Heidegger, *Being and Time*, trans. Joan Stambaugh (New York: SUNY Press, 1996), 258. "Thus we define the formal existential idea of 'guilty' as being-the-ground for a being which is determined by a not—that is, *being-the-ground of a nullity*" (261; original emphasis). "Primordial being guilty cannot be defined by morality because morality already presupposed it for itself" and "Being guilty constitutes the being that we call care. Da-sein stands primordially

together with itself in uncanniness. Uncanniness brings this being face to face with its undisguised nullity, which belongs to the possibility of its ownmost potentiality-of-being" (264).

43. Simon Critchley, "The Null Basis-Being of a Nullity, or Between Two Nothings," in *Phenomenologies of the Stranger: Between Hostility and Hospitality*, ed. Richard Kearney and Kascha Semonovitch (New York: Fordham University Press, 2011), 150.

44. Throughout his metaxological trilogy, *BB*, *EB*, and *GB*, Desmond distinguishes four senses of being: the idiotic, the aesthetic, the erotic, and the agapeic. It is fundamentally the last two that take us beyond self-affirmation and mediation to intermediation, that is, to what I have called a *prosopic* relationship.

45. This is the case particularly for the Book of Hosea. Of sin as adultery, see also Ricoeur, *The Symbolism of Evil*, 57.

46. Ricoeur, *The Symbolism of Evil*, 76.

CONTRIBUTORS

John R. Betz is Associate Professor of Systematic Theology at the University of Notre Dame. He specializes in systematic and philosophical theology, with a particular interest in German philosophy and theology from the eighteenth century to the present. In addition to articles in journals such as *Modern Theology* and the *Journal of the History of Ideas,* his publications include a monograph on Hamann titled *After Enlightenment: The Post-Secular Vision of J. G. Hamann* (Blackwell, 2009) and a translation, in collaboration with David B. Hart, of the 1962 edition of Przywara's *Analogia Entis* (Eerdmans, 2014). He is currently working on a monograph on Przywara as part of a larger project to recover the relevance of early twentieth-century Christian metaphysics to theology today.

Christopher R. Brewer (PhD, St Andrews) is Visiting Scholar at Calvin College, Grand Rapids, Michigan, and website content manager for www.giffordlectures.org. He has edited or coedited three volumes, including *God in a Single Vision: Integrating Philosophy and Theology* (Routledge, 2016) and *Divine Generosity and Human Creativity: Theology through Symbol, Painting and Architecture* (Routledge, 2017).

Patrick X. Gardner (PhD, Notre Dame) is Lilly Postdoctoral Fellow in the Humanities, Valparaiso University. He specializes in fundamental theology, modern philosophy of religion, and French Catholic thought of the twentieth century. His dissertation was on atheism and the theology of history in the works of Henri de Lubac.

Joseph K. Gordon is Assistant Professor of Theology at Johnson University, Florida. He has published essays on Aquinas, Augustine, and von Balthasar, which have appeared in *Nova et Vetara*, *Stone-Campbell Journal*, and *Theology in the Present Age: Essays in Honor of John D. Castelein* (ed. Christopher Ben Simpson and Steven Cone [Pickwick, 2013]).

Renée Köhler-Ryan is Senior Lecturer in Philosophy at the University of Notre Dame Australia (Sydney). She earned her PhD at the Katholieke Universiteit Leuven (Belgium) under the supervision of William Desmond, with a dissertation titled "Sacred Space as the Expression of Religious Experience and Imagination." She has also lectured in Rome, Italy. Currently Köhler-Ryan teaches subjects that reflect her main research interests and publications: philosophy of the human person, political philosophy, medieval philosophy, and aesthetics.

D. Stephen Long is Professor of Systematic Theology at Marquette University and has also held positions at Garrett-Evangelical Theological Seminary, St. Joseph's University, and Duke Divinity School. He is an ordained United Methodist and has served churches in Honduras and North Carolina. Long has published eight books, including *John Wesley's Moral Theology: The Quest for God and Goodness* (Kingswood, 2005), *Calculated Futures* (Baylor, 2007), *Theology and Culture* (Cascade, 2007), and *Speaking of God: Theology, Language and Truth* (Eerdmans, 2009).

John Panteleimon Manoussakis is the Edward Bennett Williams Fellow Associate Professor at the College of the Holy Cross. He was born in Athens, Greece, and received his PhD from Boston College. His research focuses on the philosophy of religion, phenomenology, ancient Greek philosophy, and Patristic thought. His articles have appeared in many scholarly journals, including *ACPQ*, *Harvard Theological Review*, and *Journal of Philosophy and Scripture*. He is the author of *God after Metaphysics: A Theological Aesthetic* (Indiana, 2007) and the editor of many books, including *After God* (Fordham, 2006) and *Phenomenology and Eschatology: Not Yet in the Now* (Routledge, 2009).

Cyril O'Regan is the Huisking Professor of Theology at the University of Notre Dame. Specializing in systematic and historical theology, O'Regan has specific interest in the intersection of continental philosophy and theology, religion and literature, mystical theology, and postmodern thought. He is the author of *The Heterodox Hegel* (SUNY, 1994), *Gnostic Return in Modernity* (SUNY, 2001), and *Gnostic Apocalypse: Jacob Boehme's Haunted Narrative* (SUNY, 2002). In addition, he has published numerous articles on such topics as the nature of tradition, negative theology, the sources of Hegel's thought, and Hegel as a theological source and on figures such as John Henry Newman and Hans Urs von Balthasar. O'Regan is currently working on books on Romanticism and Gnosticism and on Han Urs von Balthasar and postmodern thought.

Brendan Thomas Sammon is Assistant Professor of Systematic Theology at Saint Joseph's University. He previously taught theology at Georgetown University and Catholic University, where he received his PhD. He specializes in the theology of late antiquity and the Middle Ages, theological aesthetics, and the intersection of a theology of beauty with human disability. Sammon is the author of *The God Who Is Beauty: Beauty as a Divine Name in Thomas Aquinas and Dionysius the Areopagite* (Pickwick, 2013) and *Called to Attraction: An Introduction to the Theology of Beauty* (Cascade, forthcoming).

D. C. Schindler is Associate Professor of Philosophy in the Department of Humanities at Villanova University. He received his PhD from the Catholic University of America in 2001 and since then has written and translated numerous articles for various distinguished publications. Schindler is the author of *Hans Urs von Balthasar and the Dramatic Structure of Truth: A Philosophical Investigation* (Fordham, 2004) and *Plato's Critique of Impure Reason: On Truth and Goodness in the Republic* (CUA, 2008).

Christopher Ben Simpson is Professor of Philosophical Theology at Lincoln Christian University. He is the author of several books and articles, including *Religion, Metaphysics, and the Postmodern:*

William Desmond and John D. Caputo (Indiana, 2009), *The Truth Is the Way: Kierkegaard's "Theologia Viatorum"* (SCM Press/Cascade, 2011), *The William Desmond Reader* (SUNY, 2012), *Deleuze and Theology* (Bloomsbury/T&T Clark, 2012), *Merleau-Ponty and Theology* (Bloomsbury/T&T Clark, 2014), and *Modern Christian Theology* (Bloomsbury/T&T Clark, 2016).

Corey Benjamin Tutewiler is Adjunct Professor at Lincoln Christian University and Greenville College, teaching classes in the Departments of Theology, Philosophy, and Education. He received his master's degree in contemporary theology from Lincoln Christian University. Tutewiler is a contributor to the Kierkegaard Research: Sources, Reception, and Resources project based at the University of Copenhagen, as well as the multivolume book series known as the Acta Kierkegaardiana. More recently, he has written on William Desmond's work in *Theology in the Present Age: Essays in Honor of John D. Castelein* (Pickwick, 2013).

INDEX